AF705873

Civil Procedure in Argentina

Published by:
Kluwer Law International B.V.
PO Box 316
2400 AH Alphen aan den Rijn
The Netherlands
E-mail: international-sales@wolterskluwer.com
Website: lrus.wolterskluwer.com

Sold and distributed by:
Wolters Kluwer Legal & Regulatory U.S.
7201 McKinney Circle
Frederick, MD 21704
United States of America
E-mail: customer.service@wolterskluwer.com

DISCLAIMER: The material in this volume is in the nature of general comment only. It is not offered as advice on any particular matter and should not be taken as such. The editor and the contributing authors expressly disclaim all liability to any person with regard to anything done or omitted to be done, and with respect to the consequences of anything done or omitted to be done wholly or partly in reliance upon the whole or any part of the contents of this volume. No reader should act or refrain from acting on the basis of any matter contained in this volume without first obtaining professional advice regarding the particular facts and circumstances at issue. Any and all opinions expressed herein are those of the particular author and are not necessarily those of the editor or publisher of this volume.

ISBN 978-94-035-3952-2

e-Book: ISBN 978-94-035-3953-9
web-PDF: ISBN 978-94-035-3954-6

© 2021 Kluwer Law International BV, The Netherlands

All rights reserved. No part of this publication may be reproduced, stored in a retrieval system, or transmitted in any form or by any means, electronic, mechanical, photocopying, recording, or otherwise, without the prior written permission of the publisher.

Permission to use this content must be obtained from the copyright owner. More information can be found at: lrus.wolterskluwer.com/policies/permissions-reprints-and-licensing

Civil Procedure in Argentina

Roberto Berizonce
Eduardo Oteiza

This book was originally published as a monograph in the International Encyclopaedia of Laws/Civil Procedure.

Founding Editor: Roger Blanpain
General Editor: Frank Hendrickx
Volume Editor: Wannes Vandenbussche

Wolters Kluwer

The Authors

Roberto Berizonce (La Plata, 1938) is an Emeritus Professor at Universidad Nacional de La Plata, Argentina, where he was professor, Head of the Procedural Law Institute and co-director of the LLM programme on Procedural Law.

Professor Berizonce served as President of the Ibero-American Institute of Procedural Law (1998–2002) and the Argentine Association of Procedural Law (2005–2009).

Eduardo Oteiza (La Plata, 1955) is full professor and director of the LLM programme on Procedural Law at Universidad Nacional de La Plata.

Professor Oteiza has been the President of the International Association of Procedural Law (since 2019). He served as the President of the Argentine Association of Procedural Law (2011–2013) and the Ibero-American Institute of Procedural Law (2014–2018).

In 2016, Professor Oteiza received the Year Award from the Fondazione Enrico Redenti.

The Authors

Co-Authors

The authors would like to thank Ornella Piccinelli and Matías Sucunza, both researchers from the Universidad Nacional de la Plata, for their collaboration during the research process and text drafting stage. Their editorial suggestions and recommendations made a significant contribution to the final order of the chapters and texts.

Ornella Piccinelli won the prize awarded to young Procedural Law specialists by the Argentine Procedural Law Association in 2017 and was a runner-up for the prestigious 'Dr. Fábrega Ponce' award made by the Ibero-American Procedural Law Institute in 2015.

Matías Sucunza was the top of his class at the Universidad Nacional de La Plata in 2008, and won a public contest to be a Researcher at the Justice Studies Center of the Americas (JSCA) (2018–2019).

We would like to thank Rafaela Gunner for her significant contributions to the final version of the texts in English. A graduate of the University of Oxford with an Honours Degree in Modern Languages, Rafaela has been working as a translator and conference interpreter in Argentina for twenty years.

Co-Authors

Table of Contents

List of Abbreviations

AC	Argentine Constitution (*Constitución Nacional*, in Spanish)
ACCC	ACCC (Código Civil y Comercial de la Nación, in Spanish)
ACCPC	Argentine Civil and Commercial Procedural Code (*Código Procesal Civil y Comercial de la Nación,* in Spanish)
ACHR	American Convention on Human Rights
ACJ	Argentine Council for the Judiciary
ACPA	Argentine Consumer Protection Act
AEP	Argentine Executive Power
AGEPA	Argentine General Environmental Protection Act
AJP	Argentine Judicial Power
AJR	Argentine Justice Regulation
AR	Argentine Republic
BAPCCPC	Buenos Aires Province Civil and Commercial Procedural Code
BAPJP	Buenos Aires Province Judicial Power
BAPSCJ	Buenos Aires Province Supreme Court of Justice
draft of the new ACCPC	Argentine Civil and Commercial Procedural Code
ECHR	European Court of Human Rights
Fallos	Official Collection of Argentina's Supreme Court of Justice Decisions
Fundamentals	Fundamentals for Civil and Commercial Procedural Reform
ICCPR	International Covenant on Civil and Political Rights
ICHR	Inter-American Court of Human Rights
ICSID	International Centre for Settlement of Investment Disputes
MERCOSUR	Southern Common Market
MJyDH	Argentine Ministry of Justice and Human Rights (Ministerio de Justicia y Derechos Humanos, in Spanish)
OAS	Organization of American States

List of Abbreviations

RFNJ	Regulations for the Federal and National Judiciary
Supreme Court	Supreme Court of Argentina
UN	United Nations

General Introduction

§1. General Background

1. The Argentine Republic (AR) has a population of 40,117,096 and a territory of 3,761,274 km^2, according to the last national census, performed in 2010. Some 90% of the population lives in urban areas. The city of Buenos Aires is home to 2,890,151 inhabitants (14,307.68 inhabitants per km^2), while the surface area of Greater Buenos Aires has 9,916,715 inhabitants (2,694.75 inhabitants per km^2). Almost a third of the country's population (12,806,866 inhabitants) resides in the urban concentration formed by the city of Buenos Aires and the ring of towns surrounding it. These figures are very different to the average population density in the rest of the country: 14.4 inhabitants per km^2.

Of its twenty-three provinces, only nine have a population in excess of one million: Buenos Aires (15,625,084), Cordoba (3,308,876), Entre Ríos (1,235,994), Misiones (1,101,593), Chaco (1,055,259), Mendoza (1,738,929), Salta (1,214,441), Santa Fe (3,194,537) and Tucuman (1,448,188).

According to the index published in the UN Human Development Report, Argentina ranks 47th among 187 countries.[1]

2. After winning independence from Spain following several years of war at the start of the nineteenth century, Argentina underwent a period of severe political and institutional instability until the adoption of the National Constitution. The first text was passed in 1853, and subsequently amended in 1860, 1866, 1898, 1957 and 1994. The Argentine National Constitution (AC)[2] takes the republican and federal form of government (Article 1). The first part enshrines a core set of rights, including equality (Article 14), the inviolability of a person's right to a fair defence in court (Article 18), the liberal principle of free will (Article 19), the principle of legality, and constitutional supremacy (Article 31).

The 1994 constitutional reform process incorporated new rights, such as those concerning the environment and consumption (Articles 41 and 42, AC). This reform process also established preferential legal protection through four special procedures (Article 43, AC). The first concerns individual protection (*amparo individual*), presented as a rapid procedure admitted whenever there is no other more

1. United Nations Development Program (UNDP), *Human Development Report 2016,* Washington D.C., United States, http://hdr.undp.org/sites/default/files/HDR2016_SP_Overview_Web.pdf.
2. The English language version of the Argentine National Constitution may be consulted at https://bibliotecadigital.csjn.gov.ar/constitucion-traduccion-ingles.pdf.

suitable legal means, brought against any act or omission by public authorities or individuals, that currently or imminently harms, restricts, alters or threatens, either arbitrarily or with manifest illegality, the rights and guarantees recognized by the AC, or enshrined in a treaty or a law. This *amparo* may also be invoked against any form of discrimination and in relation to the rights protecting the environment, competition, users and consumers. The second, known as collective redress or representative action, is used to request guardianship in the case of a violation of collective rights. This collective redress can be invoked by the persons affected, the Defender of the People,[3] and any associations promoting these purposes, as long as it has been legally registered. The third procedure, called habeas data, may be filed by anybody for the purposes of accessing information about its purpose, when it is held in public records or databases, or private databases set up to provide reports. The claim may also be filed in cases of falsehood or discrimination to demand that data be suppressed, rectified, kept confidential, or updated. The fourth procedure is habeas corpus, which refers to instances when the right to physical freedom is infringed, restricted, altered or threatened, or when illegitimate aggravation occurs in the form or conditions of detention, or when the forced disappearance of people takes place.

The Federal Government enjoys the independence to exercise legislative, executive and judicial powers. The AC establishes a system of checks and balances through which functions are distributed among the Legislative, Executive and Judicial Powers. Argentina's Supreme Court of Justice (Supreme Court) is the head of the Judicial Power of the Nation (JP) and exercises a diffuse control over the constitutionality of the laws and acts of the Executive Power of the Nation (EP). It is also an instance whereby the rulings issued by the superior courts of the provinces may be revised when a federal question arises in a case.

The institutional structure of the AC rests on the principle of the separation of powers and the adoption of a federal system. According to the AC, provinces may retain all powers not delegated to the Federal Government (Article 121), dictate their own constitutions under the representative and republican system, and guarantee the administration of justice (Article 5). The constitutional principle underlying the preservation of all nondelegated powers has an evident effect on procedural matters, since it is a nondelegated attribution vested in the Argentine Congress. The provinces dictate their procedural codes and the laws of judicial organization. Provincial constitutions consider the judiciary to be one of the powers and therefore

3. The 1994 reform incorporated the Defender of the People. According to Article 86 of the AC, the Defender of the People is an independent body in the orbit of the Congress which acts with total functional autonomy without receiving instructions from any authority. The institution's task is to defend and protect human rights as well as all the other rights, guarantees and interests enshrined in the Constitution and the laws, in the face of deeds, acts or omissions committed by the administration. It is also tasked with overseeing the exercise of public administrative functions. Its members are appointed and removed by Congress with a two-thirds of the votes in both chambers. The Defender enjoys the same privileges and immunities as lawmakers and a five-year mandate, which may only be renewed once. The post has been vacant since 1999. The functions of this institution are enshrined in Law 24,284 (1993), subsequently modified by Law 24,379 (1994).

organize their justice systems under a court or superior court. One of the main functions of these courts is to standardize the interpretation of national and local law.[4]

The 1994 constitutional reform endowed the city of Buenos Aires with its own autonomous government regime, powers of legislation and jurisdiction (Article 129). Prior to the 1994 constitutional modification, the city of Buenos Aires was the Federal Capital and thus the seat of National Government, but it lacked a status similar to that of the provinces. Despite the fact that Article 129 of the AC grants the city sufficient autonomy to allow it to organize its own justice system, this selfsame norm established that a later law should guarantee the interests of the national State for as long as the city is the capital of the Nation.[5]

The 1994 constitutional reform established, among other significant changes, that treaties outrank laws, and thus assigned constitutional hierarchy to the following: the American Declaration of the Rights and Duties of Man; the Universal Declaration of Human Rights; the American Convention on Human Rights (ACHR); the International Covenant on Economic, Social and Cultural Rights; the International Covenant on Civil and Political Rights (ICCPR) and Its Optional Protocol; the Convention on the Elimination of All Forms of Discrimination Against Women; the Convention Against Torture and Other Cruel, Inhuman or Degrading Treatment or Punishment; the Convention on the Rights of the Child; the Convention on the Prevention and Punishment of the Crime of Genocide; the International Convention on the Elimination of All Forms of Racial Discrimination; the Inter-American Convention on the Forced Disappearance of Persons; the Convention on the Non-applicability of Statutory Limitations to War Crimes and Crimes Against Humanity; and the Convention on the Rights of Persons with Disabilities (Article 75 (22), AC).

Although the ACHR acquired constitutional hierarchy with the 1994 reform, Argentina had already ratified the Convention as early as August 1984, recognizing the competence of the Inter-American Court of Human Rights (IACHR).[6]

Regarding regional integration, Argentina is a member of the Organization of American States (OAS), the United Nations (UN), the World Trade Organization, the Latin American Integration Association and the Southern Cone Common Market (MERCOSUR).

MERCOSUR Member States established a Permanent Review Court to settle disputes and give advisory opinions on legal questions that might arise regarding the integration process. The Permanent Review Court may intervene in the first and only instance. It may also do so as a review instance for an Ad hoc Institutional Arbitration Tribunal, upon the request of a State involved in a dispute. Additionally,

4. Local law is dictated by the provincial authorities. It differs from national law in that this is the attribution of Congress (Art. 75 (12) of the AC).
5. Law 24,588 (1995) restricted the autonomy conferred on the city of Buenos Aires. Art. 8 of Law 24,588 allowed national judges based in the Autonomous City of Buenos Aires to continue with their jurisdiction and competence as established prior to the constitutional reform. The Constitution of the Autonomous City of Buenos Aires establishes a Judicial Power headed by the Superior Court of Justice (Art. 107). It also establishes that it is up to the City's Judiciary to hear and decide on all cases dealing with points governed by this Constitution, as regards any rules underwritten, substantive codes, and all national and local laws and regulations. The authorities of the Federal Government and the Autonomous City of Buenos Aires have held various discussions on how to transfer national justice, but have so far not reached an agreement.
6. Law 23,054 (1984).

the possibility of resorting to the Permanent Review Court was acknowledged in cases where an Advisory Opinion is sought or when State Parties activate the procedure established for Exceptional Emergency Measures.

With regard to the protection of foreign investments, Argentina ratified the 1965 Washington Convention (Law 24,353 (1994)), creating the International Centre for Settlement of Investment Disputes (ICSID), which also establishes an institutional arbitration system. The Bilateral Treaties ratified by Argentina with a significant number of nations, directly submit the settlement of any disputes to ICSID arbitration, or refer to the most-favoured-nation clause.

3. In the Argentine legal system, traditional European continental law converges with common law.

The influence of European continental law is part of Argentina's historical legacy and stretches back to colonial times. The Spanish colonization period covered a long process lasting over three centuries, which began during the reign of the Catholic Kings. The territories of the West Indies were assigned to the Castilian Crown when the Treaty of Tordesillas (1494) legitimized the dominion of the lands conquered by the Crown in the Americas. When the Archduke of Austria, Charles V from the House of Habsburg (1517-1556), the founder of Spanish absolutism, took the throne, he set himself to consolidate dominance in America as part of a drive to expand 'the empire on which the sun never sets'. One of the legal expressions typifying the period of the House of Austria is the Compilation of Laws of the Kingdom of the Indies (1680). This was an attempt to order the provisions in force at different times, which were devoid of any systematicity, but nonetheless inspired by the Roman code, particularly the Corpus Juris Civillis by Justinian. During the Bourbon dynasty (seventeenth century), the Río de La Plata Viceroyalty (1776) was added to those of Mexico and Peru.

In 1810, in the midst of the crisis sweeping through the Spanish monarchy as a result of the Napoleonic invasions, the May Revolution broke out, giving way to the process of Argentine independence, achieved in 1816. The concepts proposed by thinkers such as Montesquieu (1689–1755) and Rousseau (1712–1778) had a profound impact on the independence movement, mostly influenced by the Enlightenment ideas which inspired the French Revolution. However, the process of institutionalization took close to three decades, dominated by the centralization debate pitting the province of Buenos Aires against the other provinces. The federalist principle adopted by the AC was slow to establish itself, due to the historic power tussle between the provinces and Buenos Aires in its bid to centralize government. The constitutional reform of 1860 brought about the union between the province of Buenos Aires and the other provinces, which at the time identified themselves as a Confederation. At all events, the entire process was superseded by the passage of Law 1,029 (1880), declaring the Municipality of the City of Buenos Aires to be the Capital of the Republic of Argentina.

The constituents based their model for the text of the AC on the Philadelphia Constitution of 1787, and in this way, Argentine constitutional law adopted the institutional system first designed for the United States.

The Argentine Supreme Court also has similar characteristics to that of the United States in that it follows the jurisprudence developed by the latter. One example of this can be seen in *Sojo*[7] (1887), where the Supreme Court ruled on its jurisdiction to hear the case, following a request from a journalist detained by the Argentine Chamber of Deputies regarding a questionable decision taken by the latter. The Argentine Supreme Court in this instance inaugurated the doctrine of judicial review. It did so expressly according to a precedent set by its American peer, in *Marbury v. Madison*[8] (1803), regarding its competence to declare laws as being unconstitutional. The Supreme Court cites the landmark *Marbury v. Madison* decision as one of the foundations for its ruling.

Despite its adherence to the North American model, the AC entrusted the Argentine Congress with the task of drawing up codes to govern civil, commercial and criminal matters, following the rationalist tradition of European continental law (Article 75 (22) AC). In addition to espousing the ideas of the Enlightenment, the inspiration drawn from the Napoleonic code had a marked influence on the way legislation was drafted after the country's definitive institutionalization.

4. The constitutional process (18531860) laid the foundations for the country's future development. The passage of Law 1,420 (1884) guaranteeing free and compulsory public education, putting the population on the road to literacy, added to the arrival of 4 million European immigrants on Argentine shores, radically changed the country's appearance, two of the factors fuelling growth over those years.

In 1912, the Argentine Republic adopted an electoral system based on universal suffrage, endowing the Rule of Law with improved representativeness and greater legitimacy.

The 1930 military coup heralded a new era for the country and for the next fifty years, until 1983, Argentina endured the cyclical alternation between civil and military governments. One of the key features of the political process stretching from 1930 to 1983 was the instability, in particular, of Supreme Court Justices, as each new coup d'état brought about a change in the composition of the Supreme Court.

The democratic process beginning in 1983 was able to withstand the early resignation of two of the presidents-elect who failed to complete their terms in the midst of serious economic crises.

In 1991, after the first succession between civilian presidents in almost fifty years, the Argentine Congress passed Law 23,744, raising the number of Supreme Court Justices from five to nine, in order to ensure a majority susceptible to political control if needs be.

The president elected in 2002 impeached several of the justices appointed during the previous government. Another five justices originally appointed in the 1990s left office, two being removed by the Senate following a process of impeachment. Between 2002 and 2004, four new justices were appointed.

Law 26,183 (2006) established a progressive reduction in the number of Supreme Court Justices, bringing the number down to five.

By the end of the administration governed by the political party in power from 2003 to 2015, there were only three justices left in the Supreme Court. The president-elect in 2015 appointed two new justices without the prior agreement of

7. *Fallos* 32:120.
8. 1 Cranch 137, 2 L.Ed. 60.

the Senate.[9] The Decree appointing these justices was based on Article 99 (22) of the AC, which empowers the President to fill such vacancies without the agreement of the Senate when it is in recess. The president's decision was widely questioned by public opinion and its constitutionality was, to say the least, dubious. The political context and weakness of the appointments meant that the justices appointed by Decree had to wait for the Senate to issue its verdict before taking office.

The instability in the composition of the Supreme Court is a phenomenon that has been repeated several times since the early 1900s. History shows that the independence of the Supreme Court is relative, and vulnerable to pressure, both external and internal. The various sectors wielding economic and political power have tried, in many different ways, to influence and limit the institution's powers. Also, the selfsame justices making up the Supreme Court have shown themselves to be tolerant of political meddling, a constitutional practice that contradicts the Supreme Court's mission and robs it of legitimacy and credibility, undermining the institutional framework and the legal system in general.

5. Notwithstanding the issues of independence and a complex relationship with the political sectors, the Supreme Court in its exercise of constitutional control has taken decisions with a high impact.[10] During the twentieth century, the role of the State in the economy and its ability to limit the free decision of individuals on how to enter into commercial relations was a frequent subject of discussion. In *Ercolano v. Lanteri*[11] (1922), the Supreme Court ruled in favour of the constitutionality of a law allowing the State to intervene in tenancy relationships, formerly considered a typically private matter. When inflation affected the parity of benefits exchanged between parties as a result of the lost value of money, as in *Vieytez de Fernández v. the Province of Buenos Aires*[12] (1972), the Supreme Court applied the principles of commutative justice. This was a way of recognizing the update of the value of benefits in the face of inflation, to balance out the reciprocal obligations between the parties. In *Smith v. the National Executive Power*[13] (2002), the Supreme Court censured government measures passed to limit the withdrawal of bank deposits, and the emergency legislation adopted, for violating constitutional guarantees. The rulings referred to above had a particular impact on the course of political events.

In another order of social conflicts, it should be remembered that once democratic order had been restored, the Supreme Court had to issue a ruling on the legal reforms allowing the Military Juntas that governed Argentina from 1976 to 1983 to be tried. In *Videla*[14] (1984), the Supreme Court declared that new legislation allowing the civil trial of crimes that before the reforms could only be tried before a military tribunal was constitutional. One of the issues that concerned Argentine society in the 1980s was the legal limitation on couples seeking divorce. Congress, under

9. Decree 83 (2015).
10. *See* the English version of the rulings believed by the Supreme Court to be of significance, at the Supreme Court of Argentina Relevant Cases 2018), https://sj.csjn.gov.ar/sj/suplementos.do?method=ver&data=fr20182eb.
11. *Fallos* 136:164.
12. *Fallos* 295:973.
13. *Fallos* 325:2002.
14. *Fallos* 306:2101.

strong pressure from the Catholic Church, was unable to obtain the necessary consensus to pass a pro-divorce law. In *Sejean v. Zaks de Sejean*[15] (1986), the Supreme Court declared the unconstitutionality of the legislation censuring the right to divorce. As for Therapeutic Abortion in the terms regulated by criminal law, in *F.A.L.*[16] (2012), the Supreme Court established that a doctor was not required to request a legal authorization to terminate a pregnancy if the woman seeking it invoked a non-consensual sexual relationship.

In *Mendoza*[17] (2006), the Supreme Court ruled on a matter of the utmost importance, the pollution of the Riachuelo river basin and its effects on the neighbouring population, as well as determining public and private responsibilities in what was the first class action with widespread repercussions. A few years later, in *Halabi*[18] (2009), the Supreme Court laid down the guidelines for filing class action lawsuits according to Article 43 of the AC.

The aforementioned rulings are just a few examples illustrating the role played by the Supreme Court's decisions in the evolution of the Argentine legal system as regards high-profile social and political matters. It would not be appropriate here to describe the most significant Supreme Court rulings in detail, as they are mentioned primarily to explain their relevance to the Argentine legal system.

§2. Delimitation of the Subject Matter

6. The breadth of the notion of civil process requires the scope applied in this instance to be described in detail. It should be noted that this notion refers to processes established by law or arising as a consequence of legal interpretations.[19] This excludes criminal law from the body of civil law but includes civil, commercial, family, constitutional, administrative, labour and social security litigation.

§3. Source of Law

7. As previously mentioned, the Argentine Congress is empowered to issue procedural rules for federal and national justice. Provincial legislatures enact their own procedural legislation, and procedural codes come under local law.[20]

15. *Fallos* 308:2268.
16. *Fallos* 335:197.
17. *Fallos* 329:2326.
18. *Fallos* 332:222.
19. The Supreme Court's jurisprudence has regulated special processes, developing standards that constitute the precepts followed when hearing court cases. One example is the Supreme Court's creation of *protection* in the case of *Siri* (1957, *Fallos* 239:459) and the guidelines for holding a class action trial in the case of *Halabi* (2009, *Ibid.*).
20. The transfer of national justice to the Autonomous City of Buenos Aires has not yet been completed in its entirety.

8. For labour and family disputes, where public, electoral, consumer defence and labour authorities are parties, the Nation and the Provinces dictate specific legislation, which usually takes the civil procedural code of the respective jurisdiction as its regulatory body of reference.[21] One example of legislation that refers to the civil procedural code is Law 18,345 (1998), which approved the regulations before the Labour Courts.[22]

In the province of Buenos Aires, procedural regulations were adopted both for the Labour Courts[23] and for lawsuits brought against the provincial authorities,[24] as well as a law containing a special procedure for consumers and users. For any matters not covered by these laws, the issue is referred to the Civil and Commercial Procedural Code of the Province of Buenos Aires (BAPCCPC).[25] In the province of Cordoba, family procedural law enshrines specific legislation referring any unforeseen issue to that province's Civil Procedure Code.[26]

However, the number of jurisdictions dictating procedural rules (twenty-four), the differences between civil procedural legislation in its strictest sense, and the adaptation of these procedures to family, labour, administrative and consumer rights disputes in each jurisdiction mean that it is advisable to take the Civil and Commercial Procedural Code of the Nation (ACCPC) as the main axis of analysis, since most of the provincial codes have replicated its structure and many of its provisions. On the other hand, it is not appropriate in terms of practical use and for the purposes of this monograph to provide a detailed analysis of the rules and practices of each jurisdiction, as only the most relevant aspects will be mentioned here.

9. The Civil and Commercial Code of the Nation (ACCC)[27] contains several procedural rules, even though this is a matter for the provinces, in accordance with Articles 5 and 121 of the AC.

The Supreme Court has validated the incorporation of procedural rules to the ACCC in consistent case law when it considers that doing so is constitutional, as and when its purpose is to ensure the effectiveness of the rights in question.[28]

---

21. This means that the civil procedure code of the respective jurisdiction applies to issues not covered by that legislation.
22. Court proceedings in electoral matters are resolved in accordance with the provisions of Law 23,298 (1985, *Organic Law of Political Parties*), and the ACCPC is applied as a substitute.
23. Law 11,653 (1995) of the Province of Buenos Aires contains provisions governing labour disputes. This rule was amended by Law 15,057 (2018), which before entering into force, requires a series of structural changes to be made to the provincial Labour Courts.
24. Law 12,008 (1997), accompanied by the reforms of Laws 12,310 (1999), 13,101 (2003) and 13,325 (2005), regulates the processes in which lawsuits are filed against the Province of Buenos Aires, the Municipalities or the decentralized entities of the provincial administration in the case of their action or omission.
25. Law 13,133 (2003) establishes a Provincial Code for the implementation of consumer and user rights, subsequently amended by Laws 13,730 (2007), 14,393 (2012) and 14,514 (2013).
26. Law 10,305 (2015) adopts the Code of Family Procedure, whose Art. 177 contemplates the application of the provisions of the Civil and Commercial Procedural Code of the Province of Córdoba in every area not expressly provided for in the aforementioned law.
27. Law 26,994 (2014).
28. This is about a line of precedents that the Supreme Court has maintained since the case of *Barnabas Correa* (*Fallos* 138:157 - 1923), followed by the cases of *Netto* (*Fallos* 141:254 - 1924) and *Real de Maciel* 1928 (*Fallos* 151:315 - 1928), to name but a few.

10. In Article 1, the ACCC provides that cases must be resolved according to the laws applicable, in accordance with the AC and the human rights treaties signed by Argentina, and the purpose of the rule in question is accordingly taken into account. The article adds that uses, practices and customs are binding whenever the laws or the interested parties refer to them, or in instances where situations are not legally regulated. Article 2 of the ACCC establishes that the law must be interpreted according to its words, purposes, similar laws, and the provisions enshrined in human rights treaties, as well as legal principles and values, in a manner consistent with the entire legal system. Finally, Article 3 establishes that 'the court must resolve the matters submitted to their jurisdiction by means of a reasonably founded decision'.

In the parliamentary discussion prior to the approval of the ACCC, the lawmakers examined the possibility of incorporating jurisprudence as a source of law in Article 1, but eventually this initiative was overruled.

11. Although the ACCC does not include jurisprudence as a source of law, its importance is undeniable, since the judges refer to rulings handed down in previous decisions. Thus, it should be borne in mind that the Supreme Court has understood that its precedents must be followed by judges, since it is as a body the ultimate interpreter of the AC.[29] However, the lack of stability in the composition of the Supreme Court, the diversity of criteria employed as a basis for judges to apply them as precedent, the case overload and the large number of rulings made annually are four factors undermining the coherence of the criteria used to take decisions. This, in turn, means that the binding nature of rulings, in both horizontal and vertical senses, is relative. At all events, the precedents established by the Supreme Court are taken into account by Argentine judges as a basis for their decisions, and the criteria it has developed are for the most part respected.

12. The AR ratified the ACHR, subsequently assigning it a constitutional hierarchy, and recognized the competence of the Inter-American Court of Human Rights (IACHR), meaning that it adheres to the IACHR's doctrine of conventionality control. According to this doctrine, should any internal provisions violate the ACHR, national judges must declare these to be invalid through conventionality control, which should be performed even without a request from the party (ex officio). When this form of control takes place, national judges must apply the ACHR as well as jurisprudence formed by the IACHR.

The doctrine of conventionality control has two significant aspects. The first is that the IACHR retains its character as the final interpreter of the ACHR, which implies consecrating a kind of *stare decisis* or precedent, which is vertically binding in terms of any earlier rulings.[30] The second is that the IACHR assumes the supremacy of its interpretations on the scope of the ACHR and the obligation of all

29. On the question of *stare decisis*, or precedent, according to Supreme Court, *see* A.F. Garay, 'A Doctrine of Precedent in the Making: The case of Argentine Supreme Court Case Law', *Southwestern Journal of International Law*, Vol. 25:2 (2019), 258 et seq.
30. The IACHR inaugurated its doctrine on conventionality control in the case *Almonacid Arellano* v. *Chile (*Ruling of 26.9.2006, in: http://www.corteidh.or.cr/docs/casos/articulos/seriec_154_ing.pdf.)

levels of the State's jurisdictions in order to apply it directly, even when this is *contra legem*, and lacks the express request of the parties. In successive rulings,[31] the IACHR has ratified the doctrine on the control of conventionality ex officio.

The Supreme Court has with some reluctance accepted the interpretation of the ACHR made by the IACHR. In *Ministry of Foreign Affairs and Worship,* also known as *Fontevecchia* (2017),[32] the Supreme Court refused to issue a new ruling at odds with that handed down by the IACHR. The situation was later resolved when the Supreme Court agreed to comply with the IACHR's new ruling ordering the Supreme Court to include a note indicating that its sentence had violated the ACHR. The rigidity with which the conventionality control doctrine was drawn up, a figure requiring an unequivocal follow-up because the IACHR has not developed a doctrine similar to that of the national margin of interpretation espoused by the European Court of Human Rights (ECHR), has strained the relationship with the Supreme Court.

13. With regard to the incidence of jurisprudence in Argentine law, it is worth mentioning that at national and federal levels, as well as in the provinces, procedural codes provide for the unification of jurisprudence through the extraordinary appeal for the inapplicability of the law, according to its many variants in each jurisdiction. Thus, the ACCPC (Article 288)[33] envisages lodging an appeal for the inapplicability of the law against a sentence that contradicts the doctrine established by any National or Federal Chambers of Appeal. Likewise, the ACCPC contemplates that any section of the Chamber of Appeal may decide on its own initiative to convene a plenary meeting in order to unify jurisprudence and avoid contradictory judgments (Article 302). The interpretation of the law established by the Chamber of Appeal's Plenary is obligatory for all sections of the Chamber and hence for the judges of first instance for whom this is a higher court, notwithstanding the fact that

31. The Case of *La Cantuta* v. *Peru. Merits, Reparations and Costs.* Sentence of 29 November 2006. Series C No. 162, para. 173, *Boyce et al.* v. *Barbados. Preliminary Exception, Merits, Reparations and Costs.* Sentence of Tuesday, 20 November 2007. Series C No. 169, para. 79, the case of *Heliodoro Portugal* v. *Panama. Preliminary Exceptions, Merits, Reparations and Costs.* Sentence of Tuesday, 12 August 2008. Series C No. 186, para. 180, the case of *Rosendo Radilla Pacheco* v. *the United States of Mexico. Preliminary Exceptions, Merits, Reparations and Costs.* Sentence of Monday, 23 November 2009. Series C No. 209, para. 339. The case of *Manuel Cepeda Vargas* v. *Colombia. Preliminary Exceptions, Merits, and Reparations. Sentence* of 26 May 2010. Series C No. 213, para. 208, note 307, *Xákmok Kásek Indigenous Community v. Paraguay. Merits, Reparations and Costs.* Sentence of Tuesday, 24 August 2010. Series C No. 214, para. 311, *Fernández Ortega et al.* v. *Mexico. Preliminary Exception, Merits, Reparations and Costs.* Sentence of Monday, 30 August 2010. Series C No. 215, para. 234, the case of *Rosendo Cantú et al* v. *Mexico. Preliminary Exception, Merits, Reparations and Costs.* Sentence of Tuesday, 31 August 2010. Series C No. 216, para. 219, the case of *Ibsen Cárdenas and Ibsen Peña* v. *Bolivia.* Merits, Reparations and Costs. Judgement of 1 September 2010. Series C, No. 217, para. 202, the case of *Vélez Loor* v. *Panama. Preliminary Exceptions, Merits, Reparations and Costs.*
32. *Fallos* 340:47 (2017).
33. Law 27,500 (2018) restored the validity of Arts 288 to 301 of the CCPCN and repealed Law 26,853 (2013) creating the National and Federal Chambers of Cassation which never finally came into operation.

the judges may have their own personal opinion. This doctrine may only be modified by means of a new court ruling (Article 303). The explicit purpose of the appeal for the inapplicability of the law is the unification of jurisprudence.

The Constitution of the province of Buenos Aires establishes that the provincial Supreme Court may intervene whenever a Chamber or collegiate tribunal issues a sentence that erroneously applies the law.[34] The constitutional provision was regulated by the BAPCCPC when it established the extraordinary appeal for the inapplicability of law or legal doctrine.[35]

For the Supreme Court of the Province of Buenos Aires, the legal doctrine referred to in Articles 278 and 279 of the BAPCCPC is the one emanating from its own rulings.[36] This reveals that it is a Cassation Court and may preserve its own interpretations and unify them. The civil procedural codes and constitutions of the other provinces also assign certain functions of cassation or of uniformity of jurisprudence to their Supreme Courts or higher courts.

§4. Evolution of Procedural Legislation

14. The laws of the Indies, which were applied in Hispanic America following its discovery in 1492, and especially, the Compilation of the Laws of the Kingdoms of the Indies (1680), constitute the historical foundations of the Argentine system of civil law.[37] Justice in colonial times was administered by ordinary mayors of first instance, who had civil and commercial jurisdiction and were appointed by the *Cabildo*. The governors were apprised of the decisions taken by the mayors when it became a matter for appeal. The Royal Hearings officiated as superior courts, ruling on the appeals brought against the resolutions taken by the governors, mayors, or other judges in their jurisdiction; and also, originally, in the cases of serious crimes or with regard to people's conditions, or in exceptional circumstances (such

34. Article 161 (3–a).
35. Articles 278–295 of the CPCCBA.
36. In the case of *Torres v. Sancor*, dated 15 July, 2015 (C. 118.968, available at https://juba.scba.gov.ar/VerTextoCompleto.aspx?idFallo=126338, Judge de Lázzari emphasized that due to the particular design of the provincial system of redress, the doctrine established by the SCBA:

> has a very high degree of enforceability (meaning its ability to constrain the judges), which is justified, from a strictly legal point of view by the need to seek and maintain the unity of jurisprudence (e.g., conf. cases Ac. 58,428, ruling of II-17-1998; Ac. 92,695, ruling of 8-III-2007; C. 116.994, ruling of 11-XII-2013), and by the need to monitor the rationality and correctness of the pronouncements.

The judge added that:

> the pronouncements of this SCJBA - meaning those making up its doctrine - show that they have (via the extraordinary recourse of the inapplicability of the law) strong binding effects compared with other instances. Hence, ruling in a way contrary to what is established therein, (which, of course, is possible) requires compelling, substantial and decisive reasons to be given in the opposite sense.

37. *See* E. Oteiza, *Civil Procedure Reforms in Latin America: The Role of the Judge and the Parties in Seeking a Fair Solution*, J. Walker & O. Chase, General Editors, Common Law, Civil Law and the Future of Categories, 224 et seq. 2009.

as cases involving minors, widows, and churches, for instance). The Royal Hearing of Buenos Aires was first created in 1661, although it was only after several vicissitudes that it was finally established in 1783. At the pinnacle of the system stood the Council of the Indies, headquartered in Spain, which exercised exclusive jurisdiction over residence trials. It also dealt with appeals in matters referred by the Royal Hearings when dealing with serious criminal cases or civil and commercial trials that exceeded a certain amount; and, lastly, in an extraordinary instance, in appeals of second supplication, annulment and notorious injustice.

After the country embarked on its process towards independence in 1810, and during the period until the national reorganization and issue of the AC in 1853, numerous ordinances were applied, which gave rise to the so-called homeland law. This was a period when colonial institutions were systematically replaced by new courts and various new regulations were put into place for the administration of justice.

Once the country had been endowed with its institutions following the adoption of the AC in 1853, in line with the Constitution of Philadelphia of 1787, the laws setting up the National Judicial Power were adopted. These set the Supreme Court as the maximum authority in the land, in charge of defining the final interpretation of the AC. Law 27 (1862), which is still in force, albeit with numerous modifications, organizes the federal courts and the intervention of the Supreme Court on appeal.

In 1863, the Supreme Court drew up two bills subsequently converted into law according to the AC. The first gave rise to Law 48, containing regulations on the jurisdiction and competence of federal justice which basically replicates the US Judiciary Act (1789) in terms of the jurisdiction of federal justice and – fundamentally – of the Supreme Court. The second Supreme Court draft bill contained a kind of procedural code for federal justice, subsequently adopted by the Congress in the form of Law 50,[38] whose main source was the Spanish legislation of the nineteenth century, mainly the Civil Procedure Law of 1855. Laws 48 and 50 show how different models were used: regarding the jurisdiction of the Supreme Court and the federal courts, the US model was followed, but for procedural regulations, the Spanish one was preferred.

When Buenos Aires was declared Federal Capital, it became necessary to adopt procedural rules for the judges in charge of deciding conflicts arising from the application of nonfederal legislation, consequently accorded the name of national judges, to differentiate them from the federal ones. Congress thus enacted Law 1893 (1886) on the organization of national justice, whose Article 318 established that national judges were to apply the code of civil procedures in force since 1880 in the Province of Buenos Aires. Like Law 50, this procedural legislation was inspired by the Spanish Prosecution Law of 1855. Until the ACCPC was adopted in 1967, a range of different procedural rules was applied in the context of federal justice (Law 50) and national justice, based in the Federal Capital (Law 1893).

38. Article 374 of Law 50, later repealed by Law 14,237 (1953), established that pre-existing laws (under the homeland law) regulating judicial procedures would be considered as supplementary norms. This rule demonstrates the continuity between colonial legislation and the one dictated after independence regarding judicial procedures.

However, procedural legislation was criticized for not responding to the challenges of its time. Law 50 on the Procedures of the National Courts in Civil and Criminal Law, passed in 1863, and the Code of Procedures in Civil and Commercial Matters, originally adopted by the Province of Buenos Aires and subsequently by the Nation in 1886, were derived from the Hispanic tradition of the first half of the nineteenth century. The Argentine Code of Procedures in Civil and Commercial Matters adopted in 1886 was partially modified by Laws 4128 (1902), 14,237 (1953) and by Decree-Law 23,398/56. It was only in 1967 that Law 17,454, the first procedural code for national and federal justice, was issued. The ACCPC was enacted by the military government in power from 1966 to 1973 and was replicated in most provinces, largely as a consequence of the military government's annulment of federalism in its attempts to centralize the organization of power.

In the Explanation of Reasons of Law 17,454, the Committee in charge of drafting held that a written procedure should be maintained and adapted to the current judicial structures, beyond acknowledging the drawbacks entailed by such systems in terms of the speed and effectiveness of civil proceedings. The ACCPC was modified by the following laws: 20,497 (1973), 21,798 (1977), 22,434 (1981), 24,573 (1995), 24,588 (2001), 26,061 (2005) and 26,589 (2010); however, they were unable to overcome the problems of the lack of speed and immediacy arising from an order designed under a scheme that only served to reproduce its shortcomings.

15. In the framework of the programme known as Justice 2020, the Supreme Court of the Province of Buenos Aires and the Argentine Ministry of Justice and Human Rights launched a joint initiative in 2016 to expand the use of oral hearings in civil procedures in the Province of Buenos Aires. The idea was to increase the quality of jurisdictional decisions through the intermediation of the judge and the concentration of evidence in oral hearings. The purpose of this initiative was thus to speed up the procedures by controlling the length of the trial period and video recording the hearings, without modifying the BAPCCPC.

The system has been adopted by the provinces of San Luis, Formosa, Mendoza, Santa Fe, Entre Ríos, Tucuman, Santiago del Estero, San Juan, Chaco, Tierra del Fuego, Cordoba, Chubut and numerous judges from the national civil jurisdiction circuit with a seat in the City of Buenos Aires. This was a reaction to the lack of immediacy in civil proceedings. The oral hearings initiative was aimed at limiting civil and commercial trials to two hearings, both personally conducted by the judge: a preliminary hearing, aimed at reconciliation, examining the evidence and dealing with any evidence-related issues; followed by a video recording of the hearing to bring all the evidence together; after which the judge issues the sentence.

At the same time as the oral hearings programme was being driven by the Argentine Ministry of Justice and Human Rights, an Expert Commission was set up to lay the foundations for the draft of a new National Procedural Code. The document entitled Fundamentals for Civil and Commercial Procedural Reform (Fundamentals) summarizes the work of the Expert Commission.[39] The Expert Commission

39. Its Fundamentals were approved by Resolution 829/2017 of the MJyDH. The aforementioned document was planned on the basis of a compilation and systematization of documentation performed by María Lilia Gómez Alonso, Eduardo Oteiza and Santiago Pereira Campos. It was circulated on the

presented a bill of the new Argentine Civil and Commercial Procedural Code (draft of the new ACCPC) to the Argentine Ministry of Justice and Human Rights, which has been in parliament since September 2019.[40] This is a regulatory text intended to replace the current ACCPC, and it should be noted that this is the first draft bill of the new Civil Procedure Code submitted for discussion by the Congress during a period in which the AC institutions are functioning in full.

It is a regulatory proposal whose main structure is based on the ordinary procedures used for hearings. The preamble details the scope of the following procedural principles: effective judicial protection, immediacy, concentration and orality, direction and impulse, economy, speed and concentration, transparency and publicity, adaptability of forms and procedural collaboration. It proposes a mixed procedure, entailing acts of proposition (lawsuit, answer and exceptions), briefs, and two video-recorded hearings which act as the oral transmission of events: first, a preliminary hearing (to refine the process of secondary aspects and preliminarily decide on the usefulness of the evidence according to the facts alleged by the parties), and then the trial hearing itself, when the evidence is produced. Special emphasis is placed on collaborative work between judges, parties, lawyers, witnesses, experts and other participants in the process, who must act with loyalty, good faith and truthfulness (without prejudice to respect for the litigant's right not to incriminate themselves criminally, their rights to privacy and professional secrecy).

The new proposal incorporates the digitization of court proceedings, the provisional enforcement of a sentence, and an immediate legal procedure for cases requiring urgent resolution or those which can be resolved in a single hearing due to their lack of complexity and ease of access.

16. It is the responsibility of the Supreme Court to issue the necessary regulations to handle conflicts in an orderly manner (Article 18 of Law 48; Article 10 of Law 4055). The Argentine Justice Regulation (AJR) governing the exercise of these powers was adopted in 1952 and is still in force with numerous modifications amending the duties, rights and obligations of officials and employees, the operation of jurisdictional bodies, and certain formalities of procedural acts. Its powers have been made compatible with the recently recognized prerogative of the Judicial Council (Article 114, paragraph 6, AC). It should be noted that, regarding the use of the aforementioned powers, the Supreme Court issued Decision 32 (2014) creating the National Register of Class Action,[41] and Agreement 12 (2016) adopting the Regulation of the Scope of Action in Class Actions. This is a more rounded

---

www.justicia2020.com.ar platform and through several meetings with academia, the legal profession, members of the Judiciary and social organizations.

40. The Executive Power submitted the draft bill to the Senate through the parliamentary process MEN-2019-178-APN-PTE. The team in charge of drawing up the text of the draft bill submitted to the Expert Commission included Patricia Bermejo, María Lilia Gómez Alonso, Mario Kaminker and Eduardo Oteiza.

41. In Agreement 32 (2014), the Supreme Court, in addition to creating the Register, established regulatory provisions regarding class action, requiring lower-level judges to rule on certain admissibility requirements of class action for the purposes of registration.

approach to this form of group litigation established in the AC, which however still lacks any kind of specific procedural law.[42]

17. Argentina is a signatory to several International Treaties on civil procedural law, as follows: the Montevideo Treaties of 1889 and 1940, on the interspatial application of procedural laws and enforcement of judgments and awards; the Treaty concluded with Italy in 1887 on serving warrants and enforcing judgments; the 1980 Agreement with Uruguay on the equality of procedural treatment and warrants; the Conventions adopted by The Hague Conference on Private International Law on civil procedure (1954) and on obtaining evidence from abroad (1970); the Agreement between the MERCOSUR countries and Bolivia and Chile on cooperation and jurisdictional assistance (Laws 25,934 and 25,935), for instance.

§5. General Characteristics of the Administration of Justice in Civil Matters

I. Principles and Rules Characterizing Civil Procedures

18. The ACCPC is structured on the following principles: (a) the establishment of a prior instance of compulsory mediation; (b) the pre-eminence of the principle under which the parties delimit the scope of proceedings; (c) the allocation of broad powers to the judge regarding the direction taken by the proceedings, its organization and instructions concerning evidence, with limited practical effects, since there is a significant difference between what is established by legislation and judicial practice; (d) structurally contradictory, predominantly written, diluted proceedings held in double instance, with few provisions to promote orality and immediacy; (e) a strong adherence to the statutes of limitation; (f) references to orality, concentration, economy and speed in handling procedures, without specific rules ensuring compliance and a judicial practice reluctant to take effective action; (g) the absence of flexibility regarding the adaptation of the rules to the case in question, and (h) sanctions for abusive conduct or behaviour contrary to the duties of loyalty, honesty and good faith.

In certain cases, the legislator has provided for the particular modulations of each of these principles in order to facilitate the defence and protection of the rights at stake, and the judges have adopted the same attitude based on the claims in litigation.

19. The requirement for mandatory prior mediation was established by Law 24,573 (1995). This was initially a temporary experience intended to last for five years, but Laws 25,287 (2000) and 26,368 (2008) subsequently extended this

42. In Agreement 12 (2016), the Supreme Court established a series of agreements aimed at ordering the way class action procedures were managed in order to avoid circumstances liable to lead to situations of institutional gravity, until such time as Congress passes a law to regulate these procedures.

period, and Law 26,589 (2010) established it definitively. To be a mediator, candidates must be lawyers with three years of experience, having received special training as established in the regulations, and registered in the National Mediation Register. All provinces except those of La Rioja and Santa Cruz employ mediation prior to the start of civil proceedings.

20. The principle under which the parties delimit the scope of proceedings manifests itself in the fact that: (a) the start of the procedure and the defence, as well as its conclusion, must answer to the will of the parties expressed when making and answering the claims, with the corresponding contribution of evidence; (b) this is a judicial practice that leaves procedural direction in the hands of the parties, without prejudice to the fact that the ACCPC imposes on the judges the duty – which is breached on a regular basis – of not holding up the procedure (Article 36, section 1, ACCPC) and of driving the process ex officio in certain cases of public interest (Article 36, section 5, ACCPC); (c) substantive law is available in the course of the procedure (search, desist, transaction), releasing the parties; (d) there are limits to the judicial decision, due to the principle of consistency (Article 34, section 4, ACCPC); and (e) the burden rests exclusively on the parties to provide facts and evidence, without prejudice to the goodwill of the judge.

21. Other precepts empower the judge to order evidence ex officio, such as deciding whether to take testimony from people mentioned by the parties in the procedural brief, or when, according to other evidence produced, they had knowledge of certain facts that could influence decision-making in the case (Article 452, ACCPC); or whether to summon experts or technical consultants, to question them about whatever is deemed necessary; or to order the addition of existing documents held by the parties or third parties (Articles 387 to 389, ACCPC). Likewise, it is up to the judge to interrogate the parties ex officio (Articles 415, ACCPC); and request explanations about the facts subject to testimonial evidence (Article 438, ACCPC); freely question witnesses (Article 442, ACCPC); handle confrontations (Article 448, ACCPC); set points of expertise and order scientific exams (Articles 460 and 475, ACCPC).

As for the direction of the judicial procedure itself, the body is empowered with certain duties as regards the concentration of acts, consolidating and economizing procedures (Article 34, section 5, ACCPC). Likewise, judges must take the measures necessary to avoid holding up the process (Article 36, section 1, ACCPC), being empowered to: impose progressive pecuniary sanctions as a way of getting the parties to comply (Article 37, ACCPC); integrate litigation when necessary in a consortium (Article 89, ACCPC); provide for the in limine rejection of manifestly inadmissible statements; accumulate procedures (Article 190, ACCPC), etc. In practice, the powers-duties of judges are only exercised exceptionally, and the prevailing culture among judges of the JP shows that in practice they tend to neglect their duties relating to immediacy.

One example of the distance between the provisions enshrined in the ACCPC and what judges do in practice is the constant breach of their duty to order the necessary evidence to clarify the truth, respecting the parties' right of defence (Article 36,

ACCPC). The vast majority of judges do not decide on evidentiary measures without an explicit request by the parties, despite the fact that the ACCPC imposes this duty on them.

22. The structure of the procedure rests on the right to be heard and legality of form, with few concessions made to the availability of the parties. It is the generic duty of the judge to ensure that the greatest procedural economy is sought when treating cases (Article 34, section 5e, ACCPC), and accordingly concentrate proceedings and ensure their celerity. The principle of finality or instrumentality (Article 169, ACCPC) acts as a palliative within the system of legality, making it more flexible so that ritual excesses can be avoided in the interests of meeting the purpose of the proceedings.

There is also a strict preclusion system in place which splits up the procedure into stages or periods (Articles 333, paragraph 1, 346, among others, ACCPC).

23. The ACCPC adopts the double instance approach, which may be accessed by means of an appeal, with very few concessions to immediacy and oral transmission, since hearings are not regulated before the judges of the Appeals Court, whether this is to lodge the appeal or to improve the arguments.

II. Fundamental Guarantees

24. Article 18 of the AC establishes the inviolability of a person's right to defence and other rights. As the 1996 constitutional reform established that human rights treaties have constitutional hierarchy (Article 75, section 22, AC), the scope of the guarantee provided by Article 18 of the AC is broadened by the provisions of Article XVIII of the American Declaration of the Rights and Duties of Man, Article 14 of the Civil and Political Rights Covenant, and Article 8 of the American Convention on Human Rights.

25. Both the constitutional provision and the rules established in the international human rights treaties were developed on the basis of the interpretation of their scope, made by the Supreme Court and the Inter-American and Universal systems for the protection of human rights.

One of the Supreme Court's first interventions regarding the guarantee of the inviolability of a person's right to defence in court took place in *Martinez* (1894),[43] where the Supreme Court considered that this guarantee is not violated when the accused has been heard in their defence within the full breadth of the ordinary procedure. Later, in *Mollo Martín* (1913),[44] it held that 'the inviolability of the defence means that the litigant must be heard and be in a position to exercise their rights in the form and with the solemnities established by the common laws of procedure'.

In this first stage, the Supreme Court understood that the constitutional parameters were met as the steps established in the procedural codes were followed. The

43. *Fallos* 63:102.
44. *Fallos* 119:156.

aforementioned interpretation of the Supreme Court underwent a substantial change in the second half of the twentieth century with the adoption of the so-called doctrine of arbitrariness of the appealed sentence, a change also reflected in different provincial jurisdictions. The Supreme Court, in numerous rulings, admitted the presentation of extraordinary resources to examine procedural questions, or flagrant and notorious misinterpretations of substantial law requiring questions of fact and evidence to be examined. One example of the breadth of meaning ascribed to the guarantee of defence, as understood in court, is *Colalillo* (1957)[45] concerning overt ritual excess. It was argued in this case that:

> the Civil proceedings cannot be conducted in strictly formal terms. This is certainly not about the performance of capricious rites, but rather the development of procedures aimed at establishing objective legal truth, which is their goal. In accordance with this, current procedural law disposes that judges may have, at any stage of the trial, the power to order the measures necessary to clarify the facts being debated.

In reference to the concept of undue and unreasonable duration in divorce proceedings initiated in 1954, where litigation could not be blocked until 1960, the Supreme Court in *Cavura de Vlaslov v. Vlaslov* (1960)[46] held that 'the constitutional guarantee of defence in trial basically assumes the possibility of appearing before a court in search of justice, something which must not be frustrated by procedural or factual considerations...' and that 'the concept of deprivation of justice may be referred to the circumstances in which it is invoked, insofar as it turns out that what is decided and appealed deprives the exercise of the right under debate of all reasonable utility'.

As for the interpretation made by the judges of procedural rules, in *Oilher* (1980),[47] the Supreme Court concluded that:

> Procedural regulations, which are both indispensable and legally valuable, cannot be reduced to the mere technique of the formal organization of procedures, but, in their specific scope, have the purpose and objective of properly ordering the exercise of rights in order to achieve the realization of the value of justice in each case, and safeguard the guarantee of the right to defence by trial. This cannot be achieved if there is no attempt to pay attention to the objective legal truth of the facts that, notwithstanding, appear in the case as being of decisive relevance for the fair decision of litigation.

The *Oilher* doctrine was thus confirmed in *BANADE v. Catella,*[48] (1994) where the Supreme Court ruled that:

45. *Fallos* 238:550.
46. *Fallos* 246:86.
47. *Fallos* 302:1611.
48. *Fallos* 317:1759.

> Procedural regulation cannot be reduced to the mere technique of the formal organization of procedures, but, in their specific scope, have the purpose and objective of properly ordering the exercise of rights in order to achieve the fulfilment of the value of justice in each case, and safeguard the right to a fair defence by trial. This cannot be achieved if there is no attempt to pay attention to the objective legal truth of the facts that, notwithstanding, appear in the case as of decisive relevance for the fair decision of litigation.

26. Lastly, mention should be made of some decisions taken by the IACHR complementing the progress made on the scope of the guarantee of due process in Argentina. At the end of 2002, the IACHR handed down its first sentence stating that the Argentine State had violated the ACHR in *Cantos.*[49]

The IACHR's sentence declared that the Argentine State had violated Articles 8 and 25 of the ACHR in relation to Article 1.1 thereof, to the detriment of Mr Cantos. In the opinion of the Inter-American Court, these violations involved legal fees and costs, which were considered true barriers to access to justice.

The *obiter dictum* of the sentence is very useful in gaining an understanding of the scope assigned by the IACHR to the obligations of the State in accordance with Articles 8 and 25 of the American Convention. Some of the more relevant paragraphs for this point are quoted below:

> States have, as part of their general obligations, a positive duty to provide guarantees with respect to the individuals subject to their jurisdiction. This involves taking all necessary measures to remove any obstacles that may exist so that individuals can enjoy the rights that the Convention recognizes. Consequently, the State's tolerance of circumstances or conditions preventing individuals from accessing adequate internal remedies to protect their rights constitutes a violation of Article 1.1 of the Convention.

The IACHR thus reinforces the concept of the violation of Article 1.1 of the ACHR by highlighting the positive duty to provide guarantees imposed upon a State to ensure that all the necessary measures are taken to eliminate barriers limiting access to internal resources for the protection of rights. It adds that Article 8 of the IACHR enshrines people's right of access to justice, which means that States may not place obstacles in the way of those seeking judges or courts with a view to determining or protecting their rights. Any internal rule or measure that imposes costs or in any other way hinders individual access to the courts, which cannot be justified by the reasonable needs of the administration of justice, must be understood as being contrary to the aforementioned Article 8.1 of the Convention.

In a case which set a precedent in 2012, that of *Furlan,*[50] the IACHR established the responsibility of the Argentine State for failing to guarantee the reasonable duration of the procedures foreseen in Article 8 of the ACHR. The IAHCR examined

---

49. Ruling of Thursday, 28 November 2002, Series C, No. 97, https://www.corteidh.or.cr/docs/casos/articulos/seriec_97_ing.pdf.
50. Ruling of 31 August 2012, Series C, No. 246. https://www.corteidh.or.cr/docs/casos/articulos/seriec_246_ing.pdf.

the reasonableness of the period which elapsed from the filing of the lawsuit to the final stage of the execution of the sentence with effective payment, a process which took about thirteen years. Accordingly, it highlighted the relevance of the operations of judicial pronouncements in the domestic sphere in the context of the functional enforcement of the principle of effective judicial protection.

Part I. Organization of the Judiciary

Chapter 1. The Judiciary

§1. Organization of the JP and the Provincial Courts

27. The Supreme Court is the highest instance in the hierarchy of the JP and before it function the General Public Prosecutor and the National Public Defender's Office General. It has appellate jurisdiction over all matters governed by the AC and the Laws of the Nation (Article 117, AC) and also enjoys original and exclusive jurisdiction over all matters concerning ambassadors, ministers and foreign consuls, as well as over those where a province may be a party. In the event of recusal, vacancy or leave of absence of any of the Supreme Court Justices, a substitute may be drawn from the roster of Chief Justices of the Federal Courts of Appeal, or otherwise from a list comprising ten lawyers selected by the EP and approved by the Senate. These are known as *conjueces* or associate judges (Article 22, Decree-Law 1285/58, according to amended Law 23,498 – 1987).

Although the Supreme Court took as its model the version detailed in the US Constitution, there are significant differences between both bodies: the US Supreme Court only rules on some one hundred and fifty cases every year, whereas the Argentine Supreme Court settles several thousands.[51]

The 1994 constitutional reform created the National Judicial Council and assigned it a number of judicial and administrative tasks, such as appointing judges and exercising a disciplinary function (Article 114, AC). The reform also created an impeachment jury answering to the National Judicial Council, made up of legislators, judges and lawyers (Article 115, AC) empowered to remove judges from lower courts.

28. The Public Ministry comprises the General Public Prosecutor's Office, headed up by the Public Prosecutor, and the Public Defender General's Office headed up by the Public Defender General. The Public Prosecutor's Office is charged with defending the public interest and legality, while the responsibility of the Public Defender's Office is to provide legal assistance. Section 120 of the 1994 constitution laid down that the Public Ministry was an independent body with functional and financial autonomy. It does not depend on the EP or it is part of the JP. Law 24,946 (1998) explains how the structure works: the Public Prosecutor's Office

51. In 2018, the Supreme Court handed down 6,814 judgments, according to the information published on its website https://www.csjn.gov.ar/datos-estadisticos/graficos-2018.

is made up of the PGN, the public prosecutors acting before the Supreme Court, and the public prosecutor in charge of administrative investigations as well as the public prosecutors acting before Courts of First Instance and other auxiliary staff. The Public Defender General's Office is comprised of the Public Defender General, official defenders acting before the Supreme Court, public defenders appointed to represent minors and incompetent persons before lower courts, as well as deputy defenders and auxiliary staff. Public guardians and curators also answer to the Public Defender's Office (Article 4, Law 24,946).

29. The 1994 constitutional reform (Article 86) created an independent and functionally autonomous body within the orbit of the Congress, the Defender of the People, which is effectively an ombudsman. Its primary responsibility is the defence and protection of human rights as well as other rights, guarantees and interests protected both by the AC and by legislation, in the event of acts or omissions on the part of the administration. It also has oversight over the exercise of public administrative functions. The AC endowed it with legal standing to represent the aforementioned individual and collective rights.[52]

30. The Congress has created several lower courts which may be classified in terms of the scope of their territorial and material jurisdiction.

In the city of Buenos Aires, the following have jurisdiction over federal matters: the Federal Courts of Appeal for civil and commercial law, administrative law, social security, and electoral law, with their respective trial courts.

There are 15 Courts of Appeal operating in the rest of the country, in the cities of La Plata, Bahia Blanca, Mar del Plata, San Martin,[53] Comodoro Rivadavia,[54] Cordoba, Corrientes, General Roca, Mendoza, Parana, Misiones, Resistencia, Salta and Tucuman.

As mentioned earlier, the 1994 constitutional reform endowed the City of Buenos Aires with the autonomy to enact its own laws and create courts (Article 129, AC). However, Law 24,588 (1997) disposed that ordinary national judges were to retain their status in the JP.

Jurisdiction in matters governed by substantive law in the city of Buenos Aires lies with three Courts of Appeal for civil, commercial and labour law, and their respective Courts of First Instance.

31. The organization of the Judicial Branches of the various provinces is regulated by the respective provincial Constitutions (Articles 1, 5 and 121 of the AC). In the province of Buenos Aires – whose institutions are largely similar to those of

52. Law 24,284 (1993) regulates the functions of the Defender of the People. In the case of the *Defensor del Pueblo v. ENARGAS* (*Fallos* 328:1652–2005), the Supreme Court recognized the Defender of the People's legal capacity to allege unconstitutionality and defend collective advocacy rights.
53. The Federal Appeals Courts of the province of Buenos Aires are in La Plata, Bahia Blanca, Mar del Plata, and San Martin.
54. The jurisdiction of certain Federal Courts extends beyond provincial lines. Please *see* the Federal Justice map at http://www.consejomagistratura.gov.ar/index.php/botonpresidencia/1654-mapa-de-la-justicia-federal

other provinces – the AC establishes the composition of the Judicial Branch, including the Supreme Court, Appeals Court, and Courts of First Instance with jurisdiction in civil and commercial law, family law and administrative law. In each department of the province of Buenos Aires, there is also a small claims court except in those locations where the headquarters of each judicial department is based or where there are trial courts in civil and commercial law in operation.

Law 15,057 (2018), currently being implemented, aims to turn the labour courts into Courts of First Instance whose rulings may be appealed before a Chamber.

The Supreme Court of the Province of Buenos Aires is presided by seven justices and the General Prosecutor, with jurisdiction over the entire province, including both original jurisdiction (in local actions based on claims of unconstitutionality, conflicts of jurisdiction), and appellate jurisdiction as a court of cassation.

The Constitution of the Province of Buenos Aires, also reformed in 1994, created the Judicial Council for the selection of judges (Article 175).

§2. Judges

I. Independence

32. The AC forbids the executive from exercising judicial functions (Article 109, AC). To ensure the independence of judges, they are guaranteed security of tenure and their salaries may not be touched. The first guarantee (*see* Articles 99, paragraph 4, and 110 of the AC) means that all judges may remain in office while observing good behaviour and cannot be removed without a prior impeachment to determine if they have incurred in any of the acts described in the AC or in the law (Articles 53, 59, and 115, AC). The 1994 reform of the AC provided that judges must tender their resignation when they reach the age of 75. Article 94, paragraph 4 of the AC establishes that when a judge reaches the age of 75, a new one must be appointed with the prior approval of the Senate.

Security of tenure also includes the right of judges not to be transferred to a different judicial district without their consent, even in those cases where their new position is not of a lower rank.

The guarantee of unencroachability of compensation enshrined in Article 110 of the AC states that judges shall receive a compensation determined by law for their services, and that such compensation may not be reduced in any way for as long as they remain in office.

Members of the Public Ministry enjoy functional immunities and their salaries are guaranteed in the sense that they may not be touched (Article 120, AC).

II. Selection Mechanisms

33. The power conferred by the AC on the president of Argentina to propose candidates for the office of Supreme Court Justice to the Senate (Article 99, paragraph 4, AC) is governed by Decree No. 222/2003. Regarding the qualifications required, the aforementioned decree established that differences in gender, expertise, and regional provenance should be taken into account when proposing candidates to the Senate. When a vacancy opens up in the Supreme Court, the Argentine president has thirty days to nominate a candidate, whose name is published in the Official Gazette and in two national newspapers, with details of their curriculum and background as well as information about their professional activity. Following this publication, citizens and nongovernmental organizations, professional associations, academic and human rights institutions have fifteen days in which to make comments and raise objections. After this deadline, the president is free to submit a nomination to the Senate which may, in a public session, confirm it if approved by two-thirds of the members present.

34. The Argentine Judicial Council participates in the first part of the proceedings to select lower-court judges. Article 114 of the AC empowered the Congress to pass the law on the composition of the National Judicial Council, requiring an absolute majority vote by the members of both Lower and Upper Houses. However, it indicated expressly that the law governing the National Judicial Council's composition should seek to set a balance between representatives of the political bodies elected by the people, judges from all levels, federal registered lawyers and representatives from academia and scientific fields. This constitutional provision was one of the central issues in the 1994 constitutional debate, as the prior political agreement recognized that the process for selecting judges proposed by EP with the approval of the Senate, enshrined in the 1853/1860 constitution, fostered mistrust concerning judges' political independence. The purpose behind the inclusion of judges, lawyers and academics in the National Judicial Council was to ensure the independence of the judiciary by setting more objective selection criteria.

Law 24,937 (1997) thus established a fixed number of representatives to include judges, lawmakers, figures from the executive power and from academia, which was subsequently modified by Laws 26,080 (2006) and 26,855 (2013). The latter substantially altered the make-up of the body by incorporating another lawyer and five academics and scientists, and altered the way the members were elected by proposing direct universal suffrage. However, the Supreme Court, when it intervened *per saltum* in *Rizzo*,[55] declared this modification to be unconstitutional, as it upset the constitutional balance by disposing that all the members of the Supreme Court would have affiliations to the party political system.

The Supreme Court maintained that the regulation undermined the principle of representation of the technical foundations by enabling the direct election of judges, lawyers, academics and scientists, thus compromising judicial independence by obliging judges to intervene in partisan differences. The effect of this would be to distort the process to select the members of a body enshrined in the AC. As a result of the Supreme Court's ruling, the summons to elections for the offices of judicial counsellors representing the judges from all instances, as well as of federally registered lawyers and figures from academia and science, were rendered null and void.

55. *Fallos* 336:760 (2013).

35. Prospective judges are selected through a process of competitive examination and assessment organized by the National Judicial Council, which appoints the jury and draws up the three-person shortlists with a quorum of two-thirds of its members (Article 114, paragraph 1 of Law 24,937, restated text as per Decree No. 816/1999, amended by Law 26,080 – 2006). The shortlist prepared by the National Judicial Council is binding for the president of Argentina, who must choose one of the three candidates proposed. Decree No. 588/2003 establishes that after the shortlist is submitted to the president, it must be published to provide citizens and non-governmental organizations the opportunity to make comments and objections during a fifteen-day period. After the deadline, the Argentine president selects the prospective judge from the three shortlisted candidates and sends the nomination to the Senate, which confirms it in a public session on the basis of the candidates' qualifications.

36. There is no set career path or formally structured legally based promotional ladder within the JP. Promotions are not pre-established, and access to different posts is enabled by competitive examination, including the assessment of candidates' qualifications and background. Judges wishing to advance in the judicial structure must take these competitive exams and be assessed by the National Judicial Council. If they make it through to the three-person shortlist, they must wait for the PEN to submit the nomination to the Senate for confirmation. Seniority is one of the factors taken into account, but it is by no means decisive.

37. To be eligible for nomination as a Supreme Court Justice, candidates must be Argentine citizens, hold a law degree from an Argentine university, must have practised for at least eight years and have the qualifications required to be a senator (Article 111, AC; Article 4, Decree-Law 1285/58). To be eligible for nomination as an Appeal Court judge, a judge on the Court of Criminal Cassation, or the Oral Court, candidates must be Argentine citizens, hold a law degree and must have practised, or held judicial office, for six years, and be at least 30 years old (Article 5, Decree-Law 1285/58). The requirements for trial court judges are basically the same, except that they only need to have four years' practice and be at least 25 years old (Article 6, Decree-Law 1285/58).

38. The General Public Prosecutor and the National Public Defender General are appointed by the Executive Branch and confirmed by the Senate by a two-thirds majority. Other officials from the Public Prosecution and the Public Defender's Office are chosen to draw up a three-member shortlist submitted to the president of Argentina by the National Judicial Council, following a competitive examination and assessment of qualifications and background. Once the shortlist is submitted to the president, the procedure for comments established in Decree 588/2003 must be followed. The requirements are similar to those established for judges.

III. Disciplinary System and Removal

39. The National Judicial Council is charged with exercising disciplinary control over judges. Law 24,937 (restated text as per Decree 816/1999, section 14, under Law 26,080) provides that the following actions taken by judges render them liable to disciplinary action. These are: (1) the violation of statutory and regulatory provisions governing prohibitions and exclusions; (2) the failure to observe the consideration and respect owed to other judges; (3) incorrect treatment of attorneys, experts, support personnel or litigants; (4) acts inconsistent with the deference owed to judges or compromising the dignity of such position; (5) repeated failure to comply with procedural and regulatory provisions; (6) repeated absence from the court or repeated failure by the court where they sit to observe its opening hours; and (7) failure to perform, or negligence in the observance of their duties and obligations as set forth in the RFJN.

The National Judicial Council Disciplinary Committee, consisting of nine members (two senators, two members of the House of Representatives, two judges, one representative of the PEN, one lawyer and one academic), is responsible for presenting the National Judicial Council, sitting as a full body, with its proposal for disciplinary actions.[56] Disciplinary offences by judges in matters relating to the effective rendering of justice may be punished with a reprimand, a warning and a fine of up to 30% of their salaries.

40. With respect to the Public Ministry, disciplinary powers over officials for failing to perform their duties are exercised by the General Public Prosecutor and the National Public Defender General, who may impose penalties including reprimands, warnings and fines. Administrative appeals may be filed against these disciplinary resolutions and when such remedies have been exhausted, an appeal may also be filed with the courts (Article 16, Law 24,946).

41. Nonfederal judges of any level may only be removed for 'misconduct or criminal offences in the performance of their duties or for common offenses' (Articles 53, 59, 60, 110, and 115, AC). In the case of Supreme Court Justices, impeachment proceedings may commence following an accusation by the Lower House, which must previously declare the admissibility of such impeachment by the qualified majority of its members. The Senate is then charged with the duty of trying the accused in public proceedings, where due process must be observed. A two-thirds majority of members present is required to find the accused guilty. The only effect of the Senate's decision is to remove the accused and, where appropriate, to disqualify them from holding public office, without prejudice to their criminal liability before nonfederal courts.

Short-term political issues, rather than an examination of whether the judge impeached had incurred in any of the instances described above, have for the most part been the reason for impeachment proceedings brought against Supreme Court Justices. In 1947, three Supreme Court Justices and the Attorney General were removed from office. The de facto government which broke the constitutional order

56. Article 8.2 of Law 26,680.

in 1943 received a number of adverse judgments from the Supreme Court, and when Perón was elected as president in the 1945 elections, he declared in his inaugural address to Congress that: 'I place the spirit of justice above the Judiciary.' These words were the preamble to a process of impeachment, ending in the removal of the Supreme Court Justices who had handed down judgments against the decisions taken by the military government of which Perón himself had been part. The Supreme Court Justices appointed in the aftermath of these impeachment proceedings clearly answered to the ruling party; they agreed to be appointed as partisan representatives to a constitutional convention that adopted the 1949 constitutional reform. Following the revolution that overthrew the Perón government, all judges were declared to be holding office on an interim basis, and the guarantee of security of tenure was overturned. The alternating civilian and military governments that followed led to the continued replacement of the Supreme Court Justices.[57]

As mentioned above (§3), two of the Supreme Court Justices were removed from office thanks to the content of the judgments they handed down in 2004 and 2005.

The National Judicial Council has the power to commence impeachment proceedings to remove lower-court judges (Article 115, paragraph 5, AC). Removal proceedings are conducted before an Impeachment Jury consisting of two judges, four representatives of Congress and an attorney (Law 23,937, restated text as per Decree 816/1999, Article 22, according to Law 26,080).[58]

IV. Liability

42. Under the general principles of the ACCC, judges are liable before private parties for any harm arising from the performance of their duties (Articles 1765 and 1766, ACCC). While impeachment does not require them to be first stripped of immunity by the political court, case law largely holds that this is in fact required, as well as the examination and assessment of the conduct with which they are charged. Some provincial laws expressly authorize their trial by a civil court, without requiring that they first be removed or suspended (Article 119, paragraph 2 of the Constitution of the Province of Santa Fe).

43. Judges may also be held criminally liable under the same conditions (for taking bribes, breach of public duties, denial and malicious delay of justice).

57. For more information about the unstable composition of the Supreme Court arising from the alternating civil and military governments, please *see* E. Oteiza, La Corte Suprema. Entre la justicia sin política y la política sin justicia, and A. Carrió, La Corte Suprema y su independencia (Abeledo Perrot, 1996), A. Garay, A, A Doctrine of Precedent in the Making: The Case of the Argentine Supreme's Court Case Law, Law, Vol. 25:2, 258, J. Miller, Judicial Review and Constitutional Stability: A Sociology of the U.S. Model and its Collapse in Argentina), Hastings International and Comparative Journal, 21:77–176 (1997).

58. According to the legal texts prior to the reform of Law 26,080, the jury comprised three judges, three legislators and three lawyers. The number of legislators rose to four following the reform while the numbers of judges and lawyers fell.

V. Exclusions

44. First of all, judicial functions are incompatible with 'any political activity' (Article 9 of Decree-Law 1285/58), meaning that they may not be 'members of political parties' and 'act in politics' (Article 8, paragraph c of the RJN).

Decree-Law 1285/58 also forbids judges from 'engaging in trade' (Article 9) and, even more generically, from performing 'any activities for profit without the authorization of the appropriate higher authority' (Article 8, (j) of the RFNJ). They are barred from teaching in primary or secondary school institutions, although they may be university professors and participate in honorary study committees, with prior authorization from the higher authority (Article 9 of Decree-Law 1285/58). Argentine judges are forbidden from gambling or from frequenting gambling premises or carrying out any acts that might compromise the dignity of their office (Article 9, cit.). Persons related by blood or marriage up to the fourth degree may not sit as judges on the same court at the same time (Article 8 of Decree-Law 1285/58).

VI. Duties

45. The basic duty falling to judges is to render duly substantiated decisions concerning the requests made by the parties, observing the rank of the laws in force and the principle of consistency (Article 34 (4), ACCPC). Any unwarranted delay in issuing rulings is considered a serious offence, and in the case of final judgments, the judge may be penalized with a fine, without prejudice to their other liabilities or impeachment, if relevant (Articles 167168, ACCPC). In the province of Buenos Aires, Article 15 of the Constitution establishes that cases must be decided within a reasonable period; any delays in handing down a sentence, as well as undue delays, if repeated, constitute a serious offence.

The principle of immediacy contemplated in Article 34 (1) of the ACCPC obliges a judge to sit at the preliminary hearing and envisages that they may only delegate procedural acts to others when expressly authorized to do so by law. Surprisingly, the 2001 reform (Law 25,488) repealed the provision to the effect that hearings not attended by a judge were invalid. Article 360, as amended by Law 25,488, provides that if the judge is not present, the hearing may not take place and a record to that effect is entered in the attendance book.

Law 25,488 also amended Article 36 of the ACCPC. According to the previous wording, the judge was empowered to take measures to avoid proceedings being held up and order those necessary to determine the truth of the matters at stake. The rewording obliged the judge to actively move proceedings ahead and investigate as an intrinsic duty.

Since the enactment of the ACCPC in 1968, successive amendments to the text expanded the powers vested in court assistants, such as clerks and deputy clerks. Articles 38 and 39 list the various procedures that court assistants may perform.

The position of a court clerk, nowadays held by a law-school graduate, has a long tradition in Argentina. Although clerks were originally confined to keeping case files in order and certifying signatures and copies, as the workload of the judges increased, these began to delegate other tasks to the clerks, such as preparing draft rulings, attending hearings and supervising lower officials, among others. Later, the clerks themselves were allowed to delegate certain court activities to lower-ranking officials. The customary organizational structure of courts now envisages a judge, a clerk and ten employees. The result of this practice is a substantial increase in delegation and the ensuing lack of immediacy on the part of the judge.

The new draft bill of the ACCPC mentioned in paragraph 15 included among its objectives the need to reverse the lack of immediacy. Article 2 highlights the importance assigned to the immediacy between the judge and the parties, together with the concrete establishment of a judicial practice aimed at concentrating procedural activity, avoiding the harmful and unnecessary fragmentation of the process. A trial hearing, with adequate oral content, has shown itself to be a technique favouring immediacy by concentrating or bringing together the different stages and procedures. This creates better conditions that help to meet the objective of concluding the trial without undue delay.

This principle dovetails with the rule foreseen in Article 45 (d) of the new draft bill of the ACCPC establishing the judge's duty to personally attend and direct the hearings. It is important to note that in order to ensure compliance, hearings must be presided uninterruptedly by the judge and will be considered invalid if the judge is not present or absents themselves during the proceedings. The nullity sanction is absolute and may not be validated; it may be deducted or declared ex officio at any procedural opportunity.

To this, it should be added that Article 90 (a) of the new draft bill of the ACCPC disposes that hearings be video recorded rather than transcribed. Video recording is a key element when it comes to ensuring that a hearing is effectively carried out in the context of immediacy, as the best way of achieving the cooperation necessary through dialogue between the judge and the parties. Article 2 of this measure on immediacy, concentration and orality complements the judge's duty to be present and ensures evidence of compliance by means of video recording, without allowing for exceptions. In turn, it dovetails with the judge's duty foreseen in Article 45 (i) to manage the hearing agenda, taking into account the order in which lawsuits are filed, their complexity, and the need to develop jurisdictional activity with sufficient agility to ensure that the dates of the hearings are of public knowledge. This also embraces the issues of transparency and publicity recognized as principles in Article 8.

The direction taken by the proceedings is left to the judge (Article 3), who is responsible for driving it forward (Article 5). However, the initiative as such corresponds to the parties involved in the proceedings, responsible for providing both evidence and proof, and the recognition of rights (Article 4). The so-called principle of cooperation preserves the notion of self-determination, meaning respect for the decisions making up the framework of individual freedoms enshrined in the AC. This recognition is clearly linked to Article 14 in that it acknowledges the right of the parties to make procedural agreements.

Chapter 2. Lawyers

§1. Practice of the Legal Profession

I. The Teaching of Law

46. Article 75 (18) of the AC entrusts the Congress with the task of drawing up 'plans for general and university education'.[59] Law 24,521 (1995)[60] governs higher education, and Decree 256 (1996) provides that a law degree may only be granted by institutions authorized to operate as universities or university institutes (Article 10). There are twenty-nine law schools attached to national or provincial universities, where enrolment is free, and a further thirty-nine in private universities. Around 30,000 new students enrol every year at all these universities, but only some 11,600 graduate as lawyers every year, while approximately 19,100 new students enrol every year at private university law schools and a yearly average of 7,053[61] graduate every year. These figures show that there are high desertion levels among students reading law, and so far no public policy has been drawn up to address this situation.

II. Requirements to Practice Law

47. Lawyers must register with both the various bar associations and the courthouses before being allowed to practice. In order to appear before the federal courts or the Supreme Court, lawyers must register with the Federal Courts of Appeal. The bar associations of the various provincial jurisdictions and the city of Buenos Aires grant licenses to practice before local courts, and lawyers usually register in all the jurisdictions where they practice. The requirement to register with the bar associations of each jurisdiction where a lawyer practices has been ratified by the Supreme Court.[62]

Professional licence is granted to lawyers holding the required degree awarded by a national or private university, as long as they are not barred from practice by being involved in the instances of conflict or exclusion established in the legislation applicable in their respective jurisdiction. Thus, an academic degree, per se, authorizes and licenses lawyers to practice, since no other specific post-graduate or speciality degrees or in-court practice are required. Nor have any examinations or revalidation procedures been established as requirements for granting a professional licence. Registration in the professional register authorizes attorneys to practice before both first instance and appellate courts, including the Supreme Court.

---

59. Article 75 (18) of the AC guarantees free state public education, as well as the independence and self-sufficiency of national bodies.
60. Partially modified by Law 27,204 (2015).
61. Statistics on the Argentine university system may be found at: https://www.argentina.gob.ar/educacion/universidades/informacion/publicaciones/anuarios, while the 2015 yearbook may be consulted at https://www.argentina.gob.ar/sites/default/files/anuario_2015_2.pdf.
62. *Fallos* 308:987 (1986).

The ACCPC establishes the obligation to be represented by a lawyer in legal proceedings (Article 56). There is a similar disposition in force at local level.

In the province of Buenos Aires, Article 93 of Law 5177 (1947)[63] establishes an exception for parties wishing to act without legal representation in certain situations. However, this provision has in practice been repealed as it has fallen into disuse.

The laws governing the exercise of the legal profession foresee situations of incompatibility. For example, judges, court personnel and employees of the judiciary may not be practising lawyers.

III. Rights and Obligations

48. Lawyers are on a par with judges as regards the consideration and respect they are owed (Article 58, ACCPC). It is their exclusive prerogative – professional monopoly – to respond to legal inquiries and represent their clients in court. Courts are, furthermore, forbidden from hearing a petition lodged by a party if not represented by a lawyer (Article 56, ACCPC).

Lawyers have the right to communicate freely with the clients they defend who are under arrest or in prison, and to be granted unrestricted access to files and administrative offices to obtain background material relating to the matters in question, except for that classified as confidential. They also have the right to obtain detailed information concerning the reasons for their client's arrest and to collect the compensation ruled in the respective legal and regulatory provisions

Their specific duties, as detailed in the Code of Ethics, are to observe professional secrecy; faithfully comply with the Constitution and the Law; accept and carry out the assignments entrusted to them by the bar association to advise and defend those unable to pay legal fees, and to act with loyalty, integrity and good faith in the practice of their profession. They are forbidden from simultaneously or successively advising or representing opposing interests in the same proceedings; from authorizing persons who, although not lawyers, carry out activities reserved for attorneys, to use their signature or name; from publishing misleading or unethical advertising, and from using paid intermediaries to secure business.

49. The fees lawyers receive for their activities both in and out of court are established in both federal and national jurisdictions[64] by Law 27,423 (2017).[65] According to the legislation, the court is responsible for calculating the fees due when issuing a ruling or when the lawyer ceases to act in representation of a party (Articles 15, 52, 53 and 12, Law 27,423). When setting fees, a court must take the following guidelines into account: the amount claimed in the case, and if it is liable to appreciate in pecuniary terms; the value, reasons, duration and legal quality of the work itself; the complexity and novelty of the issue at stake, the responsibility

63. *See* the text passed by Decree 2885 (2001), incorporating the modifications introduced by Law 13,419 (2006).
64. Each one of the 23 provinces has different rules regarding legal fees, which are nonetheless similar.
65. Laws have been passed at provincial level to regulate the various aspects of legal fees.

accruing to the professional regarding the specifics of the case; the results obtained, and how likely it is that the resolution reached will have repercussions for future cases; the moral and economic relevance of the issue at stake for the parties involved, and the minimum amounts established (Article 16, Law 27,423).

50. Law 27,423 establishes a Rate Measurement Unit (*Unidad de Medida Arancelaria*, or UMA), which is equivalent to 3% of the basic fee assigned to a federal judge of first instance, and specifies the number of units to be awarded according to the professional task involved.

If the trial pursues the object of determining rights that can be measured in economic terms, the law establishes a table of legal fees as a percentage which is proportionally reduced as the amount of the value of the trial increases, given in the aforementioned Rate Measurement Units.[66]

The Supreme Court has ruled that such percentages may be reduced when excessively burdensome. In *Provincia de Santa Cruz v. Estado Nacional,*[67] it ruled that fee scales may not be used to legitimize a solution representing an absolutely irrational profit.

Lawyers are authorized to agree with their clients on a percentage of the amount of the judgment, which may not exceed 40% (Law 27,423, Article 6, section b). However, this form of agreement is prohibited in proceedings where provisional, spousal or child support, or family rights are involved. It is also forbidden to set fees based solely on the length of the proceedings (Law 27,423, Article 4).

IV. Oversight of Professional Ethics

51. Bar associations refer to their own established Codes of Professional Ethics. The Public Bar Association of the City of Buenos Aires, established in 1985 by Law 23,187, adopted its current Code of Ethics in May 1987. The basic mission of the legal profession is to establish justice and defend the rule of law and human rights (Articles 7 and 8 of the Code of Ethics). Inherent to the exercise of the profession are obligations to comply with the following: to employ the rules of law to resolve conflicts, founded on the principles of loyalty, probity and good faith; to receive on-going professional training; not to advertise services in an unseemly, excessive or misleading manner; to observe the secrecy of all privileged communications; to defend the privacy of their firm and of the documents entrusted, and to respect the dignity of the legal profession. With respect to their colleagues, lawyers must respect their standing, comply strictly with agreements, not solicit cases or clients working with another lawyer, give notice of the appointment of another lawyer, and refrain from entering into agreements without the participation or knowledge of the lawyer involved therein. Lawyers' duties towards their clients include the following: to advise them truthfully, without creating false expectations or providing any

66. The base rate corresponds to matters where the value involved is not in excess of a specific sum and may be established between 22% and 33%. When the value involved is at the higher end, the legal fees may be calculated between 12% and 15% (Art. 21).
67. *Fallos* 320:495 (1997).

guarantee of the desired outcome of the case; to provide sufficient information on the course of the proceeding; to refrain from disposing of third-party monies or property; to render accounts of the monies and property received; to deal personally with the proceedings; to refrain from advising or representing opposing interests, and to not put their own interests before those of their clients. Lawyers have the right to accept or reject cases, without needing to explain themselves, unless assigned by the court on its own initiative to defend persons in need and unable to afford legal assistance.

As far as the administration of justice is concerned, lawyers must conduct themselves with dignity, not use offensive language to refer to judges or employees, litigate in good faith without resorting to recklessness or delaying tactics, and not use false evidence.

The Disciplinary Tribunal, a body of peers set up within each bar association, is empowered to assess the conduct of lawyers as to the performance of their legal duties and compliance with the rules of professional ethics, without prejudice to the powers specifically granted to judges to apply procedural sanctions to lawyers for their conduct during proceedings. These include disciplinary sanctions (Article 35, ACCPC) or those for actions involving malicious intent (Articles 34, paragraph 6, and 45 et seq., ACCPC).

The Disciplinary Tribunal acts in accordance with the regulations governing disciplinary procedures.[68] It receives complaints from private parties or lawyers, investigates the facts, receives admissible evidence provided by the parties, and decides on the merits of a case through a final resolution, which may be appealed before the court determined by law, thereby causing its execution to be stayed during the appeal process. In the city of Buenos Aires, resolutions may be appealed before the Court of Appeal for Federal Administrative Litigation Matters, while in the province of Buenos Aires they are heard before the Courts of Appeal for Administrative Litigation in a full and fair hearing.

The sanctions established by Law 23,187 (1985) range from a reprimand, a warning in the presence of the Board of Governors and fines, to the suspension of up to one year from practising law, or exclusion from the professional register (Article 45). There are similar dispositions in force regarding the exercise of the legal profession in the provinces.

52. The ACCPC imposes on the parties the duty of loyalty, integrity and good faith[69] and provides that parties, their counsel or both, may be penalized for reckless conduct or acting with malicious intent.[70] Reckless conduct has been described as litigating while being aware of the absence of a valid cause of action, whereas malicious intent involves any manoeuvre made with the intention of delaying proceedings. Article 18 of Decree-Law 1285/58 empowers judges to penalize lawyers, court representatives *(procuradores)*, and other persons found to be obstructing the course of justice, committing breaches or not respecting their authority or person at

68. Regulation passed by the Bar Association of the City of Buenos Aires in November 1988.
69. Article 34, para. 5d.
70. Article 45.

hearings, in appeals or communications of any kind. They may be issued with a reprimand, a warning, a fine, or imprisonment of up to five days.

The ACCPC also contains a number of provisions envisaging negative consequences or fines for those acts considered by legislators to be delaying tactics. Thus, with respect to execution proceedings, Article 551 provides that if the defendant litigated without valid grounds, or otherwise obstructed the normal course of the proceedings with arguments that are clearly inadmissible; or if they delayed the proceedings without due justification, they may be fined in favour of the plaintiff-creditor. The sum involves between 5% and 30% of the amount of the debt, depending on the effect their procedural misconduct had on delaying the proceeding. In terms of legislative policy, the ACCPC provides for instances where the parties delay the normal course of the proceedings and establishes consequences for such actions. Thus: (i) it defines the standards of conduct in the proceeding and provides that the parties must act with loyalty, integrity and good faith; (ii) it censures reckless or delaying actions; (iii) allows the court to set *astreintes* or penalty payments when parties are reluctant to comply with a court order;[71] and (iv) it selects specific instances where misconduct is likely to occur.

Regarding the powers of the court to penalize lawyers, in *Speter*[72], the Supreme Court found that the unjustifiably lengthy appeal signed by the lawyers, which was, for the most part, unintelligible and lacked any legal basis, not only showed ignorance of the law but also constituted a repetition of inadmissible arguments hampering the work of the court. It thus merited a warning.

In *Kasdorf v. Provincia de Jujuy,*[73] the Supreme Court also held that, pursuant to the provisions of Article 58 of the ACCPC, lawyers:

> are on a par with judges, not only in the practice of their profession as regards the respect and consideration owed to them, but also as regards their duties, applicable to all actions during the course of the proceedings, which acquire the characteristics of reciprocity between the lawyers representing the parties in the proceedings … The function of legal counsel is a necessary and essential service for the dispensation of justice. The courts therefore have the power pursuant to the provisions of Article 34, paragraph 5 d) of the Procedural Code to take such preventive measures as required to ensure the proper conduct of the proceedings and ensure compliance with the ethical standards to be observed by the parties and their counsel.

As for the penalizing powers of judges and the Disciplinary Tribunal of the Bar Association, in *Soldini de Torio,*[74] the Supreme Court held that the purpose of the disciplinary powers wielded by judges when hearing cases was to safeguard the propriety of the administration of justice. Whereas, the reason behind the disciplinary powers given to bar associations concerns the generic oversight of ethical behaviour in the practice of law.

71. Article 37.
72. *Fallos* 313:956 (1990).
73. *Fallos* 308:2217 (1986).
74. *Fallos* 249:559 (1961).

§2. BAR ASSOCIATIONS

53. Argentine lawyers have a long tradition of establishing professional associations. The first bar association in Argentina was created on 18 August 1858 in the province of Buenos Aires. The mandatory association of lawyers in a bar association, with sole control of the professional register and disciplinary powers over members failing to observe the canons of ethics, was enshrined in Law 5177 of the Province of Buenos Aires. In *Ferrari*,[75] the Supreme Court held that:

> delegation to professional entities of the control over the performance of [lawyers'] work and a proper disciplinary regime is admissible, as its reasonability is supported by the direct interest of its members in maintaining the prestige of their profession, and because such entities must be empowered to oversee ethical conduct in the practice of such profession. This delegation now extends to many aspects of the practice of law.

In Argentina, there are bar associations created by law – public bar associations – and private law entities for legal professionals. Public associations – such as public bar associations – may be found in the various jurisdictions. These are nongovernmental entities governed by public law with limited powers delegated to them by the State for the achievement of their public purpose. Membership of such institutions is mandatory, they are democratically organized, and their authorities are elected by government organs. Their main powers concern the organization and control of the professional register and the exercise of disciplinary powers. Institutional powers, which are also duties, relate to specific cooperation in the administration of justice through the organization and support of free legal clinics for those who cannot afford legal aid, drawing up proposals and draft bills to improve the judicial system. These powers also include oversight over the actions of judges and their impeachment, participation in the Judiciary Council (including, in the Province of Buenos Aires, since the 1994 constitutional reform). These bar associations are also empowered to defend their members with a view to ensuring that they are free to practice their profession.

The Public Bar Association of the City of Buenos Aires answers to the following governing bodies: the Members Assembly, the Board of Governors and the Disciplinary Tribunal, whose powers are set by the law.

Although membership is mandatory and a condition for legal practice, there are no restrictions on the principle of free association, including the membership of a union as enshrined in the Constitutions. Accordingly, in parallel to the entities governed by public law, there are scores of union institutions organized as private associations in the various jurisdictions, some of which were created before the laws providing for mandatory membership were enacted. Practically all such public and private bar associations – currently over eighty – are members of a private entity, the Argentine Federation of Bar Associations, which acts as their spokesperson vis-à-vis the federal authorities in all matters relating to the practice of law and the administration of justice.

---

75. Id. *Fallos* 308:987 (1986).

Bar associations have recently taken on new roles to comply fully with their institutional aims, primarily as regards the training of lawyers, the organization of conciliation and arbitration services and participation in the selection of judges.

§3. Nongovernmental Organizations

54. In the past ten years, nongovernmental organizations have begun to play a major role in promoting and protecting various rights. Their action and intervention has made an impact on the government's agenda and put sectoral or general claims on the map. The extraordinary degree of legitimacy they enjoy, foreseen in Article 43 of the Constitutions, has also helped to forge one of their principal tools: strategic litigation. They also carry out vital training and monitoring tasks. Their work has done much to advance the cause in the areas of class action, justice in general, environment, gender, and the right to economic, social and cultural rights, for instance. These include, among others: Asociación Civil por la Igualdad y la Justicia, Asociación por los Derechos Civiles, Centro de Estudios Legales y Sociales, Instituto de Estudios Comparados en Ciencias Penales y Sociales, Fundación Poder Ciudadano, Fundación Ambiente y Recursos Naturales, and Unión de Usuarios y Consumidores.

§4. Government Lawyers

55. Public defence is entrusted to the National Public Defender General's Office, headed up by the National Public Defender General (Article 129, paragraph 26, AC).

Public defenders have the duty, before courts of all levels: (a) to care for minors and those who are incapacitated or mentally unfit in their charge, endeavouring to ensure that minors are duly educated, and, in the case of those suffering from mental illness, drug addiction or alcoholism, to seek their recovery and, where appropriate, to apply to courts of any level for their discharge from guardianship; (b) to legally represent incompetent persons; (c) defend persons who own no property in proceedings to declare them legally incompetent; (d) defend persons and their rights whenever required in criminal and other cases when such persons are poor or are not present.

Public bar associations, for their part, have the legal duty to contribute to defending the rights of those unable to afford legal assistance. The laws governing the profession require that they set up free legal clinics and organize the legal aid and defence of such persons (Law 23,187, Articles 55 to 57 and the applicable provincial laws). To this end, they adopt the regulations governing the operation of the clinic and free legal representation and set conditions to be met by those requesting such services, as well as how the lawyers providing these services are to be appointed, and the range of penalties for non-compliance. Lawyers' services are free of charge and they are obliged to accept these appointments and provide the required services.

There is a long tradition in Argentina of lawyers defending people living in poverty *pro bono*, which was confirmed in 1878 by the Supreme Court,[76] with respect to criminal cases. This task has been required from lawyers as a legal duty since the middle of the last century, but it is very clear that the various mechanisms in place to provide official defence, the legal aid provided by practising lawyers and even by public bar associations, are all inadequate. The system is subjective and continues to determine the beneficiaries of the certificate of indigency authorizing them to proceed *in forma pauperis*, regulated by the ACCPC (Articles 7886) and by local procedural codes. In addition, the duty to provide assistance is often undermined as it is entrusted to younger and less experienced lawyers, which ultimately frustrates the right of the beneficiaries to access the legal system on the same footing as those able to pay for it. It is generally held that a substantial transformation is required to redress the organization of legal aid and enable it to gradually provide comprehensive social security coverage. The idea is to complement the official defence provided by the Public Ministry with legal aid provided by practising lawyers. This includes providing information and advice with a view to preventing disputes through means such as conciliation, mediation and arbitration, managed by professional associations on the basis of an objective scheme to determine who is eligible for such aid (e.g., on the basis of monthly income).

Different public and private university law faculties as well as NGOs also offer free legal advice clinics to litigate strategic cases for individual or class action. The MJyDH also offers free legal assistance and counsel through offices and programmes designed for this purpose. Some provincial jurisdictions do the same. The Supreme Court itself has a Woman's Office which coordinates and offers resources and information organized with other state functions to promote and protect women's rights and include a gender perspective (Agreement 13/2009 and Laws 26,585 (2010), 26,364 (2008) and 26,061 (2005)).

As said earlier (*see* paragraph 2), another key player in the constitutional structure is the Defender of the People, an independent organ in the orbit of the Congress. Its mission is to defend and protect human and other rights, guarantees and interests enshrined in the Constitution and the laws in the face of the State's action or omission (Article 86, AC and Law 24,284 (1993) amended by 24,379 (1994)). It thus has a broad-based *locus standi*, and its constitutional relevance has been conditioned by political powers, to the point where the position of the head of the institution is vacant. This figure is present in several different provincial and municipal jurisdictions and shares the same faculties.

76. *Fallos* 20:373 (1878).

Part II. Jurisdiction

Chapter 1. Jurisdiction and Venue

§1. Judges and the Exercise of Jurisdiction

56. In its Preamble, the Constitution (AC) makes express reference to its purpose to 'ensure justice is done' (paragraph 41), which guarantees the right to a defence in court (Article 18), recognizes the right to a fair trial, and affords the American Convention on Human Rights constitutional rank (Article 75 paragraph 22, AC; Article 8, ACHR), enshrined in 'the efficient administration of justice' (Article 114, paragraph 3, in the last part of subsection 6).

Therefore, in the interpretation and application of laws, special attention must be paid to constitutional maxims protecting access to the courts, ensuring that court proceedings are humanized, and that effective judicial protection (in terms of both time and cost of proceedings) of the guarantees established in the Constitution and the treaties.

57. Now, which are the principles established by the Constitution governing the adequate exercise of jurisdictional powers? The main role of the judges is to administer justice through the decisions handed down in each particular case. This involves applying a set of rules of procedure, including both the method for the formal organization of proceedings and the tool providing for the orderly enforcement of rights. This means paying due attention to the determination of the facts brought by the parties and attempting to reach a fair and objective decision regarding the case.[77] A court may not ignore the constitutional provisions requiring cases to be decided 'within a reasonable period of time' without affecting the right to a 'quick and effective legal decision'.[78]

58. The concept of 'adequate administration of justice', according to the Constitution, includes the following: (i) the proceedings must be conducted in compliance with the principle of equal opportunity to be heard and avoid excessive form; (ii) the judge should not depart from the truth concerning the facts; (iii) the final

77. The Supreme Court has developed this line of interpretation concerning the object of the trial in numerous cases. *See Colalillo*, *Fallos* 238:550 (1957) and *Ohiler*, *Fallos* 302:1611 (1980).
78. *Fallos* 256:491 (1963), 257:132 (1963), 261:132 (1965), 265:147 (1966), for instance.

decision must be issued within a reasonable time; (iv) this decision must be intrinsically fair; and (v) fully executed in a reasonable period of time. Each of these premises enshrines the public purpose of jurisdiction, and their infringement, whether through action or inaction, violates all legally protected interest.

59. In the legal vocabulary employed in Argentina, jurisdiction refers to the adjudication of the power conferred upon judges to decide in those legal cases they hear according to the rules of the distribution of competences, which here relates to jurisdiction. The term 'competence' is used to identify the specific power to cases adjudicated within the different state subdivisions (provincial, national, or federal). Judges have the power, whether in the provincial, national or federal sphere, to decide (jurisdiction) on certain conflicts inasmuch as the law invests them with the competence to do so. Thus, competence refers to the kind of jurisdiction attributed to the judge according to the different criteria employed by the law to assign tasks and distribute power within a federal structure.

§2. Jurisdiction

60. The Constitution makes a first and fundamental distinction between federal and nonfederal court jurisdictions (*see* paragraphs 2731). Nonfederal court jurisdiction depends upon the autonomy of the provinces and their powers to organize their own provincial judicial systems. The jurisdiction of federal courts is vested in the Judicial Branch of the Nation. In order to establish which judge or court has jurisdiction in a particular case, it must first be determined whether the conflict concerns a federal or nonfederal court. Then, in either of these forums, the jurisdiction or venue where the case is heard must be established, and after that, which courts have jurisdiction by reason of the subject matter, its function or degree, and the amount of the claim.

61. There may be either a *relative* or an a*bsolute* jurisdiction of the courts, depending on whether jurisdiction can be extended or waived by the parties. Federal jurisdiction is in principle absolute, reserved and in the public order. As for ordinary or local jurisdiction, the procedural code only permits a change of venue when the case involves claims against a defendant's assets. In international cases (*see* paragraph 89), the ACCPC explains that the extension may even be admitted in favour of foreign judges or arbiters acting outside the bounds of the national territory, except when Argentine courts have exclusive jurisdiction over the matter, or when such an extension is prohibited by law (Article 1). The dispositions enshrined in international treaties and the hypothesis contemplated in Article 12 of Law 48 concerning the extension of jurisdiction of federal courts over the persons are left untouched. Any extension of jurisdiction can be expressed according to the agreement reached between the parties or is otherwise tacit if the parties take any action implying a waiver of the jurisdiction of the court provided by law. At all events, to define jurisdiction, the main issue is to observe the statement of facts given in the lawsuit, its objective and the reasons giving rise to it, as well as the legal relationship between the parties. Last, but not least, inasmuch as it is relevant to the case, attention must be paid to the right invoked as its legal basis.

62. The power to exercise jurisdiction cannot be delegated, but judges from other districts may be entrusted with the performance of specific acts or proceedings (Article 3 (1), ACCPC) determined on the basis of the nature of the cause of action (Article 5).

63. There are two procedural stages at which a judge may declare whether or not the case falls within their jurisdiction. The first is when the action is filed in court; if the allegation of facts reveals that the court where the action is filed lacks the jurisdiction to hear the case, the judge must decline jurisdiction *sua sponte* (Article 4). The second is when the judge must rule to dismiss a challenge to the court's jurisdiction (Article 347, paragraph 1). Once a resolution disallowing the challenge to a court's jurisdiction is final and conclusive, the parties may no longer challenge it, or may the judges themselves decline it (Article 352). The only exception to this rule is the lack of jurisdiction of the federal courts, which may be declared by the Supreme Court when it intervenes in the original instance, and by federal courts seated in any of the provinces, at any procedural stage.

I. Ordinary Jurisdiction: Territory, Subject, Rank and Amount

64. Territorial jurisdiction is provided for both in the ACCPC and in the body of procedural laws, establishing different rules according to whether the court case is dealing with rights in personam or rights in rem. In actions in rem, jurisdiction is determined depending on whether actions involve real estate or personal property. In the first case, by virtue of the principle of *forum rei sitae*, the court where the item in dispute is located has jurisdiction to hear the case. If more than a single issue is involved, or one located in different jurisdictions, any of these can act as the jurisdiction of the court, provided that the defendant is domiciled there. Otherwise, it can be the location of any of these, at the discretion of the plaintiff (Article 5, paragraph 1). If a legal action in rem is brought in respect of personal property, jurisdiction lies with the place where the property is located or where the defendant is domiciled, at their own discretion (Article 5, paragraph 2, ACCPC).

In the event of actions in personam, jurisdiction lies with the court located where the obligation, whether expressly or impliedly established in the facts alleged in the lawsuit, should have been performed. Otherwise, this may be at the plaintiff's own discretion, such as the court with jurisdiction over the place where the defendant resides, or over the place where the agreement is supposed to be executed, provided always that the defendant resides or happens to be in the specified location when the notice is served (Article 5, paragraph 3). Thus, the principle of the jurisdiction of *forum solutionis* applies as provided for in Articles 1215 and 1216 of the ACCC.

If the issue concerns actions in personam arising from torts, committed either intentionally or through negligence, jurisdiction lies with the court where action occurred or the place where the defendant is domiciled, at the plaintiff's own discretion (Article 5, paragraph 4, ACCPC).

As for actions in personam in general, the ACCPC establishes that whenever there are several defendants, and joint or indivisible obligations involved, jurisdiction lies with the court where any of the defendants resides, at the plaintiff's own discretion (Article 5 (5), ACCPC).

Finally, the ACCPC includes specific actions in personam involving assets, such as the rendition and approval of accounts, tax collection, rates and fines, and actions arising from corporate relationships (Article 5, paragraphs 6, 7 and 11).

Filings for partial divorce, divorce, and marriage annulment, as well as legal action related to marital possessions, may be filed either with the court where the couple was domiciled or at the domicile of the defendant spouse, at the plaintiff's own discretion, or at that of either of the spouses in the case of a joint filing (Article 5, paragraph 8, ACCPC, and Article 717, ACCC). This rule also establishes specific requirements for court action involving children and teenagers, common-law marriage, living allowances, filiation action and legal disability statements in the cases of insanity, deaf and muteness, as well as rehabilitation (Articles 31, 32, 47, 48, 705 712, 716, 718, 719, and 720, and in corroborative articles, of the ACCC). The remaining provisions concerning jurisdiction over such matters are provided for in general and specific substantial law.

Finally, as regards actions involving a relationship between the parties outside the lawsuit (voluntary jurisdiction), the ACCPC articulates the general principle whereby, except for probate, or as otherwise provided, jurisdiction lies with the court where the person in whose interest the proceedings are being developed is domiciled (Article 5, paragraph 12).

65. The jurisdiction of nonfederal courts is divided into the following main areas: civil, commercial, labour, consumer, social security, and criminal matters. Courts of First Instance and appellate courts for civil, commercial, consumer-related and labour matters hear cases involving any of the first four areas, while labour courts have exclusive jurisdiction over social security matters.

Decree-Law 1285/58 establishes the jurisdictional boundaries of civil and commercial courts based on the nature of the act or event in question but also includes various exceptions.

66. Functional jurisdiction or by rank means that proceedings are divided into various stages, entrusting cognizance of the case to different courts. Argentina's nonfederal courts' system for civil, commercial, labour, consumer and administrative litigation matters consists of a two-tier court structure, where initial cognizance of the case corresponds to single-member bodies (one-judge courtrooms), whose resolutions may be appealed with collegiate courts (courts of appeal).

67. In the Argentine system, there is no special system for small claims courts. This jurisdiction usually exists in most provinces and in some cases, it is entrusted to judges who are members of the bar or Justices of the Peace (province of Buenos Aires) or lay judges (province of Santa Fe).

68. The exceptions to these rules of jurisdiction involve the consolidation of claims on the grounds of commonality or legal connection between them (Articles 188, 87 and 6, ACCPC), and cases involving the ancillary jurisdiction inherent to all universal proceedings involving probate or bankruptcy proceedings, laid down in substantive laws.

II. Jurisdiction of Federal Courts

69. The AC establishes the matters over which federal courts have jurisdiction, made up of the Supreme Court and lower courts. Article 116 says that:

> The Supreme Court and the lower federal courts of Argentina are empowered to hear and determine all cases arising under this Constitution, under the laws of Argentina, except as specified in Article 75, paragraph 12 of this Constitution, and according to the treaties signed with foreign states; all cases of admiralty and maritime jurisdiction; controversies to which Argentina is a party; controversies between two or more provinces; and between a province or the citizens thereof and foreign States or citizens.

In these cases, the Supreme Court has appellate jurisdiction according to the regulations and exceptions ruled by Congress. However, in cases involving ambassadors, ministers and consuls, and those where a province is a party, the Supreme Court has original and exclusive jurisdiction (Article 117, AC).

Various organic laws have since regulated these constitutional provisions, limiting the scope of original jurisdiction given to the Supreme Court and establishing the jurisdiction of federal lower courts.

Federal jurisdiction is limited and unique (in the sense that it is exclusive of provincial courts), and it cannot be extended to other courts (if so required because of the subject matter).

70. The jurisdiction of federal courts sitting in the provinces over civil, commercial, and administrative litigation matters is governed by Article 2 of Law 48 (1863) and Article 55, paragraphs b), c) and d) of Decree-Law 1285/58. In the City of Buenos Aires, federal jurisdiction over such matters is vested in judges sitting in Federal Courts of First Instance for civil and commercial matters according to Article 111 of Law 1893 (1886), and Article 42 of Decree-Law 1285/58 and in those judges sitting in Federal Courts of First Instance for administrative litigation matters.

71. Federal courts have jurisdiction over subject matter and may thus hear and rule on:

1. Cases governed exclusively by the Constitution (Article 116, AC; Article 2, para. 1, Law 1893; Article 111, para. 1, Law 48), where the right at stake is directly founded in a constitutional norm.[79]
2. Cases governed exclusively by the Constitution (Article 16, AC; Law 48; Article 111, para. 1, Law 1893). These are the laws enacted by Congress in the exercise of the powers conferred upon it by Article 75 of the Constitution, to be applied throughout the territory. These do not include matters corresponding to the civil, commercial, criminal, mining, labour and social security codes (Article 75, para. 12, AC). These include laws governing services, institutions and activities throughout Argentina.[80]
3. All cases governed by treaties made with foreign states (Article 116, AC; Article 2, para. 1, Law 48; Article 111, para. 1, Law 1893).
4. All cases of admiralty and maritime jurisdiction (Article 116, AC), including those involving acts or events occurring at sea, and any acts and contracts concerning navigation (Article 2, paras. 710, Law 48; Article 111, paras. 69, Law 1893).
5. All cases involving acts, events and contracts relating to land transportation, except those involving damages complaints brought in connection with losses derived from torts, whether intentionally or through negligence (Articles 55, para. b and 42, para. b, Law 13,998), heard and determined by federal judges sitting in the provinces, and federal judges of the city of Buenos Aires.[81]

72. Federal courts have jurisdiction to hear and determine:

(1) All controversies in which the Nation is party (Article 116, AC; Articles 2, paragraph 6 and 11, paragraph 5, Law 48). This applies to the Federal Government, decentralized agencies, and state-owned companies, including tax collection agencies.
(2) All civil actions where both the resident of the province where the incident prompting the lawsuit occurred, and the resident of another province, are parties (Article 116, AC; Article 2, paragraph 2, Law 48). Article 11 of Law 48 (1863) says that:

> For the purposes of jurisdiction, a person is considered a resident of a province after having lived continuously in that province for two years; or because they own real estate, or an industrial or commercial establishment there, or because they have settled in the province, and show intent to remain there.[82]

79. *Fallos* 26:233 (1883); 43:234 (1891); 96:347 (1902); 115:167 (1911).
80. *Fallos* 181:326 (1938); 248:781 (1960); 250:236 (1961).
81. *Fallos* 243:372 (1959).
82. *Fallos* 137:337 (1922).

(3) All civil actions involving an Argentine citizen and a foreign citizen (Article 116, AC; Article 55 paragraph C, Law 13,998; Article 111, paragraph 3, Law 1893). The fact that a case is handled by a federal court by reason of diverse citizenship of the parties is a privilege granted exclusively for the benefit of a foreign person, and may accordingly be waived expressly or implicitly by that party, although a foreign defendant in a federal court may not waive the jurisdiction of that court. Foreign states may also be sued in federal courts, provided they forgo their right to exemption by that jurisdiction.

(4) All cases relating to the private business of foreign consuls and vice consuls (Article 116, AC; Article 55 c, Law 13,998; Article 111, paragraph 3, Law 1893).

73. Federal court jurisdiction by reason of place refers to the scope of powers granted to the Federal Government enshrined in Article 75, paragraph 30 of the Constitution, enabling them to exercise legislative, administrative and judicial powers in those places acquired by purchase or assignment in any of the provinces for the purposes of establishing property assigned for a public purpose.[83]

74. Federal judges sitting in any of the provinces also have appellate jurisdiction to review resolutions issued by administrative agencies. Such powers are vested in them under special statutes such as agricultural defence, health control, phytosanitary controls, arms and weapons.

III. Jurisdiction of the Supreme Court

75. The Supreme Court's jurisdiction is regulated by Decree-Law 1285/58: it has both original and appellate jurisdiction, with original jurisdiction applying to those persons party to the proceedings and appellate jurisdiction due to the person, subject matter, and particular circumstances of the case.

76. The Supreme Court has original and exclusive jurisdiction:

1. In all cases involving two or more provinces, and in civil cases involving a province and a resident or residents of another province, or citizens or foreign nationals (Article 24, paragraph 1, LOPJN). The Supreme Court has original jurisdiction in controversies between two or more provinces, regardless of the nature of the matters involved, except for cases over disputed boundaries, which must be

83. Provincial jurisdiction may only be excluded inasmuch as its exercise may interfere, directly or indirectly, in the duty to satisfy the services rendered in the public interest as required by the public institution (*Fallos* 201:536 (1945); 215:250 (1949); 240:311 (1948); 248:824 (1960); 259:414 (1964); 293:287 (1975); 296:449 (1976); 301:856 (1979), among others). This doctrine was explicitly adopted by the 1994 constitutional reform whose Art. 75 para. 30 refers to the 'specific purposes of the establishments of national use and disposes that the provincial and municipal authorities retain the power to police and control these establishments as long as they do not interfere with the aforementioned purposes'.

settled by Congress (Article 75, paragraph 15, AC). However, if a case arises between a province and a foreign national, or a resident from another province, this should be treated as civil law.[84]

2. In cases between a province and a foreign state (Decree-Law 1285/58). In these cases, the Supreme Court has jurisdiction *ratione personae*, but no action brought against a foreign State will be prosecuted without having first requested and obtained consent from the State against whom the case was filed from its Diplomatic Agent through Argentina's Foreign Relations Ministry.

3. In all cases affecting ambassadors or other diplomatic ministers, persons making up their legation and members of their families, so that a Court of Law may decide the case in accordance with public international law (Article 24, paragraph 1, Decree-Law 1285/58). These include cases concerning ambassadors or plenipotentiary ministers who are directly affected as this concerns their respective rights or liability, those pertaining to the members of their families, the embassy or delegation staff according to the aforementioned rules given in Article 24, subsection 1, paragraph 5 where the corresponding foreign authority is obliged to conform.

4. In cases concerning diplomatic privilege and immunity of foreign consuls in the course of their duties, according to the aforementioned Article 24. These are cases concerning acts or events committed during the course and scope of their duties, as and when their civil or criminal liability is at issue.[85]

77. The Supreme Court has 'extraordinary appellate jurisdiction' when it hears extraordinary appeals (Article 14, Law 48 and Article 6, Law 4055) and motions to admit an extraordinary appeal that has been formerly dismissed (Article 24, paragraphs 2 and 4, Decree-Law 1285/58).

78. The Supreme Court has ordinary appellate jurisdiction when it hears:

(1) Ordinary appeals on final judgments from Courts of Appeal in the following cases: (i) all controversies to which Argentina is a party, be it directly or indirectly, when the final amount debated, not including any related costs and expenses, exceeds a certain amount in Argentine pesos; (ii) cases of extradition of criminals to foreign states; and (iii) cases involving the capture or imposition of maritime embargos in times of war, military salvage, and actions involving the vessel's nationality, licence, or registration papers (Article 24, paragraph 6, LOPJN).

---

84. In the Barreto case (*Fallos* 329:759–2006), the Supreme Court reformulated the criteria traditionally applied to the scope of the term 'civil case'. It limited its significance by reason of institutional policy, to its minimum expression. Henceforth, civil case is only used to refer to litigation ruled exclusively by private law principles or norms, except for those whose solution requires local public law rules to be applied, or when the application of private law rules is subsidiary or analogue.
85. *Fallos* 10:324 (1871) and 29:66 (1885), among others.

(2) Direct appeals following the dismissal appeals detailed above (Article 24, paragraph 4, Decree-Law 1285/58).

79. Finally, the Supreme Court has jurisdiction to hear and rule on the following:

(1) Motions filed to complain about delay in the administration of justice on the part of Appellate court administration of justice (Article 24, paragraph 5).
(2) Issues of jurisdiction and conflicts arising during the proceedings between judges and courts lacking any common hierarchically superior court able to rule on the case,[86] unless such questions or conflicts arise between Nonfederal Courts of First Instance, in which case they will be decided by the appellate court corresponding to the judge who first took cognizance of the case. They also determine which judge has jurisdiction in cases where this decision is fundamental to prevent the actual deprivation of justice (Article 24, paragraph 7).

IV. Questions of Jurisdiction

80. A question of jurisdiction may be raised in the light of either of the following procedural avenues: 'a ruling of lack of jurisdiction, or a motion for improper jurisdiction', and in addition, questions of jurisdiction may also be raised by judges on their own initiative. In the first case, the defendant appears before the judge of the court serving notice upon them to request that a ruling of lack of jurisdiction be issued. In the second case, the defendant appears before the judge of the court believed to have jurisdiction, to request the court to declare its jurisdiction over the case, and to send an official letter or letters rogatory to the court hearing the matter, to ensure that the latter court desists from the proceedings.

81. The parties may avail themselves of either procedural option, unless the issue involves judges with the same territorial jurisdiction. In this case, only a ruling of lack of jurisdiction is admitted. It should be noted that in both cases, the parties must not have consented earlier to the jurisdiction of that court. Furthermore, the exercise of one of the motions precludes the exercise of the other (Article 7, ACCPC). A motion for the court to issue a ruling of lack of jurisdiction may be filed like any other preliminary defence, and if upheld, the case must be turned over to the court believed to have competent jurisdiction (Article 8, ACCPC).

As to motions for improper jurisdiction, the aforementioned Article 8 establishes that these may be filed before raising a defence or filing an answer to the complaint, unless the proceeding requires these to be filed as preliminary defences.

86. Provincial authorities may not avail themselves of what is enshrined in their own laws to obstruct the actions of judges making up the Judicial Branch (Art. 20, Decree-Law 1285/58: *Fallos* 242:480 (1958); 244:457 (1959); 245:61 (1959), et al.

If the court before which the motion for improper jurisdiction is filed declares that it has jurisdiction to hear the case, it issues and sends an official letter or letters rogatory, attaching a certified copy of the brief whereby the motion is filed, the judgment rendered, and any additional information required as grounds for exercising jurisdiction. The requested court must also request that the records of the case be forwarded to them, or to any other body held competent to decide the case. This resolution may only be appealed if the court maintains that it lacks jurisdiction to hear the case (Article 9, ACCPC).

As to formalities, following reception of the official letter or the letters rogatory, the requested court must rule on its own jurisdiction. A judgment holding that it has jurisdiction over the case may be appealed, and if not contested by the parties within the statutory time limit, it will have the effect of res judicata. The court must then forward these proceedings to the requesting court and summon the parties to appear before it.

If, on the contrary, after appealing, the requesting court is held to have jurisdiction, the requested court will send the records to the applicable higher court to decide, asking the requesting court to act in the same way (Article 10, ACCPC).

82. Questions of jurisdiction are heard in the form of ancillary proceedings and are not grounds for suspending the proceedings, which continue as scheduled before the court that first took cognizance of the case, unless the issue of jurisdiction involves territorial aspects (Article 12, ACCPC).

Article 11 of the ACCPC provides that the hierarchically superior court must, within five days of receiving the records of proceedings, rule on the issue and turn the records over to the court with jurisdiction, notifying their decision to the other court by means of an official letter or letters rogatory. If the court that filed a motion for improper jurisdiction fails to forward the proceedings within a reasonable time, the higher court will, at its own discretion, demand the former to do so in a term not to exceed within fifteen days, depending on distance, with the attached warning that otherwise the claim will be deemed abandoned.

Chapter 2. International Jurisdiction

§1. Brief Overview of Argentine Statutory Provisions Regarding International Jurisdiction

83. Although the terms 'international jurisdiction' or 'international jurisdiction and/or venue' are often used interchangeably, when judges are authorized to rule on a case involving more than one State, it is appropriate to use the term 'international jurisdiction'. This is because we are not only dealing with the apportionment of jurisdiction at international level but also facing the problem of determining whether an Argentine judge can hear a dispute (jurisdiction) involving elements from international law. After determining that Argentine courts have international jurisdiction to hear a case, the domestic rules for the establishment of jurisdiction must be applied to determine which Argentine court is competent to deal with that case.

84. The issue here is primarily about direct international jurisdiction, understood as the power of Argentine courts to decide conflicts involving multinational or foreign elements. In this chapter we do not cover the subject of indirect international jurisdiction, which occurs when an Argentine court must determine whether or not to recognize the international jurisdiction of foreign courts.

85. Prior to the enactment of the ACCC, there was no formally structured body of general laws in Argentina regarding international jurisdiction.

86. Article 2601 of the ACCC recognizes that in the absence of international treaties and when there is no agreement between the parties in cases where the extension of jurisdiction is permitted, Argentine judges may enjoy international jurisdiction according to the rules established in the code and in the special laws of application.

87. One of the assumptions harboured by Argentine international jurisdiction involves the reasonable relationship between a multinational case and the judicial sphere. If there are no appropriate points in common, the Argentine court must disregard their international jurisdiction in order to ensure that the ruling issued is not disregarded outside Argentina. In one of the Supreme Court's first interventions in this area, in *Marciano Molina v. Morton*,[87] it upheld as a principle of international private law that a national court may only exercise jurisdiction directly over people and things in its own territory, as beyond its boundaries, it lacks the powers to enforce its rulings. This makes it hard for Argentine courts to exercise their powers and dictate precautionary measures in proceedings applicable to goods and people not in the country (Article 2603, sub-paragraph a), ACCC). This is why the conventional framework, reciprocity of treatment and international cooperation are so important (Articles 2611 and 2612).

87. *Fallos* 7:267 (1869).

88. When resolving cases involving different national legal systems over which Argentine courts enjoy international jurisdiction, the ACCC states that legal norms applicable are determined by the relevant international treaties and conventions in force and, in the absence of international norms, by the rules of Argentine domestic private international law (Article 2594). Likewise, it recognizes that in those cases when foreign law is applicable to a legal relationship, private international law of that country is also applicable. Similarly, when parties in a legal relationship have chosen the law of a certain country, it is understood that they have also elected to abide by the domestic laws of that State, unless expressly stated otherwise (Article 2596). For the application and interpretation of foreign law, the judge must follow the guidelines stipulated in Article 2595. In exceptional cases, the right designated by a conflict rule is not applied when the factual circumstances of the case indicate clearly that the situation has little relevance to that right and very close links to the right of another State, whose application may be foreseen and under whose rules the relationship would be established as valid. This provision is not applicable when the parties have chosen the right for the case (Article 2597). In all cases, international imperative norms and Argentine public order must be taken into consideration, as these elements condition the exercise of free will and the application of the law chosen by conflict norms or by the parties, particularly in those cases of legal fraud.[88]

89. The ACCC regulates the assumption of international lis pendens. In this sense, it specifies that when an action with the same object, cause and subjects as one previously initiated abroad is pending resolution, the Argentine court must suspend the proceedings pending in this country when it is likely that the foreign decision will be acknowledged. The proceedings resume when the foreign court declines its jurisdiction, or if the procedure concludes without there being a resolution on the merits of the matter, or when the sentence issued abroad is not subject to recognition in the country (Article 2604).

90. A change of venue, upon the parties' decision to submit any dispute to the jurisdiction of a particular court, is permitted in cases involving property. The ACCPC of 1968, as originally drafted (Article 1, Law 17,754), banned the extension of jurisdiction to foreign courts or arbitrators. Subsequently, Law 21,305 (1976) amended the ACCPC, permitting a change of venue in cases involving property, provided Argentine courts do not have exclusive jurisdiction over the case, and an agreement concerning such jurisdiction was made before the occurrence of the events leading to the controversy. Law 22,434 (1981) again amended Article 1 of the ACCPC, eliminating the need to agree to an extension before the disputed events occurred. The National Commercial Chamber, in *Neufron v. Gambro Sales*,[89] resolved that it was not appropriate to accept the tacit extension of international jurisdiction, as it understood that an explicit declaration of submission to the foreign court was necessary. The third paragraph of Article 56 of the 1940 Montevideo

88. *See* Arts 2598, 2599 and 2600 of the ACCC.
89. Section A, judgment of 14.9.88, in the *Commercial Law Review of Obligations*, Buenos Aires, 1988, pp. 169 et seq.

Treaty establishes the territorial extension of international jurisdiction, in the case of proprietary actions in personam, if the defendant admits this voluntarily after the lawsuit has been filed, expressing their will to accept it in a positive way.

The Protocol of Buenos Aires on International Jurisdiction in Contractual Matters was signed within the MERCOSUR framework (1994)[90] establishing that in conflicts arising in international civil or commercial contracts, the competent courts will be those in the State to whose jurisdiction the contracting parties have agreed to submit, provided that this agreement is not obtained in an abusive manner. It is also possible to agree to the extension in favour of arbitration tribunals (Article 4).

The ACCC has ratified in proprietary and international matters the freedom of the parties to extend the jurisdiction of judges or arbitrators outside of Argentina, except when the Argentine judges have exclusive jurisdiction or the extension is prohibited by law (Article 2605). Without prejudice to the provisions of special laws, it is understood that they have exclusive jurisdiction over real property rights located in Argentina. This also applies to matters related to the validity of inscriptions in an Argentine public registry and to cases regarding the inscription or validity of patents, trademarks, industrial designs and models and other similar rights subject to deposit or registration in the country (Article 2609). The extension of jurisdiction may be express or tacit, according to whether it has been expressly agreed by the parties, or accepted by the plaintiff when filing their lawsuit, or by the defendant when answering it, or when failing to do so, or when opposing exceptions without making a plea (Article 2607). The court chosen by the parties has exclusive jurisdiction, unless they expressly decide otherwise (Article 2606).

91. Based on *Vlasov v. Vlasov*,[91] the Supreme Court developed the idea of attributing international jurisdiction to Argentine courts when there is the possibility that justice will be denied in another State, based on the right to due process or guarantee of defence in court, enshrined in the Constitution (Article 18). In this case, the issue concerned a divorce lawsuit in which the wife claimed separation from her husband, alleging that he had left home and committed adultery. The husband had moved to Europe and it was established that it would be very difficult to file a lawsuit against him while abroad. In the event of a possible deprivation of justice, the Supreme Court recognized the international jurisdiction of the Argentine court. This principle is referred to as a 'forum of necessity' when faced with the possible denial of justice. Article 2602 of the ACCC includes this institute and states that although the rules of the code do not attribute international jurisdiction to Argentine courts, they can nevertheless intervene exceptionally in order to avoid an event involving the denial of justice. As a condition, it establishes that it would be unreasonable to demand that the lawsuit be filed abroad, given that the private situation presents sufficient contact with the country, the right of defence in trial is guaranteed, and the desirability of achieving an effective sentence is taken into account.

---

90. Approved by Argentina through Law 24,669. The Member States party to the Treaty are Argentina, Brazil, Paraguay and Uruguay.
91. *Fallos* 246:87 (1960).

92. The principle of equality between people is enshrined in the AC (Article 16) as well as in other international declarations and conventions signed by Argentina. As previously mentioned, the conventions have constitutional hierarchy and contain express provisions that establish the principles of equality and non-discrimination: the Universal Declaration of Human Rights (Articles 2 and 7), the Covenant on Civil and Political Rights (Articles 2 and 26) and the American Convention on Human Rights (Articles 1 and 24). Hence, foreigners are protected by the principle of equality when acting before Argentine courts. The aforementioned principle of equal treatment has two aspects that must be analysed: the limits to access to justice for economic reasons and the regulation of the exception of *arraigo* by the ACCPC (Article 348).

Given the economic difficulties that may limit a person's right to access justice, it must be remembered that Argentina is a signatory to the 1954 Hague Convention on Civil Procedure (ratified by Law 23,502 of 1987[92]). Article 20 of the Convention on Civil Procedure establishes that nationals from each Contracting State may benefit from free defence in all Contracting States on an equal footing with their nationals, in accordance with the legislation of the State where the benefit of free defence is sought. The Protocol for Cooperation and Assistance in Civil, Commercial, Labour and Administrative Matters (ratified by Law 24,578 of 1995) was approved within the scope of MERCOSUR, recognizing the principle of equality for the purposes of free access to jurisdiction for the defence of rights (Article 3).

Article 2610 of the ACCC includes this institute, establishing that citizens and permanent residents abroad may enjoy free access to jurisdiction to defend their rights and interests under the same conditions as citizens and permanent residents of Argentina. This equality is also dispensed to legal entities constituted, authorized or registered in accordance with the laws of a foreign State. In its Articles 79 et seq., the ACCPC regulates specific proceedings, which may be undertaken through ancillary proceedings to determine whether the benefit of litigating without expenses can be granted, given a person's inability to bear costs and legal fees. The official defenders and the Bar Associations make up two parallel systems of legal assistance for people unable to meet the expenses involved in technical defence (paragraph 55).

The ACCPC establishes that the defendant may raise the possibility that the procedure cannot continue when the plaintiff has no domicile or property in Argentina as a previous exception in the process of knowledge (Article 348). Article 17 of the Hague Convention on Civil Procedure establishes that no bond or deposit may be required due to a person's condition as a foreigner or lacking domicile or residence in the country, from the nationals of one of the Contracting States domiciled in one of those States acting as plaintiffs or parties before the courts of another State. The aforementioned Protocol of Cooperation and Jurisdictional Assistance in Civil, Commercial, Labour and Administrative Matters of MERCOSUR also establishes the prohibition on imposing the *iudicatum solvi* (Article 4). Article 2610 of the ACCC establishes that no surety or deposit, whatever its name, may be imposed because a person is a citizen or permanent resident in another State. Therefore, those

92. The number of the Member States signatories to the Convention and the scope of its ratifications may be found at www.hcch.net.

able to declare that their respective States are parties to either of the two conventions, or to a specific bilateral treaty,[93] or who enjoy the status of citizen or permanent resident of another State, do not have the obligation of *arraigo*. Other parties are covered by the exception provided in the aforementioned Article 348 of the ACCPC.

§2. International Subject Matter Jurisdiction

I. Cases Involving Personal Rights

93. As mentioned previously (see paragraphs 85, 92), Chapter III of Title IV of the ACCC organizes the different cases covered by international jurisdiction and the rules applied by the court when ruling on conflicts involving multinational or foreign elements, depending on the subject (Articles 26132671). The sixteen sections systematized cover: human persons (where it deals with the points of contact made regarding their attributes), marriage, cohabitation, food, affiliation by nature and by assisted human reproduction techniques, adoption, parental responsibility and protection institutions, international restitution of children, probate, forms of legal acts, contracts, consumer contracts, civil liability, securities, property rights and statutory limitation periods.

94. The domicile is the point of contact indicated by international jurisdiction for the resolution of issues related to individual factual and legal capacity. The ACCC considers that, for the purposes of private international law, a human person is domiciled in the State where they reside, with the intention of establishing their habitual residence and themselves in the State where they live and establishing long-lasting relationships. Likewise, it recognizes that a person may not reside at several addresses at the same time, and that if they do not have a known address, that this is where they reside habitually, or, failing that, their simple residence (Article 2613). In general, the ACCC establishes that, excepting specific provisions, actions in personam must be filed before the court where the defendant has their domicile or habitual residence (Article 2608).

As for the protection of minors, the ACCC establishes that the court where those exercising parental responsibility reside should hear the case. When this exercise is plural and those responsible live in different States, the minors involved are considered to have their legal domicile where they have their habitual residence. The only exceptions to this rule concern minors illegally abducted or retained, and who thus do not acquire the domicile of the place where they have been abducted (Article 2614).[94]

The ACCC exceptionally recognizes that Argentine courts may adopt the requisite urgent measures of protection considered necessary for minors, incapacitated

93. Argentina has signed bilateral treaties with Italy, Brazil and Uruguay that exempt the need for *arraigo*.

94. *See* Art. 2639 of the ACCC.

persons and/or their assets in Argentine territory. This measure must be immediately communicated to the competent authorities in the domicile or of the nationality of the person in question, except in the case of refugees (Article 2641).

Argentina is a party to the Inter-American Convention on the Restitution of Minors,[95] which establishes the international jurisdiction of the courts of the State where the minor has their habitual residence prior to transfer or retention. Whoever files an application for the return of a child may choose to request the intervention of the court where the illegally transferred or retained minor is, or is supposed to be, at the time of the application. Article 2642 of the ACCC establishes that current conventions apply in this matter. Beyond its scope, Argentine courts have a duty to adapt the principles contained in such agreements to the case, ensuring the best interests of the child. In the event of an imminent entry into the country of a child or adolescent whose rights may be under threat, they also have the duty to adopt measures in advance to ensure their protection, as well as, if appropriate, that of the adult accompanying the child or teenager.

The habitual domicile or residence is the point of contact used for matters involving persons subject to guardianship or other forms of protection (Article 2615),[96] the capacity of adults (Article 2616), a person's name as their human right and attribute (Article 2618) and for the declaration of absence with presumption of death (Articles 2619 and 2620). If the alleged absentee has not been domiciled or resident in the country, the court where there are abandoned goods, or the one which could have prevailed if these goods were found in various different jurisdictions (Article 16, Law 14,394), has international jurisdiction, although an Argentine court may assume jurisdiction in the event of a legitimate interest in Argentina (Article 2619).

In matters related to marriage, its validity, nullity, dissolution and effects, the court in the last effective marital domicile (where they lived together), or that of the defendant spouse's domicile or habitual residence (Article 2621) has international jurisdiction.[97] In matters of cohabitation, it is the court in the common effective domicile of those constituting the relationship, or the defendant's domicile or habitual residence (Article 2627). As for maintenance allowance claims, the ACCC establishes that they should be filed by whomsoever requires them with the court in their domicile or habitual residence and with the defendant or, if judged reasonable according to the circumstances of the case, before the court in the place where the defendant has assets. Regarding maintenance allowances between spouses or cohabitants, actions must be filed before the court in the last conjugal or cohabitation domicile, or that in the domicile or habitual residence of the defendant or the court which ruled in the case of the dissolution of the bond. In the event of a maintenance agreement, the respective actions may, at the option of the plaintiff, be

95. Law 25,358 (2000). This Convention has been ratified by: Antigua and Barbuda, Argentina, Belize, Bolivia, Brazil, Costa Rica, Ecuador, Mexico, Nicaragua, Paraguay, Peru, Uruguay, Venezuela (1989).
96. *See* Arts 2617 and 2640, ACCC.
97. *See* Arts 2622–2626, ACCC.

lodged before the court in the place where the obligation is to be fulfilled or where said agreement is to be executed, if it coincides with the defendant's residence (Article 2629).[98]

95. Regarding claims related to paternity determination and challenges, the plaintiff may choose between the courts where the person filing the paternity suit is domiciled, or the court where the parent or alleged parent is domiciled. In the event of recognition, international jurisdiction is held by the court where the person making the recognition is domiciled, where the child is domiciled, or the court where they were born (Article 2631).[99] In the matter of adoption, the ACCC regulates that Argentine courts have exclusive jurisdiction to declare a child's adoptability, to decide on a guardian for adoption purposes and to grant an adoption, provided that the children are domiciled in the country. For the annulment or revocation of an adoption, it is the court in the place where the adoption was granted or the domicile of the child adopted which has jurisdiction (Article 2635).[100]

96. Argentine probate legislation follows the principle of unity and bestows jurisdiction on the court where the deceased was last domiciled. If the deceased was domiciled abroad, but owns real estate in Argentina, according to the *lex situs*, the Argentine courts have international jurisdiction over the assets (Article 2643).[101]

II. Assets and Patrimonial Relations

97. In order to determine international jurisdiction in matters of property, the ACCC distinguishes based on the type of property and whether it can be registered or not. Thus, it determines that the court of the State where the assets are located has jurisdiction over real estate actions concerning immovable property, specifying that the quality of immovable property is determined by the law applicable in the place of situation (Articles 2663 and 2664). Registrable assets that are not immovable are governed by the court of the state where they were registered (Article 2665). When assets are not registrable, actions must be filed before the court where defendant is domiciled or at the location of the assets in question (Article 2666).[102]

98. In contractual matters, the parties may agree on the choice of the judicial seat. When there is no valid agreement, the ACCC grants the plaintiff the power to file actions before the court of the defendant's domicile or habitual residence (if there are several defendants, then that pertaining to any one of them), or the court where any of the contractual obligations were performed, or where an agency,

98. *See* Art. 2630, ACCC.
99. *See* Arts 2632–2634, ACCC.
100. *See* Arts 2636–2638, ACCC.
101. *See* Arts 2644–2648, ACCC.
102. *See* Arts 2667–2670, ACCC.

branch or representation of the defendant is located, provided that the latter has participated in the negotiation or conclusion of the contract (Article 2650).[103]

In relation to consumer contracts, the ACCC has specific protective provisions for this group. It foresees that claims related to these relationships may be filed, at the consumer's choice as follows: before the court where the contract was concluded or the provision of services fulfilled; where the goods were delivered and the obligation guarantee fulfilled; the defendant's domicile; the place where the consumer performed the acts necessary to conclude the contract; or where the defendant has a branch, agency or any form of commercial representation, as long as they have intervened in the conclusion of the contract or when the defendant has mentioned them for the purposes of the fulfilment of a contractual guarantee. Likewise, it establishes that the action brought against the consumer by the other contracting party may only be lodged with courts in the State where the consumer is domiciled, thus prohibiting agreements of choice of forum (Article 2654).[104]

99. In matters relating to civil liability, beyond the aforementioned assumptions, international jurisdiction corresponds to the court where the defendant lives, or where the event causing the damage occurred, or where it had direct harmful effects (Article 2656).[105] The 1940 Montevideo Treaty (Article 56) confers international jurisdiction on the court whose law is applicable or the one where the defendant is domiciled, at the choice of the plaintiff.

100. The court of the State where the obligation must be fulfilled or where the defendant is domiciled, at the choice of the plaintiff, has international jurisdiction over all controversies arising in the area of securities, except for those concerning cheques. Here, international jurisdiction pertains to the court where the bank from which the cheque was drawn is domiciled or where the defendant is domiciled (Article 2658).[106]

103. *See* Arts 2651–2653, ACCC.
104. *See* Art. 2655, ACCC.
105. *See* Art. 2657, ACCC.
106. *See* Art. 2659-2662, ACCC.

Part III. Actions and Claims

Chapter 1. Actions

§1. Definitions

101. The concept of action is intrinsic to the right of every individual to access justice as established in Article 18 of the Constitution, which refers to the inviolability of the right to defence in court. Article 8 of the ACHR, as previously stated, enshrines the right to due legal process (*see* paragraph 26). Both are constitutional hierarchy rules recognizing the right to petition the judicial authorities to resolve a case or a conflict.

102. However, action may be used in more than one sense. It is frequently used in Argentine law to identify a type of proceedings. Thus, the *amparo,* or protection action, and habeas corpus are enshrined in the Constitution (Article 43). The ACCC establishes rules for paternity suits or actions (Articles 576 et seq.), the annulment of marriage (Article 714), divorce settlements (Article 717) or possessory and real actions (Articles 2238 et seq.), among others. The discussion in European law about the difference between action in the abstract and in the concrete sense led to the widespread acceptance of the notion of claim and of the object of the proceedings in Argentina. The claim encompasses both what the plaintiff is requesting from the court by instituting proceedings and the oppositions of the defendant who wishes these to be recognized in the judgment. The sentence is linked to the specific petition, which is what the persons appearing in court want to either promote or oppose, and which needs to be resolved. Article 330 of the ACCPC includes among the requirements intrinsic to the lawsuit the need to designate as precisely as possible what is the subject of the suit (section 3) and the request in clear and positive terms (section 6). Article 163 of the ACCPC regulates the content of the sentence and establishes that the court must express itself in a positive and precise manner concerning the claims brought in the proceedings (section 6).

The Argentine Civil and Commercial Procedural Code, for its part, often uses these terms interchangeably. It refers to accumulation (Article 87) or connection (Article 88) between actions when in fact it should speak of accumulation or connection between claims.

103. The lawsuit is the procedural act giving rise to the proceedings, whose object is the procedural claim (Article 330, ACCPC).

§2. Admissibility of Complaint

104. The procedural notion of admissibility refers to the requirements whose existence must be verified before analysing whether or not the claim is well founded. These have been classified as extrinsic and intrinsic.

I. Extrinsic Requirements

105. Law 26,589, in force since 2010, establishes that a prior and mandatory instance of mediation is a prerequisite for the admissibility of the complaint (Article 1). Mediation, as we will see later, is confidential (Article 7) and is carried out in the presence of mediators who must be law graduates with three years of legal experience, registered with the National Mediation Registry (Article 11). The maximum term of the mediation procedure is sixty days, counted from the last notification made to the other party (who then takes the character of the defendant in the proceedings initiated if the mediation fails.) The legislation identifies which proceedings are excluded from the mediation, such as criminal cases, divorce proceedings, disability, protection, and executive lawsuits, for instance.

106. The application must be submitted in writing (Article 330, ACCPC) and written in the national language (Article 115, ACCPC). Both the plaintiff and the defendant must be identified with their corresponding addresses. For the purposes of the proceedings, the plaintiff must establish a domicile within the perimeter of the city where the court is located and also provide their real domicile (Article 40, ACCPC).

In its Agreement 14/2013, the Supreme Court mandated the use of the Lex100 management system, which allows users to consult all the data and activities occurring during judicial proceedings. As of May 2015, all those taking part in the judicial proceedings must notify their Electronic Judicial Identification (IEJ, for its acronym in Spanish) to enable them to participate in the cases corresponding to them, which means that in addition to a person's physical addresses, their IEJ must also be notified.[107]

If the plaintiff has no domicile or assets in Argentina, the defendant may request them to supply a guarantee set by the judge to cover legal expenses and fees involved in the proceedings, in accordance with Article 348 of the ACCPC regulating the so-called exception for *arraigo*.[108]

Argentina is a signatory to international treaties that limit the possibility of requiring a guarantee to sue based on the nationality of the parties. It has adhered to the 1954 Hague Convention on Civil Procedure (enacted by Law 23,502), limiting the

107. The BAPCCPC modified Art. 40, which has a similar wording to Art. 40 of the ACCPC according to Law 14,142 (2010), which established the requirement for an email address, being the same as the one officially assigned to the lawyer in attendance, allowing writs to be served which neither require paper support nor the intervention of the Notifying Officer. The ACCPC also establishes that it is incumbent upon the lawyer to establish their electronic address (Art. 30).

108. The draft of the new ACCPC does not contemplate exception for *arraigo* among those that the defendant may adduce in the proceedings.

application of the *cautio judicatum solvi* (Article 18). Consequently, it may not require any guarantee for the purposes of litigation when the plaintiff is a national of another State signatory to the aforementioned Convention. The Member States of MERCOSUR signed the Protocol of Cooperation and Jurisdictional Assistance enshrining equality between the citizens of the States party to the Treaty regarding their ability to litigate in any of the national jurisdictions (Article 3). Argentina adhered to the Protocol through Law 24,578. Article 2610 of the ACCC establishes that no surety or deposit may be required simply because a person is a citizen or permanent resident of another State.

107. A petition must be filed before a competent judge, as previously indicated (paragraph 63). Jurisdiction in terms of the matter, degree, value and territory in extra-patrimonial matters is non-extendable and the court must declare itself incompetent ex officio, before transferring the suit. Territorial jurisdiction regarding matters that exclusively concern property, and federal jurisdiction in personam, are both extendable. A judge may only declare themselves incompetent if the opposing party moves to dismiss for lack of jurisdiction (Article 347.1 and Article 1, ACCPC) or when responding to the request for recusal (Article 9, ACCPC).

108. The plaintiff and the defendant must have civil and procedural capacity. Civil capacity is linked to the ability to acquire rights and contract obligations (Articles 22 and 23 et seq., ACCC). Minors, or people whose capacity is limited due to mental illness, are provided with a legal representative (Articles 26 et seq., ACCC). Legal entities act through their necessary representatives (Articles 141 et seq., ACCC). Procedural capacity is the power to legitimately petition in the proceedings on behalf of another. This refers to the voluntary representative authorized by a party to act on their behalf.

When the parties act through a necessary representative, as in the case of legal entities, or a volunteer, they must present the respective documents enabling them to do so (Articles 46 and 47, ACCPC).

The code authorizes those without conferred representation to present themselves when urgent procedural acts are required and certain facts prevent the party obliged to comply with them from doing so (Article 46, ACCPC). If, within forty judicial working days counted from the presentation of the representative, which the law calls the administrator, the instruments substantiating representation are not provided, or the party in question does not ratify the role of administrator, everything decided upon so far in terms of representation will be rendered null and void.

The defects of the parties' procedural capabilities, or of their representation, may be pointed out by the judge or the defendant through an objection raised on the grounds of lack of legal status (Article 347.2, ACCPC).

109. The plaintiff when suing must specify the details of their claim. The ACCPC establishes that the lawsuit must designate the 'particularized claim' with complete accuracy (Article 330.3). It reiterates in the aforementioned article that the petition must be identified 'in clear and positive terms' (Article 330.6). Judges may reject lawsuits ex officio (in limine) when the claim is not covered by law.

In claims where the object involves financial repair, the amount claimed must be specified, except when the plaintiff cannot determine this at the time of filing the suit, because of the circumstances of the case. Another exception is because the estimate depends on circumstances not yet established, making it necessary to file the lawsuit to avoid the statute of limitations affecting the rights claimed (Article 330.6, ACCPC).

110. The lawsuit must contain 'a statement of the facts on which it is based, clearly explained' (Article 330.4, ACCPC). The ACCPC requires a detailed account of the background supporting the claim. The defendant may file an objection on the ground of legal defect (Article 347.5, ACCPC) requiring the plaintiff to clarify the description made in the lawsuit, in case their description of the facts is confusing.

111. The legal case must be 'succinctly stated; avoiding unnecessary repetitions' (Article 330.5, ACCPC). All that is required is the identification of the legal norm considered affected. Argentine procedural legislation follows the *iura novit curia* principle (the judge knows and understands the law). Although the statement of the facts must be given in detail, it is sufficient to identify which right has been considered to have been violated.

112. A lawsuit is thus inadmissible when there is another pending, previously filed, where the elements – subject, object and cause – are the same, which enables an objection to be raised on the grounds of lis pendens (Article 347.4, ACCPC).

113. If a sentence has formerly been passed in another court case with the same subjects, object and case, the principle of res judicata will prevail, which may be declared by the judge informally or at the request of the opposing party. The opposing party may object to the exception on the grounds of res judicata either based on a previous ruling or when there is a judicial resolution in favour of the transaction, conciliation and withdrawal of the right.

114. The signing of the writ constitutes one of the requirements in accordance with Articles 288 et seq. of the ACCC. Article 288 adds that for digital instruments, the requirement for a person's signature may be deemed satisfied if a digital signature is used, which ensures the authorship and integrity of the instrument.

115. Technical legal assistance is required to perform the range of procedural actions, including filing the lawsuit (Article 56, ACCPC). Any document which is signed by a lawyer will not be admitted by the judge and instead returned to the signatory (Article 57, ACCPC).

116. The judge must require the plaintiff to pay court fees before summoning the defendant. Law 23,898 (1990) establishes the regulatory framework for court fees, calculated proportionally to the amount claimed in the lawsuit. In cases which can be quantified, the rate is 3% of the amount claimed (Article 2). Certain figures are exempt from paying court fees: the National State, the provinces, the municipalities, official banks, etc. The judge may dispense with the payment of court fees in cases of people able to prove that they cannot bear the expenses of the proceedings according to the incidental procedure regulated as 'litigation *in forma pauperis*' (Articles 7886, ACCPC).

117. The lawsuit must be accompanied by documentary evidence and offer any other evidence that the parties intend to use. When documentary evidence is not available, the interested party must make this clear and indicate its content, location, file number, and the public office or person in whose possession it is. When documentary evidence is duly offered, the representing lawyers may, after the suit has been filed, directly request private entities to send any relevant documentation or an authenticated copy. They do not need a prior judicial request, and only need to send a letter, including a transcription of this article, directly to the secretariat, with a transcript or copy of the brief. If witness evidence is offered, the points to be proved with the statement of each witness will be indicated. In the case of expert evidence, the interested party will propose the points of expertise (Article 333).

II. Intrinsic Requirements

118. Intrinsic requirements are dealt with according to their relationship with the subjects or with the lawsuit. The subjects (plaintiff and defendant) in addition to their generic aptitudes – civil and procedural capabilities – must prove their condition as 'legitimate parties'. Procedural interest is also a requirement of admissibility related to the subjects (paragraph 120).

119. As for the claim, it must be legally possible to achieve, in the sense that it is not expressly excluded by law. In these cases, the claim may be considered objectively improbable and the judge is empowered to reject it in limine (Article 348, ACCPC).

A. Procedural Interest

120. The jurisdictional function does not contemplate abstract declarations unrelated to either the case or the conflict to be resolved, as court jurisdiction is limited to ruling on the issues raised by the parties. The notion of a judicial case presupposes the existence of the interest of one of the parties in obtaining a decision to protect the right that they hold was affected by the other party. If there is no concrete and current interest, then the exercise of the court's jurisdiction collides with the political branch, invading its constitutional faculties to the detriment of the principle of separation of powers.

121. The Supreme Court has zealously guarded this basic rule, maintaining that 'the essence of the Judicial Power is to decide on effective collisions of rights, and that it is not for the judges to make general or abstract statements'.[109] It has also argued that 'the interest must be current, so that eliminating the reason for the litigation is a requirement of the jurisdictional function incumbent upon the judges, which they must verify ex officio'.[110]

122. Procedural interest is different from substantial interest, which is the one at stake in the legal relationship binding the parties and becomes manifest when it is necessary to appeal to the court to require the protection of a right. However, there are certain cases where procedural interest is configured without there being any non-compliance with a provision, due to a situation of uncertainty regarding the existence or non-existence of a right. Article 322 of the ACCPC envisages filing 'a merely declarative action' to put an end to the state of uncertainty regarding the existence, scope or modalities of a legal relationship, as and when this lack of certainty has the potential to harm the plaintiff. Likewise, there is procedural interest when situations able to modify a state or legal relationship, which only a judicial pronouncement can declare and constitute, can be verified (e.g., marriage annulment, restricted capabilities or disability).

123. The content of procedural interest goes beyond what is purely economic and may have an exclusively moral substance such as the guardianship of non-patrimonial or personal rights, or an institutional one, such as the right to information, public ethics.

B. Standing

124. The concurrence of this requirement requires there to be a coincidence between the people intervening in the process and those whom the law specifically empowers to both file a claim (active legitimation) and contradict it (passive standing) regarding the matter in question.[111] Procedural standing derives, as a rule, from the active or passive ownership of the substantial legal relationship in controversy in the proceedings, except in cases of extraordinary or anomalous standing, configured in cases of procedural substitution or oblique action (Article 1196, ACCC). For various reasons, the law grants anomalous or extraordinary standing for the protection of collective advocacy rights (*see* §2). In the absence of active or passive standing, objection on the grounds of lack of standing is appropriate, and if it is manifest,

109. *Fallos* 199:213 (1944), 218:590 (1950), 221:215 (1951); 229:460 (1954); 236:673 (1956), among others.
110. *Fallos* 257:227 (1963).
111. The Supreme Court has pointed out that the existence of 'case', 'cause' or 'matter' presupposes, according to Art. 116 of the Constitution, the 'parties', and thus it is necessary to determine whether there is a logical link between the status affirmed by the litigant and the claim they are seeking to satisfy. That is, the 'party' must demonstrate that the alleged grievances affect them in a 'sufficiently direct' or 'substantial' manner, meaning that they possess sufficient specificity and immediacy 'to be able to achieve said process' (*Fallos* 306:1125 (1984); 308:2147 (1986); 310:606 (1987); 328:2429 (2005), among others).

it must be resolved in a prior instance; otherwise, this only needs to be decided when the judgment on merits is ruled (Article 347 (3) of the ACCPC).

§3. Civil and Criminal Action Deriving from the Same Events

125. Civil and criminal claims arising from the same event may be filed independently. However, in those cases where a harmful act may be considered a crime, the civil claim may be filed with a criminal court, according to the provisions enshrined in procedural codes or special laws (Article 1774, ACCC).

126. Likewise, the point at which a criminal lawsuit is filed affects the civil process, because if the former precedes it or is filed while it is pending, the defendant cannot be sentenced in the civil proceedings before the accused is convicted in the criminal proceedings. This is the case, except when: (i) the criminal case is concluded; (ii) the criminal proceedings in fact frustrate the right to compensation; or, (iii) if the civil action is based on the factor of strict liability (Article 1775, ACCC).

127. None of this places any limits on filing a civil action or on the continuation of the proceedings, only on the passing of the sentence, as a pronouncement in criminal proceedings is taken as res judicata in civil proceedings regarding the existence of the main event and who is at fault. Hence, if the criminal sentence considers that the act does not constitute a criminal offence or does not compromise a person's criminal responsibility, this fact may be freely discussed in the context of civil liability (Articles 1776 and 1777, ACCC). Nor do grounds for criminal justification affect the civil claim, unless otherwise foreseen by law (Article 1778, ACCC).

128. On the contrary, they prevent the repair of harm, the proof of the truth of the reputed slanderous deed, or, in crimes against life and limb, having been a co-author or an accomplice, or not having prevented the deed when able to do so (Article 1779, ACCC). Thus, a criminal sentence issued after the civil one has no effect upon the latter, except in the case of review. This procedure may be brought when the civil judgment assigns the scope of res judicata to issues resolved by criminal law, and the latter is reviewed on the basis of these (unless it arises from a change in legislation); if the person convicted in civil action for strict liability is acquitted in the criminal trial based on the absence of the act or the lack of authorship, and in other cases foreseen by law (Article 1780, ACCC).

§4. Summons of the Defendant

129. The judge must analyse compliance with the formal requirements of the lawsuit and may, if it does not comply with the rules established, reject it in limine, expressing its defects (Article 337, ACCPC). If the court considers that the requirements established have been met, it may notify the defendant to allow them to reply within fifteen days. When the defendant is the Nation, a province or a municipality, the term provided to answer the suit will be sixty days.

The summons to the defendant will be issued through a certificate delivered to their current address. If the defendant is not present, they will be left a notification at their home address advising them to wait until the next day and if they are not found then, the notification will be delivered to another person in the house, department or office, or to the manager of the building. In case it cannot be left to any of these parties, it may be attached to the door corresponding to their domicile.[112]

130. Once a suit has been filed, the plaintiff may not modify it. However, it may also increase the amount of the claim if new terms or quotas relating to the same obligation expire before the judgment (Article 331, ACCPC).

§5. Abusive and Reckless Lawsuits

131. In Argentine law, there are legal regulations that may be considered in their entirety equivalent to what in Anglo-Saxon law is called vexatious litigation. Various standards make it possible to hold the party and misconduct liable for misconduct in terms of the consequences of their reckless and malicious action in the proceedings, or for taking advantage of the proceedings for abusive purposes and to the detriment of the opposite party. In addition to common responsibilities, formal law foresees the imposition of sanctions on reckless and malicious conduct in the course of the proceedings, whether on the part of the lawyers or their clients. Furthermore, in relation to the former, there are disciplinary charges. Certain kinds of conduct may give rise to prosecution and criminal penalties.

I. Civil Liabilities

132. General substantive rules on tort liability allow claims to be made for damages arising from the unlawful action of the litigants when this causes material or moral damages. According to Articles 1067, 1109, 512 et seq. of the ACCC, the concurrence of intent, fault or negligence is required in order to impute the harmful consequences of certain actions to the subject, as well as the demonstration of a precise causal link between their actions and the concrete harm caused. This is the case with lawsuits, which are objectively improbable (*see* paragraph 118), whether they have been rejected in limine or in the judgment on merit, due to the 'frivolity' of the grounds giving rise to concrete harm to the other party, according to the circumstances of the case. The ACCPC regulates those specific cases of civil liability involving a party granted a precautionary measure when it can be shown that the

112. *See* Art. 339 of the ACCC.

petitioner abused or exceeded the right granted by law. In this case, the judge ordering this measure to be lifted may themselves also order this party to compensate the other, at their request, for the damages caused (Article 208).[113]

II. Procedural Liabilities

133. The ACCPC establishes that the parties must prove loyalty, probity and good faith and requires courts to 'prevent and punish any act contrary to that duty' (Article 34, paragraph 5). It refers, when the final sentences are issued, to any recklessness or malice on the part of the litigants or professional lawyers involved (Articles 34, paragraph 6; 163 paragraph 8). Article 45 makes explicit these faculties when it stipulates that if either of the parties is found guilty of malicious or reckless conduct, the judge will impose on them and/or their lawyer a fine of between 10% and 50% of the amount at stake in the judgment in favour of the other party, with a limit of ARS 50,000, now out of date as a result of inflation.

134. Other precepts establishing similar sanctions in the process of execution tend towards the same objective, when the party whose goods have been executed has: litigated without valid reason; or has obstructed the normal course of the proceedings with manifestly improper articulations; or has in any way unreasonably delayed proceedings (Article 551, ACCPC); or in the preparation of the executive route, falsely deny their own signature (Article 528, ACCPC); or if they deliberately ignore the signature of the document attributed to them with malicious intent (Article 528, ACCPC); or if they cause unnecessary delays in complying with the executive sentence (Article 594, ACCPC).

135. Furthermore, the conduct observed by the parties during the substantiation of the proceedings may constitute an element which can be used to corroborate the conviction of the evidence for the purpose of judging the origin of the respective claims (Article 163 (5), ACCPC).

136. Recklessness is understood as the attitude of someone who affirms facts without due grounds, or conducts themselves unreasonably, in full awareness that they are doing so in order to take advantage of the proceedings and jurisdiction to cause harm to the other party. Malice, on the other hand, refers to invaluable action during the proceedings when any of the parties, even the one that ultimately wins, hinders, delays, or prompts manifestly inappropriate expressions, with the sole purpose of delaying the proceedings.[114]

113. Even when the party calling for an embargo is entitled to request the measure, they must answer for the damages caused, arising from negligence in the preparation of the notification which gave rise to the attachment (BAPSCJ, Ac. 38,706, 25-8-92); or if the attachment was applied to assets of a much higher value than the credit being claimed (BAPSCJ, Ac. and Sent., 1963-III, p. 584).

114. The rule enshrined in Art. 45 of the ACCPC, according to repeated decisions, is not contrary to the guarantee of defence (Supreme Court, *Fallos* 291:251 (1975), among others), nor to equality before the law (SCBA, Ac. and Sent., 1974-III, p. 649), as it may be applied ex officio by the court (Supreme Court, *Fallos* 289:162 (1974); 295:700 (1976)). However, if the attitude criticized did

137. Finally, it should be noted that the parties' procedural liability for their reckless or malicious actions is different from the responsibility for the costs caused by the proceedings (Articles 68 et seq., ACCPC). These are generally awarded objectively with regard to the losing party and not related to abusive procedural conduct, which creates a certain aggravated responsibility for the damages caused to the opponent.

III. Responsibility of the Lawyer

138. According to Article 45 of the ACCPC, the lawyer may be sanctioned for recklessness or malice as a result of their own actions, regardless of the attitude of their client. The conduct demonstrated by the lawyer during the proceedings must be shown to be unjustifiable in terms of the duties of the defence, while the intent to wilfully obstruct the progress of the proceedings or pursue improper purposes according to a reasonable application of the law must be demonstrated. In these cases, a lawyer may also be held jointly and severally responsible for the costs.

139. The code of professional ethics also imposes disciplinary sanctions on lawyers for their conduct when this contravenes the principles of loyalty, honesty and good faith (*see* paragraph 48).

IV. Criminal Liability

140. The Criminal Code sanctions the reduction of the value of an estate with deliberate intent to avoid complying with the obligations claimed in court. Article 179 of the Penal Code details sanctions against those who maliciously destroy, render useless, damage, conceal or make disappear assets from their patrimony, or fraudulently diminish their value, during the course of proceedings, or after the conviction, and thus frustrate, in whole or in part, the fulfilment of their corresponding civil obligations. Beyond these typical assumptions, there is no other criminal liability arising from the malicious or fraudulent use of civil proceedings foreseen in Argentine law.

---

not in fact exceed the limits of the exercise of defence, the qualification and corresponding sanction for reckless conduct may be excessive (Supreme Court, *Fallos* 302:464 (1980)).

Chapter 2. Claims and Defences

§1. Defence of the Merits and Procedural Exceptions

141. The clerk's office sends a certified copy of the complaint along with other preparatory documents to the defendant at the address given by the plaintiff. When a defendant is served a lawsuit, they have the option to either appear or ignore the summons.

If they decide not to appear, the plaintiff may request that the process proceeds without their intervention and that the judge declares them in default (Article 59, ACCPC). Declaring someone in default refers to proceedings carried out when one of the parties is absent. Default constitutes a presumption of the truth of the lawful acts affirmed by the opposing party (Article 60 of the ACCPC) and precautionary measures may be decreed against it, at the request of the other party. Another consequence of declaring someone in default is that the offender in this case is notified of the resolutions on Tuesdays or Fridays. Excepted from notification on those days are: (i) the resolution declaring in default, and (ii) the final judgment. Those decisions must be notified by writ.

If the defendant decides to appear, they have the option of agreeing to the plaintiff's claim (Article 307, ACCPC), thus releasing them from paying costs of the proceedings, as and when this concession is unconditional, total and made in timely fashion (Article 70, ACCPC).

142. The ACCPC dedicates two chapters to the right of defence. The first of these covers prior exceptions and the second to the answer to the claim.

143. Prior exceptions are nominated defences, whose enumeration responds to the fact that the legislator has considered that it is convenient to resolve them before the proceedings progress to the stage of producing evidence. Exceptions must be made in tandem with the answer to the claim, or the counterclaim, and the court must resolve these before continuing with the proceedings.

Within Articles 346, 347 and 348 of the ACCPC, there are means of defence pursuing different purposes: (i) those are related to the regular constitution of the proceedings, such as lack of jurisdiction, or of legal status, lis pendens, legal defect and *arraigo*; (ii) those that refer to the requirements of the suit, preventing the court from ruling on whether the grounds for this are the lack of manifest legitimation, prescription, res judicata and temporary defences; and (iii) those attacking the plaintiff's substantive right, including the transaction, conciliation and withdrawal of the right.

Article 347 of the ACCPC establishes the following exceptions:

(1) Lack of jurisdiction: the court must state that it has jurisdiction when the suit or claim is filed or otherwise request the party to rule on it in case this is doubtful (Articles 4 and 337, ACCPC).
(2) Lack of legal status: this exception raises questions about the civil capacity to act in the proceedings, or the scope of the representative's power to act on behalf of the person they claim to represent.

(3) Obvious lack of standing: this may be raised with respect to the aptitude of the person suing, or to the person being sued regarding the right being claimed. For the case to proceed, this must be evident; otherwise, its resolution may be postponed until the time when the sentence is passed.
(4) Lis pendens: the notification of the lawsuit leads to lis pendens and therefore no other proceedings may be validly initiated following it. Lis pendens assumes the existence of an identity, between the elements of the claims deduced in two proceedings: subjects, object and cause.
(5) Legal defect: this allows the claim to be clarified concerning its more obscure points, or when it fails to respect the requirements established in Article 330 of the ACCPC.
(6) Res judicata, transaction, conciliation and withdrawal of the right: this prevents the plaintiff from returning to an issue that has already been definitively resolved.
(7) The various temporary defences enshrined in general law include, for example, that of excussion, which may benefit the guarantor (Articles 1583 et seq., ACCC), the fulfilment of the convictions of the possessor by the defendant intending to file a petition (Article 2272, ACCC), the nine days' mourning period following the death of the plaintiff which rule out the possibility that they may present a claim against the heir to accept or refuse an inheritance (Article 2289, ACCC) and the lack of prior execution of the assets of a company in the case of Article 125 of the General Companies Law.[115]
(8) The statute of limitations (Article 346, ACCPC) may be an exception if the issue on which it is based can be resolved without the need to produce evidence.[116]
(9) *Arraigo* (Article 348 of the ACCPC) whose characteristics have already been discussed (*see* paragraph 91).

All prior exceptions must be based on the brief answering the claim, accompany the instrumental evidence and offer any others that the opponent tries to use. In ordinary proceedings, all exceptions tend to be resolved as a prior and special pronouncement,[117] except for the lack of legitimation, when this is not manifest, or the statute of limitations, when this cannot be resolved as a matter of law, whose treatment will be deferred at the time of sentencing. This is so because the ease with which they can be proven makes their substantiation with the remaining underlying issues involved in the proceedings inadequate.

The court checks the admissibility of the objections and verifies that the supporting documentation has been duly presented (Article 349, ACCPC) before permitting the opposing party to intervene (Article 350, ACCPC). Once the writ has been

115. Law 19,550 (1972), text ordered by Decree 841/84, denomination according to Law 26,994 (2014).

116. The ACCC (Arts 2551 and 2553) establishes that a statute of limitations may be opposed as an objection until the moment when a claim has to be answered in the discovery process.

117. In summary proceedings, all objections are resolved with the final decision (Arts 346, 347, 350 and 498, subsection. 1, ACCPC).

notified, the court may proceed to examine the evidence, after which it will decide on the merit of the objections brought (Article 351, ACCPC).

The court primarily deals with declination and lis pendens, and their admission renders any pronouncement on the remainder useless.

A resolution on prior exceptions may be appealed, except if any postpones the treatment of the lack of legitimacy for not being manifest, or if one decides that the facts referring to the statute of limitations require evidence to be produced.

Once the resolution giving rise to the prior exceptions is firm, the judge may proceed according to the nature of each one. In the case of lack of jurisdiction, depending on whether the case comes under national justice or not, the judge may send it to the competent court, or archive it if the conflict comes under provincial justice.[118] They may also order the file to be archived when admitting the exceptions of res judicata, lack of legitimate standing, statute of limitations or lis pendens. Regarding the lack of legal status, legal defect or *arraigo*, the court will set a term for the objections to be rectified. If this mandate is not met, it will be considered abandoned, and fees will be charged. Once the errors indicated have been corrected, the pertinent notifications will be made or the period for answering the lawsuit will be resumed (Articles 352, 353, 354 and 354 (bis), ACCPC).

Civil proceedings are designed on the basis of a first stage dedicated to objections, which must be concluded before the judge receives the parties at the preliminary hearing, which effectively postpones the necessary immediacy. This stage is not managed by the judge and it may take up an inordinate amount of time. For this reason, the Preliminary Draft foresees the possibility, according to the characteristics of the issues debated as objections, that the court may resolve them before or during the preliminary hearing (Article 415).

144. The concept of defence includes, generically, the different kinds of oppositions that the defendant may formulate to counteract the procedural claim filed against them. The opposition is the procedural act wherein the defendant makes statements aimed at refuting the claims brought against them. This is grounded in the exercise of a person's constitutional right of access to justice, the inviolability of the right to defence by trial, and due legal process (Article 18, AC, and Article 8, ACHR). The opposition defines, together with the plaintiff's claim, the *thema decidendum* to be resolved by the judge when passing sentence, according to the principle of consistency (Article 34 (4), ACCPC).

145. The answer to the claim is the act by means of which the defendant may materialize their defence, and in which they may provide the arguments to be used in their defence. This act completes the legal and procedural relationship, once the facts covered by the evidence are established, together with the subject matter of the litigation. The deadline for answering the suit is fifteen days in ordinary proceedings, and five in summary proceedings, plus any corresponding extension due

118. The Supreme Court departed from the rule requiring the proceedings to be archived given the declaration of lack of jurisdiction based on the principle of procedural economy. In the case of *Leon Zalchner v. Munro Finance* (*Fallos* 307:852 (1985)), it resolved that the proceedings initiated in the Province of Buenos Aires should continue before federal justice.

to distance.[119] When the defendant is the State, the term will be sixty days for ordinary proceedings, and for summary proceedings, the deadline is set at the court's discretion (Articles 158, 338 and 355, ACCPC). This term is not suspended due to the opposition of prior exceptions, except in the case of lack of legal status, *arraigo* and legal defect.

146. In the answer to the suit, the defendant shall:[120]

(1) Formulate all previous or substantive objections and remaining defences.
(2) Recognize or deny, categorically, clearly and explicitly each of the personal and essential facts given in the lawsuit,[121] as well as the authenticity of any accompanying documents and the receipt of any writs addressed to them. Silence, evasive responses or the general and indeterminate denial of the facts may be considered as the acknowledgement of the same. The court will in this case evaluate these attitudes in accordance with the elements of conviction provided in the case. In relation to documentation, if this has not been categorically denied, it will be considered to have been recognized.
    For certain subjects, the procedural burden may be satisfied by manifesting ignorance or giving answers in expectation. This is the case with the official defence counsel and defendant intervening in the process as an inheritor, as they can argue that they have no knowledge of the facts of the person or cause, meaning that the power to rule definitively on these may be reserved until after the evidence has been produced.
(3) Clearly specify the facts alleged as the basis of their defence.
(4) Observe, as applicable, the requirements of the application, such as its wording in the official language, the complaint, and the constitution of domicile or the reference to the law applicable.
(5) Add the documentary evidence in their possession or identify their location and offer any remaining evidence to be used to prove defence. Once the lawsuit has been answered, documents dated either later or earlier may only be admitted, under oath of not having previous knowledge of these (Articles 333, 335, 356 and 358, ACCPC).

147. Failure to answer a suit can imply the acknowledgement of the documents but does not oblige the court to admit the facts invoked by the plaintiff. In principle, this does not exempt the plaintiff from having to produce the evidence required to support the facts.

---

119. If a defendant is not domiciled in the city where the court hearing the case sits, Art. 158 of the ACCPC extends the terms of the proceedings at the rate of one day per 200 km or fraction not below 100.
120. *See* Art. 356 of the ACCC.
121. There exists a widespread practice of denying each of the facts asserted by the plaintiff regardless of whether they are true or false, in view of the risk that they will be recognized. The Preliminary Draft places the burden of corroborating the veracity of the facts alleged in the lawsuit on the defendant who must give their version in this regard (Art. 418 -a-). This provision is complemented by the duty to tell the truth established in Art. 15 (c) of the Preliminary Draft.

§2. ACCUMULATION OF CLAIMS

I. General Background

148. The accumulation of claims may be original or successive, depending on whether they are brought at the beginning of the process or incorporated as it evolves. In turn, the original claim may be divided, taking into consideration the plurality of claims or the plurality of subjects. The principle of successive accumulation may operate when a new claim is brought within the framework of proceedings which are already under way.

II. Successive Accumulation of Claims

149. The objective accumulation of claims involves the joint presentation, within the same lawsuit, of the different claims that the plaintiff is bringing against the defendant, so that these can be substantiated and resolved in a single set of proceedings. In this case, the justification for accumulation lies in the possibility of reducing costs and maximizing time and resources.

150. The plaintiff may exercise this power before being notified of the lawsuit. However, to do this, they must be able to show that the claims: (i) are not contrary to each other and thus mutually exclusive; (ii) correspond to the jurisdiction of the same court; and (iii) may be substantiated through the same procedures (Article 87, ACCPC).

151. As for the first requirement, it has been stated that incompatibility between different claims does not prevent their eventual accumulation, which occurs when a claim is filed as the principal complaint and another in a subsidiary fashion, whose resolution is subject to the rejection of the first. This may occur successively when a claim is filed with the condition that another one presupposed by it is accepted first. Likewise, there are cases where accumulation is expressly prohibited by law (Articles 1083 et seq., ACCC). With regard to jurisdiction, the accumulation of claims involving different courts due to the subject matter is excluded. The purpose of substantiation through the same procedures is to prevent the accumulation of claims under various different proceedings. The nonobservance of the requirements detailed may be denounced by the defendant when they file their opposition with the answer to the demand, through either legal defect or lack of jurisdiction.

152. The subjective accumulation of claims occurs when claims related to the cause or the object are substantiated in the same process, between more than one actor or defendant (active or passive accumulation) or between more than one actor and more than one defendant (mixed accumulation). In this case, the issue is not only one of economy but also the need to avoid the risk of contradictory pronouncements. This type of accumulation is admissible as long as the claims are connected depending on the cause, the object or both at the same time (Article 88, ACCPC).

That is to say, whenever an identical legal relationship or the same factual situation appears as the basis for these, or the immediate and mediate objects claimed happen to coincide.

153. Subjective accumulation adds an exception to the rules of attribution of ordinary jurisdiction by reason of civil and commercial matters. This is not the case with territorial variables, since the defendant may request to be allowed to litigate at their own domicile, unless the different defendants are bound by joint or several obligations, in which case the claim may be brought before the court of the domicile of any of them (Article 5, paragraph 5, ACCPC).

154. Successive accumulation by insertion may come from the plaintiff in the event of the expansion of the claim, or from the defendant in the case of a counterclaim, or from a third party, in cases of exclusive third-party intervention.

155. Supplementing the complaint operates when the plaintiff accumulates other claims against the defendant, after the suit has been filed but before the writ is served. Once a writ has been served, no further new claims may be brought within the same proceedings (Article 87, ACCPC).

156. The counterclaim is the claim that the defendant can bring against the plaintiff, provided that it is derived from the same legal relationship or is connected with the one stated in the lawsuit. The characters, elements and requirements specified in any claim may be applied.

157. The counterclaim must be raised in the brief answering the claim. It cannot be brought later, unless this is in the context of another trial. It is inadmissible within the framework of the summary process (Articles 357 and 498, paragraph 2, ACCC). In addition to the extrinsic and intrinsic requirements of the claim, a counterclaim must be able to show the following: the material competence of the intervening judge, their relationship or connection with the original claim, the possibility of it being substantiated by the same procedure and its main points, as well as the accompanying documentary evidence. These will be notified to the plaintiff, who, if they decide to answer, must observe the rules governing the statement of defence (Article 358, ACCPC). A counterclaim cannot be counterclaimed. If the response to the counterclaim alleges facts which have not been originally considered in it, the counterclaimant may offer evidence on them, and the documents incorporated must be notified (Articles 334 and 356, paragraph 1, ACCPC).

158. In cases of exclusionary and third-party intervention, a new claim may be brought by persons who are not the original parties, making them passive subjects of the former. The ACCPC acknowledges third-party domain and best law. The first is based on the domain of the assets attached. The second is founded on the right of the third party to be paid in preference to the attaching party (Articles 97 et seq., ACCPC).

159. Successive accumulation occurs when several claims are added together, meaning when two or more proceedings with related claims have to be substantiated together, at the risk of incurring contradictory judgments. In other words, there are various accumulating claims which lead to the material union of the various proceedings where they are aired.

160. Article 188 of the ACCPC dictates that the accumulation of proceedings corresponds when the subjective accumulation of claims is admissible and, in general, when the sentence handed down in any one of them has the effect of res judicata on one or more of the others. In addition, it must be proven that: (i) the proceedings are taking place in the same instance and can be substantiated by the same procedures, so that proceedings subject to different procedures may only be accumulated when necessary, due to the effects of res judicata which the sentence ruled for one may have for the others. In this case, the court will determine the proceedings to be followed; (ii) the court hearing the accumulated processes has jurisdiction because of the subject matter and may assimilate civil and commercial cases to this effect. In cases of different territorial jurisdiction, it is necessary to obtain the consent of the litigant empowered to extend jurisdiction; and (iii) the status of the cases allows for their joint substantiation, without causing any detrimental and unjustified delays in the proceedings of those cases which are further ahead.

161. The accumulation of proceedings may be arranged at the request of a party, when answering a claim, or afterwards, or ex officio. To do so afterwards means that a claim can be filed at any stage of the process, up to the point when a sentence is about to issued, unless this causes a detrimental delay to those proceedings which are already well under way.

162. A late claim may be brought before the court due to rule on the subject or otherwise refer it, as it will substantiate the request with the remaining litigants and will require or refer action depending on the case.

163. Once the late claim has been brought or communicated to the other judges all proceedings will be suspended, except for urgent measures. Any decision rejecting the request may be appealed, not so a decision admitting it. Accumulation may also be applied to a case that it would otherwise have prevented, unless the courts involved in the proceedings had different jurisdictions because of the amount involved, in which case the one handling the largest amount prevails.

164. In the case of conflicts of jurisdiction, when the court does not see fit, it is up to the Chamber drawing up the appeal to decide on the origin of the accumulation. Accumulated processes shall be substantiated together, unless this becomes difficult due to the nature of the issues raised, when the judge may order them to be substantiated separately. The principle of unity of pronouncement obliges the court in all cases to issue a single decision.[122]

122. Articles 89, 190-194, ACCPC.

§3. ACCUMULATION OF PARTIES

I. Joinder of Parties

165. When there is active or passive co-ownership in relation to a single claim or a connection between different claims, in such a way that the proceedings involve more than one more person in the role of party, it is called a joinder of parties. The joinder of parties may be active, passive or mixed, depending on the role taken by the plurality of subjects. Likewise, it may be optional or necessary, depending on whether it is constituted by the free will of the parties or through a legal imperative, or because of the type of relationship making up the cause for the claim.

166. A joinder is necessary when the judgment may only be handed down usefully in front of all those making up the substantial legal relationship discussed in the proceedings. Hence, its effectiveness depends on the summons of these persons (Article 89, ACCPC). In certain cases, the law imposes the constitution of a joinder, for example, in marital affiliation cases (Articles 582 et seq., ACCC). In others, it is the nature of the relationship or legal status that is the subject of the controversy, common and indivisible to several people, that determines the need for a single judicial decision (e.g., in the cases of the division of a condominium, inheritance partition or the declaration of simulation of a contract). In necessary joinder litigation, there is a single claim that can only be filed by or against those entitled to do so. When proceedings are not properly integrated, objection on the grounds of lack of action is admissible. Likewise, the court may order the due integration of the litigation ex officio or at the request of a party (Article 89, ACCPC). The reason for this would be to safeguard the right of defence by trial for all co-interested parties, to whom the res judicata of the sentence would be extended.[123] Among other effects, this type of joinder results in the following: (i) the proceedings or the defences brought by any of the joinder litigants, whether these are based on common or individual facts, favouring the others; (ii) the acts in the proceedings carried out by one of them do not have any consequences until such time as the others adopt similar behaviour; or, (iii) the legal action brought by one takes advantage of or harms everyone involved.

167. The option for a litigation consortium has its origins in the existence of a connection linking various claims, or in the adhesion or opposition that a third party may pursue in relation to a claim already brought (Articles 88 and 90, paragraph 2, ACCPC). The joinder litigants in this case enjoy autonomous procedural standing, which is why the result of the proceedings may be different for each of them. The effects may include the following: (i) the proceedings may conclude for certain joinder litigants and continue for others; (ii) the petition brought by one party does not benefit the rest, except when there is an objection; or, (iii) the evidence has to be analysed based on the common or individual facts of each joinder litigant.

123. Supreme Court, Rulings 252–375; 256–198.

II. Third-Party Intervention

168. The intervention of third parties occurs when people other than the original parties join the proceedings, either spontaneously or because they are induced to do so in order to assert their own interests which are also related to the object or cause of the claim. Once the admissibility of the third-party intervention is declared, they become a party, even when this does not happen in autonomous form.

169. Voluntary intervention occurs when the third party, freely and spontaneously, takes part in the process, be it as principal, as a joinder litigant, or in simple form. In the principal intervention, the third party is asserting their own right through a claim which is incompatible with, or exclusive to the one filed by the plaintiff, as a party. The ACCPC does not regulate the institution, although different provincial legal systems do. When acting as a joinder litigant, the third party participates in the process of asserting their own right against one of the parties, adhering to the role assumed by the other. The ACCPC defines a joinder litigant as one who, according to substantive norms, could have been entitled to sue or be sued in the proceedings (Article 90, paragraph 2, ACCPC). Thus, they act as a joinder litigant with the main party and enjoy the same procedural faculties (Article 91, paragraph 2, ACCPC). When acting as a simple litigant, the third party does not have the character of an autonomous party as they have a right which is related to, or dependent on, the claims brought in the proceedings. Hence, they may only collaborate in the procedural efforts made by any of the parties, as their action is ancillary and subordinate to that of the party they support, and they may neither allege nor prove whatever was prohibited for the party in question (Article 91, paragraph 1, ACCPC). In order to intervene, summary evidence must be provided that the sentence may affect own interests (Article 90, paragraph 1, ACCPC).

170. The request for intervention must be formulated in writing and comply, as appropriate, with the requirements of the claim. After the parties have been duly notified, if there is any opposition, this will be substantiated in a single hearing, after which the court will decide. Any decision rejecting the request may be appealed, not so a decision admitting it. The volunteer who is intervening may join the proceedings at any stage, without this intervention rolling back, or suspend the proceedings. The sentence issued after the intervention or summons of the third party affects them as the main litigants. This implies that the decision may be enforced against them, unless at the time of making the request for intervention or answering the summons, they allege and are able to prove the existence of defences or rights that cannot be the subject of debate and decision in court (Articles 92, 93 and 96, ACCPC).[124]

171. Coactive intervention occurs when the court, at the request of a party or ex officio, orders a third party to be summoned to take part in the proceedings, so that

124. This was the criteria established by the Supreme Court in the case *Gandolfi de Vanetta,* Rulings: 321–769 (1998).

the sentence ruled may be imposed on them. The parties may request the intervention of the third party with whom they believe they share the controversy, in their statements of claim and defence. Otherwise, the judge may order the integration of the litis (Articles 89 and 94, ACCPC). This type of intervention may occur both in those cases in which the party, if defeated, has a claim for return against the third party and in the cases of *nominatio auctoris* (Article 2255, ACCC), third party plaintiff (Article 904 paragraph b, ACCC), or in an eviction notice, which is specifically regulated by the ACCPC (Articles 105 et seq., of the ACCPC and 1044 et seq., ACCC). The third party involved will take on a role as a party. Unlike a volunteer, they must be able to fully exercise their right of defence within the proceedings to which they are summoned, hence their summons suspends the proceedings until they appear, or until the expiry of the period established for it (Article 95 of the ACCPC). As for the effects of the sentence, the same rules specified for the volunteer apply to this type of intervention.

Chapter 3. Sanctions on Procedural Irregularities

§1. Scope

172. The ACCC establishes a difference between absolute and relative nullities. According to Article 386, acts that contravene public order, morality or good customs are null and void. Those acts on which the law imposes this sanction are only of relative nullity when it comes to protecting the interests of certain people. Absolute nullity may be declared by the court, even without a request from the party, if it is manifest at the time of sentencing (Article 387, ACCC). Relative nullity can only be declared at the request of those persons for whose benefit it has been established (Article 388, ACCC). The nullity of procedural acts is a sanction wherein the law deprives a procedural act of its effects due to the flaws inherent to it. The main flaw concerns the defects intrinsic to the act which end up limiting the right to submit a rebuttal.

173. When what is raised is the nullity of the resolution or sentence, questions should be raised by means of filing an appeal to contemplate questioning the flaws affecting the decision. The appeal for annulment is inherently implicit.

174. Nullity may also be considered as: (i) an objection to the executive judgment in view of the hypothesis that the rules established to prepare the executive route will not be complied with (Article 545, ACCPC); and, (ii) an autonomous action aimed at obtaining the total or partial nullity of the proceedings. The latter is an exceptional tool referred to by the ACCPC in relation to the award of amiable composition when it is alleged that the ruling has been handed down after the deadline, or is on uncommitted points (Article 771). This also refers to those cases where it is maintained that the proceedings constitute legal fraud, or that the proceedings were not conducted correctly.[125]

175. The principles governing procedural nullities according to the ACCPC are:

(1) *Legality or specificity*. In order to declare nullity, the law must contemplate such a sanction with respect to the flaw invoked, but it may only proceed when the act lacks the requirements indispensable to obtaining its purpose (Article 169).
(2) *Validation or rectification*. Procedural annulments may be remedied by the express or presumed consent of the parties harmed (Articles 170 and 172).

125. The Supreme Court developed the doctrine of fraudulent res judicata in the case of *Campbell Davidson* (*Fallos* 279:59 (1971)). In its Art. 2564 (f), the ACCC recognizes autonomous action taken to review res judicata and establishes that this must be exercised within a period of one year to avoid the statute of limitations. The Preliminary Draft of the new ACCPC regulates the claim to review res judicata on the basis of the nullity of the final judgment in its Art. 129. It establishes that in the lawsuit pursuing the purpose of requesting the review of the res judicata, the plaintiff must bear the burden of demonstrating the flaw in question and the harm caused, and it is up to the court in case of doubt to dismiss it.

(3) *Relevance.* The party requesting nullity must declare what damages have been suffered as the basis for their interest in obtaining such a declaration, and must also mention, where appropriate, the defences they have not been able to oppose (Article 172).
(4) *Protection.* The party whose actions gave rise to the call for annulment may not request their act to be held invalid (Article 171).
(5) *Causation or independence of the acts.* The nullity of an act does not affect the previous or successive annulments independent of this act. The nullity of a part of a legal action does not affect the other parties which are independent of it (Article 174).

176. The following precondition the declaration of nullity of a procedural act: (i) the existence of a flaw in any of its elements; (ii) that despite this flaw, the act has failed to achieve its purpose; (iii) the demonstration of legal interest in invalidating action; (iv) the unimputable nature of the nullity to the person calling for it to be declared; and, (v) failure to validate the flawed act (Articles 172 and 173, ACCPC).

§2. Proceedings

177. Nullity may be declared either at the request of a party or ex officio, as long as the flawed act is not consented. The request for nullity will be processed as an incidental claim for nullity. An incident is the only way in which the nullity of any procedural act performed in the course of the proceedings no can be brought, even when, as a consequence of an irregular procedure, an interim or final judgment has already been issued.

178. The party driving this must explain the flaw in question, the damage caused, which is motivating their interest in obtaining the declaration and detailing the defences they were unable to oppose. If these requirements are not met in detail, the petition will be dismissed forthwith by the court (Article 173, ACCPC). The incidental proceedings must be brought within a period of five days from the date when the interested party was made aware of the flawed legal action (Article 170, ACCPC).

179. The court must allow the counterparty to respond to the incidental proceedings, except when the nullity is manifest, in which case this is not necessary. However, when a request for nullity is manifestly inadmissible, the court may reject it in limine. When recording the processing of the incident, the rules regarding incidental proceedings in general will apply (Articles 175187, ACCPC).

180. The declaration of nullity of a legal act means it has no effect. The nullity of an act does not affect the previous ones nor the subsequent ones, which are independent of that one. The nullity of one part of an act does not affect others which are independent of it (Article 174, ACCPC) or does it prevent them from producing the effects for which the act is qualified unless otherwise expressly provided for by the law.

Part IV. Proceedings

Chapter 1. Proceedings in First Instance

§1. Adversary Proceedings

I. Ordinary Proceedings

181. The ACCPC has a general and a special part. The general part contains provisions on courts, the parties, proceedings, general contingencies and the different ways in which a case may be concluded before a ruling. The special part deals with the different types of proceedings. It regulates the processes of: (i) ordinary proceedings, (ii) execution proceedings, (iii) special proceedings, (iv) probate, (v) arbitration, and (vi) non-contentious proceedings. The central axis, the ACCPC's structure, is supported by the general provisions and the rules of plenary proceedings, which are of two types: ordinary and summary proceedings.[126] Conflicts not governed by any specific procedural norms must be handled according to the provisions established for ordinary proceedings (Article 319, ACCPC). Expedited summary proceedings are reserved for minor matters and when a claim is brought against an individual's act or omission which currently or imminently harms, restricts, alters or threatens with manifest arbitrariness or illegality, any right or guarantee explicitly or implicitly recognized by the Constitution, or a treaty or law. This is so in those cases when the urgent repair of the harm or the immediate cessation of the effects of the action is necessary, and the matter, due to its nature or by legal provision, cannot be substantiated by any other proceedings (Article 321, ACCPC).[127] The other proceedings concern the rules established in the general part and apply to ordinary proceedings. Execution proceedings are aimed at obtaining the enforcement of a previously recognized right. The ACCPC dedicates Book III

126. Before its modification in Law 25,488 (2001) the ACCPC regulated summary proceedings. The original idea of those drafting the law was to establish intermediate proceedings, shortening certain deadlines and limiting some of the powers of the parties to speed up the process. Law 25,488 repealed summary proceedings. Some provinces maintain three forms of plenary proceedings. This is the case of the provincial codes that maintained the provisions enshrined in the 1967 ACCPC such as the BACCP (1968, Arts 319, 320 and 321), the Civil, Commercial, Labour, Rural and Mining Procedural Code of Ushuaia (1994, Art. 336), or the Civil and Commercial Procedural Code of Chubut (2010, Arts 322 and 323).

127. Article 498 of the ACCPC establishes the particular rules of expedited summary proceedings with respect to ordinary proceedings, which are intended to provide greater simplicity and to shorten certain timeframes. Some provincial codes refer to these proceedings as 'highly abbreviated', but they basically respond to the same legislative technique.

of the special part to execution processes, regulating in successive chapters the proceedings to execute judgment (Chapter 1), executive proceedings (Chapter 2) and special executions (Chapter 3). Although special proceedings are known to take place, there are different requirements according to the type of conflict to which they refer. The distinctive note of non-contentious proceedings is that decisions are taken in favour of the petitioner without prejudice to the rights of third parties. The ACCPC dedicates Book V to probate, VI to the arbitration process and VII to non-contentious proceedings, providing, among others, the authorization to marry, as well as for guardianship and conservatorship, which must be applied in accordance with the regulations enshrined in the ACCC (Articles 100, 104, 138 and 498 et seq.).

182. Ordinary proceedings involve four stages: preparatory, evidentiary, decisive and recursive. The principle of preclusion prevails during the development of the proceedings, ensuring that procedural acts are carried out at the stage assigned and preventing the procedure from returning to a phase that has already been concluded.

A. *Preparatory Stage*

183. After the mediation phase has finalized (*see* paragraph 534), the claim is filed (Article 330, ACCPC), although in certain cases the proceedings may be prepared by requesting preliminary proceedings (Article 323, ACCPC), in order to reassure the parties of the opportunity to state their claims as precisely as possible. Pretrial evidence may also be requested, aimed at preventing the loss of certain evidentiary elements (Article 326, ACCPC).

184. Preparatory proceedings must be followed for all ordinary proceedings as their objective is to obtain a series of data or elements necessary to formulate the claim or the defence, without which these could not be carried out. These include, for example, a sworn statement regarding the facts related to legal status without whose verification the trial could not begin; exhibition of the *movable goods*; the exhibition of the will when the applicant believes they are the heir; the appointment of a guardian or curator for the trial in question; that the eventual defendant constitutes domicile if they have to leave the country, etc. Whoever seeks to file a claim and use the information obtained through most of the pretrial evidence must bring the respective action within thirty days. Otherwise, if there is no apparent interest or diligence shown in bringing the claim, the possibility of using it expires (Article 323, ACCPC).

185. Pretrial evidence (Article 326, ACCPC), on the other hand, allows for evidence to be incorporated when there are justified reasons for fearing that it could be impossible or very difficult to produce later. This can take place in three instances: before the lawsuit is filed, before it is notified, and after the defendant's answer, but before the trial is opened. Although evidence is admitted with respect to all kinds of evidence, confession only applies when proceedings have already been initiated. In the event that the evidence is granted, the party opposed must be summoned to participate in its production, unless this is impossible for reasons of urgency, in which case it is the official defender who must intervene as a guarantor of the adversary. The production of evidence is governed by the general rules of each type. A resolution denying interim measures may be appealed.

186. The new draft bill of the ACCPC makes pretrial evidence more flexible as it provides for the court to authorize it at the request of one of the parties with oversight by the opposing one, when this is considered to be reasonable given the circumstances of the case, for reasons of procedural economy, or given the likelihood of conciliatory solutions (Article 203). In addition, the new draft bill of the ACCPC foresees procedural agreements, allowing the parties to enter into a pre-lawsuit phase (Article 14).

187. The ACCPC foresees that after the lawsuit is filed, the counterclaim and the answer to both must be accompanied by the documentary evidence that the party is trying to use and any remaining evidence must be offered. When documentary evidence is unavailable, the interested party must make this clear and indicate its content, location, file number, and the public office or person in whose possession it is (Article 333, ACCPC). The principles of concentration and procedural good faith apply, aimed at avoiding the disadvantage of ignoring the existence of any document that might be fundamental to the defence during the trial of the party in question. Once the claim has been brought, the ACCPC does not allow any more documents to be added, except in the case of those which are dated later or earlier, and only when the parties state under oath that they did not have prior knowledge of these. In such cases, the other party must be notified and they must comply with the duty imposed on them by Article 356 (1) of the ACCPC, meaning that they must recognize or refute the authenticity of the documents; otherwise, the court will deem them to be authentic.

188. Filing a claim effectively interrupts the course of statute of limitations, even if brought before a judge with no jurisdiction over the case or is null due to defects in form (Article 2546, ACCC). The intervening court must rule on their jurisdiction (except in the case of venue by agreement, where such a declaration is not pertinent).

189. If the court considers that a lawsuit may be admitted, it issues a resolution requiring the defendant to appear and answer it within fifteen days.[128] Fulfilling this

128. However, it is interesting to note that if the claim is brought against the national State, a province or a municipality, the term given to answer it is sixty days in ordinary proceedings (Art. 338, ACCPC). In expedited summary proceedings, the notification period is shorter, being only five days (Art. 498, ACCPC). In some provincial codes of summary proceedings, the regulation of the *ordinary proceedings* merely imposes the burden of producing documentary evidence to accompany the claim while the offer to produce the remaining means of evidence is deferred to the first ten days of the evidentiary period (e.g., Arts 332 and 365, BACCPC).

procedural act of communication materializes the principle of contradiction and places a double burden on the defendant: that of appearing in the proceedings and that of answering the claim.

190. In cases where the defendant is not domiciled in the territorial jurisdiction of the intervening court, the summons must be sent in the form of a letter or a warrant to the judicial authority of the town where they are to be found, without prejudice to the provisions enshrined in the law of uniform procedure on warrants. By virtue of an agreement concluded between the Nation and the province of Santa Fe on 9 October 1979, enacted by Law 22,172 (to which all the provinces have adhered), this procedure may be dispensed with when issuing notifications, citations and intimations or making requests for reports in another territorial jurisdiction. In cases where a province is a party, the summons must be made in an official letter addressed to the Governor and the State Prosecutor or official with those faculties (Article 341, ACCPC).

191. Due to the relevance of the effects deriving from this communication, it was ruled exceptionally that, in the case of persons of uncertain identity or whose domicile was unknown, a notification can be supplemented by the publication of edicts both in the official gazette and in a newspaper of broad circulation, when any efforts aimed at investigating their whereabouts are shown to be unsuccessful, under oath. In these cases, if the statement made by the party saying they had no information about the domicile were found to be false, or if this information could be verified in the process of due diligence, procedural legislation provides for the annulment at their expense of everything decided subsequently, and penalty fees are imposed.[129]

B. *Evidentiary Stage*

192. After the application stage, the phase dedicated to proving the facts begins. This is a contingent phase, as it only takes place when there is no agreement between the parties concerning the facts related to the issue to be resolved. Its purpose is to form the court's conviction of the existence or non-existence of the facts supporting the claims of both parties.

193. In the current structure of ordinary proceedings, there is a kind of hinge between the application and the evidentiary stage, constituted by the preliminary hearing provided for in Article 360 of the ACCPC.[130] Law 24,573 (1995), which

129. *Fallos* 316:2247 (1993). It has been pointed out that if the ACCPC authorizes this form of notification based merely on oath of the party, it does so in the conviction that people must act according to the standards of rectitude and good faith governing the exercise of their actions before the judicial organs (*Fallos* 306:392 (1984)), especially when this concerns the summons of the defendant, which is of critical importance in the proceedings, as it is closely related to the constitutional guarantee of defence by trial.

130. Expedited summary proceedings also foresee a preliminary hearing which must be scheduled within ten days of the claim being answered or the deadline for this step.

introduced compulsory mediation, incorporated the preliminary hearing in Article 360 of the ACCPC, which had to be carried out under penalty of nullity in the presence of the judge. Although the idea was to move forward in the implementation of orality in civil proceedings, the reform did not achieve the results expected as the courts either omitted to call it or delegated it to their clerks. Law 25,488 (2001) abolished the nullity sanction foreseen by the aforementioned Article 34 in cases where the judge was not present at the preliminary hearing. Article 360 of the ACCPC, according to the wording of Law 25,488, establishes that a judge may not delegate the hearing and that if they are not present, the hearing will not take place, and this must be recorded in the court attendance records. Article 34 of the ACCPC establishes that it is the judge's duty to be present at the preliminary hearing.

Several provincial procedural codes have incorporated preliminary hearings. This is the case with the Tierra del Fuego Civil, Commercial, Labour, Rural and Mining Procedural Code (1994, Articles 369 and 8),[131] the Civil and Commercial Procedural Code of the Province of La Pampa (1999, Articles 343 and 35 (2)),[132] the Formosa Civil and Commercial Procedural Code (2002, Article 358),[133] the Civil and Commercial Procedural Code (2007, Article 346),[134] the Civil, Commercial and Mining Code of the Province of San Juan (2008, Article 321),[135] the Civil and Commercial Procedural Code of the province of Rio Negro (2011, Articles 361 and 34),[136] the Civil and Commercial Procedural Code of the Province of Santa Cruz (2016, Article 338),[137] the Civil and Commercial Procedural Code of the Province of Chaco (2016, Article 371),[138] and the Civil, Commercial and Tax Procedural Code of the Province of Mendoza (2017, Article 173).[139]

The new draft bill of the ACCPC in Article 2 highlights the importance assigned to the immediacy between the judge and the parties. This principle dovetails with the rule foreseen in Article 45 (d) of the new draft bill of the ACCPC, establishing the judge's duty to personally attend and direct the hearings. It is important to note that in order to ensure compliance, hearings must be presided uninterruptedly by the judge and will be considered invalid if they are not present or absent themselves during the proceedings. The nullity sanction is absolute and may not be validated, although it may be deducted or declared ex officio at any procedural opportunity. To

131. Article 8 establishes that evidentiary hearings will be held in the presence of the judge who may not delegate them under pain of irremediable nullity.
132. Article 35 establishes the nullity of the hearing if the judge fails in their duty to be present.
133. Article 358 foresees that the judge will preside over the hearing on a non-delegable basis.
134. Article 346 (1) establishes that the preliminary hearing will be presided over by the judge, and may not be delegated. If the judge is not present, the hearing will not be held, and the appearance of the parties must be recorded in the court attendance records.
135. Article 321 does not require the hearing to be called, but instead establishes that it may be held at the judge's discretion.
136. Article 34 establishes the sanction of nullity in the event that the judge does not attend the hearing.
137. Article 338 also provides that the preliminary hearing must be held in full in the presence of the judge, who will preside over it and may not delegate it.
138. Article 371 establishes that the preliminary hearing will be presided over by the judge, and they may not delegate it. If the judge is not present, they will be liable to the fines established by the regulations.
139. According to Art. 173, the initial hearing must be conducted in a non-delegable manner and under penalty of nullity, by the judge hearing the case.

this, it should be added that Article 90 (a) of the new draft bill of the ACCPC disposes that hearings be video recorded rather than transcribed. Video recording is a key element when it comes to ensuring that a hearing is effectively carried out in the context of immediacy, as the best way of achieving cooperation as a consequence of the dialogue between the judge and the parties. The measure conjugates immediacy, concentration and orality to complement the judge's duty to be present and ensures evidence of compliance by means of video recording, without any exceptions. In turn, this dovetails with the judge's duty foreseen in Article 45 (i) of the new draft bill of the ACCPC to manage the hearing agenda, taking into account the order in which lawsuits are filed, their complexity, and the need to develop jurisdictional activity with sufficient agility to ensure that the dates of the hearings are of public knowledge.

194. According to the ACCPC, in the preliminary hearing, the judge should strive to bring about conciliation between the parties. If this is not possible, they should try to simplify evidentiary activity, receiving oppositions to discovery proceedings and, eventually, deciding whether the issue should be resolved as a purely legal question. In this case, the judge is in a position to pass the sentence. Otherwise, they must determine which are the facts at issue leading to the judgment, on the basis of the evidence; receive a declaration concerning the facts under scrutiny from the parties; and concentrate testimonial evidence in a single hearing.[140]

195. The evidentiary stage ends when all the evidence has been produced, or when the parties desist from producing any more, if any remains pending. This is when the ACCPC foresees the provision of the case file to the parties for ordinary proceedings (which is expressly prohibited in expedited summary proceedings), so that they can, if they wish, present their arguments on the merits of the evidence produced. This is a written statement whose form is not determined by law and whose purpose is to analyse the evidence presented, on the basis of the facts at issue, indicating the conclusions that may be derived from it in order to reaffirm a position and convince the judge. Each of the parties has a period of six days in which to do so as well as withdraw the case file, a term that runs as from the day after the court issues the order for the final arguments. If the party returns the case file after the six-day period conferred, they lose the right to argue.

C. Judgment

196. In this case, the decision will be taken following the completion of the evidentiary stage, when the evidence has been added to the case file, the closing arguments have been produced, or the period has elapsed for such purposes, the judge will issue a resolution opening the period for issuing the sentence (Article 483,

140. In the provincial codes where a hearing of this type is not foreseen, the lawsuit is opened to evidence if there are controversial facts on which evidence must be produced, together with the brief answering the claim, or the counterclaim, where appropriate. If the matter is one of pure law, a new notification is generally foreseen by order, before the case is concluded for a final sentence.

ACCPC). The notification of this procedural act has a number of effects: (i) it precludes any discussion without further briefs being presented or more evidence being produced (except for the steps necessary to clarify the truth of the facts that the judge is empowered to order pursuant to Article 36 paragraph 4, ACCPC, without prejudice to the parties' right of defence, and in a single act Article 484, ACCPC); (ii) the burden of momentum driving the process and weighing on the parties ceases, meaning that subsequent actions are carried out informally (including the notification of the judgment;[141]) (iii) it marks the beginning of the period granted by the law to the judge to issue the sentence, which in ordinary proceedings is expected to be forty or sixty days (depending on whether it is a single voice or collegiate body).[142]

197. The constitutional guarantee of a person's defence in court includes the right to obtain a prompt ruling within a reasonable time.[143] For this reason, in addition to setting the deadline by when the judgment must be pronounced, the procedural rule refers to the delay of justice, indicating that the judge or court must notify the higher court of the delay ten days in advance of its expiry when in the case of an ordinary trial, and five days in other cases, stating the reasons for such a delay. The Courts of Appeal or the Supreme Court are in charge of setting the term by which the judgment must be pronounced, by the judge or court, or by another court in the same jurisdiction, when exceptional circumstances so advise. It also contemplates the possibility that a judge who has not sent the communication to the Court of Appeal in a timely manner, or who, having done so without just cause, does not pass judgment within the term set, will be liable for a fine not in excess of 15% of their basic remuneration, and the case may be referred to another judge within the same jurisdiction for sentence. Based on these regulations, it was decided to order a court that had, in response to the request of the interested party, showed unjustified delays in providing the appropriate legal channel for the proceedings in a timely fashion, to resolve the issue within forty-eight hours, as this represents a veritable case of delay of justice.[144]

1. The Final Judgment: General Points

198. A judgment is an act of authority, emanating from a judge in the exercise of their jurisdiction, issued by means of a trial in proceedings that declare the rights of the parties and that may condemn or absolve in whole or in part, or constitute new legal instances by putting an end to the declarative stage of the proceedings.

141. Once the sentence has been passed, it will be notified ex officio, within three days by means of a certificate issued with a transcription of the operative aspects. One simple copy of the judgment signed by the secretary or by the first clerk will be delivered to the litigant who requests it.

142. In expedited summary proceedings, the sentence must be pronounced within twenty or thirty days, depending on whether it is a one-person or collegiate court. When this concerns *amparo* processes, the term will be ten and fifteen days, respectively.

143. *Fallos* 287:248 (1960); 289:181 (1974); 300:1102 (1978); 305:913 (1983); 315:2173 (1992), among others).

144. *Fallos* 328:218 (2005).

199. When the ACCPC refers to the judgment of first instance, it does so under the name of a 'final judgment of first instance' (Article 163, ACCPC). The adjective 'definitive' does not refer to whether or not it can be modified (we shall see that the final judgment may be appealed) but rather to the result of the procedural act that normally concludes the instance, resolving the merits of the issue at stake.[145]

200. If we look at the function predominantly fulfilled by judgments, these may be characterized as follows: (i) statement: they resolve the conflict by ratifying the existence of a right or legal situation; (ii) conviction: in addition to containing a statement, they require the fulfilment of a benefit (to give, to do or not to do), they become enforceable in a coercive manner; (iii) constitutive: they either modify or extinguish legal relationships, determining a new status. The classification is of practical interest as regards the analysis of the effects of each one over time.

2. Formal Aspects and Content of the Judgment

201. The sentence must conform to the requirements set for procedural acts in general. It must be written in the national language in black ink (Article 115, ACCPC). The law requires (as in the case of simple and interlocutory decisions) that the date and place be recorded (Article 163, paragraph 1, ACCPC), in order to determine the application of the act in temporal and spatial terms. A sentence is composed of three parts: (i) the findings, (ii) the recitals and (iii) the ruling or operative part. The ACCPC regulates the various aspects making up each section indicated, although without referring to their location (Article 163, ACCPC). The findings play a predominantly informative role, based on a sequence that refers to the background to the procedure in objective terms, following the chronological order of events. The name and surname of the parties and the succinct account of the issues constituting the object of the trial are given in this section (Article 163 (2 and 3), ACCPC). The recitals are the most important part of the decision-making act, as their purpose is to specify the factual and legal reasons for the decision. The court must consider the issues making up the object of the claim, in light of the assessment of the evidence provided in the file. In the sentence, the judge is empowered to take into consideration the procedural conduct of the parties and those presumptions not established by law, as and when these are based on real and proven facts and when, due to their number, precision, gravity and concordance, they lead to a conviction according to the nature of the trial, and the rules of sound criticism. Once the context of events has been determined, the facts must be included in the legal norms applicable to the case. Article 3 of the ACCC establishes that the judge must

145. From that perspective, it differs from simple resolutions, which only serve, without substantiation, the development of the process or order acts which merely have to be executed. They do not require any other formalities than their written expression, date and place, and the signature of the judge or president of the court, or the secretary, if applicable (*see* Art. 160, ACCPC). Interlocutory judgments resolving issues requiring substantiation, raised during the course of the proceedings, but which do not address the main bone of contention. These, in addition to the requirements set forth for simple orders, must state the grounds for the judgment and specify the express, positive and precise decision of the questions raised as well as rule on the costs.

resolve the matters submitted to their jurisdiction by means of a reasonably founded decision. The obligation to have sufficient grounds for judgments is an unavoidable requirement of constitutional validity. The AC establishes the inviolability of a person's right to defence, as well as other rights. This guarantee includes, for those resorting to justice, the right to obtain a judgment that is a reasoned derivation of current law, according to the famed expression coined by the Supreme Court when it concluded that any judgments deviating from said rule of interpretation are arbitrary.

202. A judge cannot refuse to resolve due to obscurity or indecision and may not absolve the instance by invoking *non liquet.* They have the duty to decide (in the operative part of the sentence) expressly, positively and precisely on the litigation, in accordance with the claims brought in the trial, qualified as appropriate by law, declaring the rights of the litigants and condemning or acquitting them of any claims or counterclaims, where appropriate, in whole or in part. The foregoing represents an application of the principle of consistency, insofar as it requires the existence of an exact correspondence between the object of the claim and what is resolved in the sentence, as a guarantee of due process and defence in court. Hence, the court may not decide less than what was asked *(citra petita),* more (*ultra petita*) or on something different (*extra petita*) in the lawsuit. However, this does not prevent the judge from deciding to make merit of certain supervening events directly related to the object of the lawsuit. This is expressly referred to in the seventh paragraph of Article 163 of the ACCPC, which recognizes that the sentence may be worthy of constitutive or modifying facts, or those which effectively discharge or extinguish the obligation, produced during the trial and duly proven, even if they had not been invoked in timely fashion as new facts. The deadline for its fulfilment must also be specified when the judgment has to be executed. Although in some cases the deadline is determined by law (e.g., Article 686, ACCPC), it is usually determined by the judge according to the obligations imposed in the judgment. Finally, the judgment must rule on the payment of court and legal fees, and also include any statement as to the recklessness and malicious intent corresponding to any of the litigants and professionals involved due to their conduct (Articles 163 paragraph 8, and 34 paragraph 6, ACCPC). The judge's signature of the judgment is an essential requirement for the existence of the procedural act as such.

3. Effects of the Judgment

203. The issuance of the judgment produces a series of effects: (i) it discharges the jurisdiction of the judge with respect to the object of the proceedings, except for any legally recognized exceptions (Article 166, ACCPC); (ii) it determines the individual rule applicable to the case; (iii) it creates certain secondary effects.

204. In relation to the discharge of jurisdiction, although procedural regulations state that once a judgment is passed, the court's jurisdiction ceases, the truth is that the same rule enables the intervening magistrate, among other things, to (i) exercise ex officio, before the sentence is notified, the power granted by Article 36, paragraph 6, of the ACCPC (material corrections to the sentence); (ii) correct, at the request of a party, within three days of the notification and without the need for substantiation, any material error, clarify any obscure concept – without altering the substance of the decision – and make up for any omission incurred in any of the claims brought and discussed in the litigation; (iii) order, at the request of a party, the pertinent provisional measures; (iv) order the annotations established by law and delivery any witness statements; (v) continue dealing with the incidents requiring a separate decision; (vi) decide on the admissibility of appeals and substantiate them, where appropriate, and determine the requests for rectification referred to in Article 246; (vii) enforce the judgment in a timely manner. Thus, in reality, when the judgment is issued, it has the effect of temporarily suspending the court's jurisdiction, which is subsequently resumed at the time of execution, if appropriate.

205. The judgment eliminates the state of uncertainty and determines the individual rule governing the conflictive situation presented. Its objective is therefore to eliminate the uncertainty about the existence, modality or interpretation of a legal relationship (a merely declarative judgment); it determines the enforcement in favour of the winner in the event of non-compliance (conviction); or if it is a determinative judgment, the corresponding legal relationship will be integrated.

206. Finally, the issue of the judgment itself also produces certain secondary effects, which are a direct consequence of some main effect, or merely of the pronouncement, of the ruling. The power to request an attachment (or any other precautionary measure) if a favourable judgment (Article 212, paragraph 3, ACCPC) is reached, and the imposition of costs on the losing party (Article 68, ACCPC), are examples of this type of effects.

207. The projection of the effects over time also depends on the type of judgment in question (*see* paragraph 249). In the case of declaratory judgments, the effects will be projected to the time when the events leading to the declaration occurred (ex tunc). However, as a rule in the case of judicial decisions, the effects occur in the future (ex nunc), although the rule is not absolute, and admits certain exceptions. When there is a guilty verdict, this point becomes relevant inasmuch as it determines from what moment interests are owed. In the case of contractual liability, the principle is that they are due as from the expiry of the obligation, as automatic default remains the rule (Article 886, ACCC). However, in the case of term obligations the judge must at the request of the party set interests using the shortest procedure provided by local law, unless the creditor chooses to accumulate a series of actions setting both terms and compliance. In this case, the debtor is regarded as delinquent on the deadline for compliance with the obligation indicated by the judgment (Article 887, ACCC). On the other hand, the course of interests in the case of liability for an illegal act commences with the production of evidence of harm in each instance (Article 1748, ACCC).

4. Res Judicata

208. A judgment when issued becomes final (for having been consented or executed) and acquires the status of res judicata. This refers to the fact that it may not be modified if action is subsequently brought against it.

209. Doctrine has developed the concepts of formal and material res judicata. Formal res judicata happens when there are no resources left which are capable of allowing what has been decided during the proceedings to be reviewed, but there is the possibility of starting other proceedings which could lead to a different result. This is the case of executive proceedings, where only the defences established by law may be exercised (Article 544, ACCPC). This limitation determines that the person convicted, once the judgments brought against them have been completed, may initiate discovery proceedings to assert all the defences and exceptions that were not admissible in the executive process by law.

On the other hand, res judicata in a material sense takes place when the judgment, in addition to not being susceptible to modifications in the proceedings during which it was issued, cannot be altered under any circumstances nor in any other proceedings. The irrevocable nature of res judicata in a formal sense is joined by the immutability of res judicata in a material sense.

210. A judgment passed under the authority of res judicata constitutes an asset which may be incorporated into the constitutional concept of patrimony, of which it cannot be deprived without diminishing the constitutional precept establishing the inviolability of property (Article 17, AC).[146]

211. Res judicata presents objective and subjective limits. The problem with the objective limits of the sentence includes issues relating to which part of the sentence acquires the force of res judicata, and the determination of which litigious issues are protected by that force. The subjective limits of res judicata, on the other hand, aim to determine who is reached by its effectiveness.

As for objective limits, traditionally the issue has been whether the quality of res judicata includes only the operative part of the judgment, or also extends to the statements made in the recitals in the same. In general, doctrine and jurisprudence maintain that, although the recitals in the judgment are not res judicata, they may exceptionally acquire that authority when there is a connection between the grounds and the decision preventing their scope from being established without reference to them.

As for the subjective limits of res judicata, these only apply to the parties in the proceedings where judgment has been passed. Parties not only refers to the plaintiff and the defendant, but to those intervening as third parties, as Article 96 of the ACCPC establishes that the sentence affects them 'as much as the main litigants'. The same rule applies in matters of procedural substitution (Article 114, ACCPC), since it is necessary to bear in mind the legal identity of the parties when determining the subjective limits of res judicata.

146. *Fallos* 307:1709 (1985); 313:1297 (1990).

There are, however, certain exceptions based, for example, on the particular relationships between the main parties and third parties. This is the case with joint and several obligations. In this context, the ACCC foresees that although a judgment passed against one of the codebtors may not be enforced against the others, these may invoke it as long as it is not based on the personal circumstances of the defendant codebtor. Likewise, although the debtor may not oppose the judgment obtained against one of them to the other cocreditors, the cocreditors can oppose it to the debtor, without prejudice to the personal exceptions that the debtor may have against each of them (Article 832, ACCC).

212. Both jurisprudence and doctrine accept the rule that judgments related to matters of the state of persons acquire res judicata authority, not only with respect to those intervening in the respective process, but also *erga omnes*. This is based on the indivisibility of civil status and the nature of public order attributed to it. However, the aforementioned stands when the legitimate primary opponents have intervened in the trial (e.g., father and son in a paternity suit), but not when secondary opponents have intervened, since their procedural activity must not affect the exercise of the rights claimed by other legitimate parties in the same position. Otherwise, anybody suing later would find themselves burdened by the consequences of the negligent or deficient performance of those who did so in first place.

5. Proceedings for Reopening of Civil Judgment

213. The effectiveness of res judicata, despite having remained firm, may be the result of an irregular procedure in which the right of defence of one of the parties may have been seriously limited. These are cases where res judicata is merely so in appearance, such as the following: (i) after the judgment has been pronounced and it has become final, the aggrieved party recovers decisive documents which were either ignored or lost due to force majeure or to deliberate manoeuvres by the other party; (ii) the judgment had as conclusive evidence documents declared false or based on testimonial or expert evidence, and the witnesses or experts are subsequently found guilty of false testimony concerning the statements made in that trial; (iv) the judge was found criminally liable for malfeasance, bribery, violence or other fraudulent schemes in the proceedings in which the sentence was passed; or, (v) the proceedings were simulated or fraudulent.

At national level, jurisprudence allows a fraudulent sentence to be annulled through the autonomous action of nullity based on rules of substantial law concerning legal defects. The claim brought thus accumulates the claim of nullity to that requiring the issuance of a new sentence. This is based on respect for due process, the contradictory exercise wherein the defeated party is given adequate and substantial opportunity for a hearing and evidence, and the fundamental idea of justice which is to prevent proven crime from yielding benefits.[147]

Article 2564 (f) of the ACCC establishes that legal action may be filed to review res judicata within a period of one year.

147. In the case of *Tibold* (*Fallos* 254:320) the Supreme Court held that:

The new draft bill of the ACCPC (Article 129) incorporates the intention to review res judicata on the basis of the nullity of a firm sentence, imposing upon the plaintiff the burden of demonstrating the flaw in question and the harm caused, as the sentence must in case of doubt be dismissed. The claim of nullity of the final judgment will not be addressed when there are allegations of defects that could have been corrected through an appeal or incidental activity, but which were not attempted in a timely manner. Its filing does not automatically suspend the process to execute the judgment passed. If provisional measures were set, the existence of the credibility and trustworthiness of the proposal drawn up and the provision of a bond to cover damage and losses will constitute sufficient provisional measures.

II. Provisional Proceedings

A. *Background*

214. Provisional measures are a form of preventive assurance of a credible right whose satisfaction is sought, in the face of the possibility that any delay in proceedings could frustrate the utility of the sentence to be issued. They are defined on the basis of certain characteristics: ancillary to the proceedings, instrumentality, superficiality, one-sidedness, provisionality, and modifiability. They constitute a pre-ordered incidence aimed at guaranteeing the utility and effectiveness of the sentence handed down in the proceedings.

> the generic admission of the institution of res judicata does not mean that its recognition cannot be conditioned to the absence of fraud in a case where the sentence was issued. This possibility, which underpins the principles of appeal for review, is also valid for disregarding the final effectiveness of the sentence passed in a trial where procedural fraud was incurred.

Also:

> The security of the final judgements, passed in the civil order, must yield to the reason of justice, which requires that the proven crime does not yield any benefits.

Subsequently, the Supreme Court, in the case of *Campbell Davidson v. Province of Buenos Aires* (*Fallos* 279:54 (1971)) stated that:

> the institution of res judicata, like all legal institutions, must be organized on bases which are compatible with constitutional rights and guarantees; not every judicial sentence can be recognized as an immutable resolution, only those preceded by a contradictory process where the loser has had an adequate and substantial opportunity for a hearing and evidence.

In the latter case, it was considered that there had been a defect in the consent given to the proceedings given the coercion on the part of the then Governor of the Province of Buenos Aires, in an attempt to ensure that the plaintiff (who had had a large piece of property expropriated), would consent to the judgment issued in the proceedings where the amount of compensation was set.

They are instrumental inasmuch as they do not constitute an end in themselves and are aimed at enabling compliance with the final judgment issued in the main trial under way or yet to be initiated, and their purpose is to ensure the effectiveness of the judgment.

Resolutions on provisional matters require the truth of facts and the law to be demonstrated (Article 199, ACCPC), and may be requested independently before the claim is brought (Article 195 ACCPC). However they expire, if, within the term of ten days after they are executed, the main proceedings do not commence (Article 207, ACCPC).

The ACCPC establishes that they be resolved without the intervention of the opposing party (Article 198, ACCPC). The rule of postponing the opposing party's intervention until the measure is executed assumes that the former could take advantage of the opportunity to frustrate the purpose pursued with the precautionary protection. The new draft bill of the ACCPC is based on another criterion as it chooses to assume that there is good faith on behalf of the parties. Hence, the principle of bilateralism is maintained, unless the applicant is able to prove that there are urgent reasons or, if the prior hearing has the potential to compromise the success of the measure (Article 153).

215. These measures are deemed provisional inasmuch as they remain in force only while the conditions for their issue continue to be current during the main proceedings (Article 202, ACCPC), and they may be reviewed in the event of a possible change in circumstances. Conversely, they cease to have effect when the circumstances which gave rise to them end (Article 203, ACCPC) or if a final adverse judgment is handed down (Article 203, ACCPC).[148]

They may also be modified at the request of the creditor (expanded, improved or replaced), or at the request of the debtor (reduced or replaced) or ex officio, where the judge may order a measure other than the one requested or a limitation to avoid unnecessary damages (Articles 203 and 204, ACCPC).

216. In the ACCPC system, nominated measures are: attachments (Articles 209220, ACCPC), sequestering (Article 221, ACCPC), judicial intervention (Articles 222-227, ACCPC), a restraint on the alienation of property (Article 228, ACCPC), notice of lis pendens (Article 229, ACCPC), the prohibition on innovating and contracting (Articles 230 and 231, ACCPC) and the protection of persons (Articles 234237, ACCPC).

---

148. The Supreme Court has understood that 'a sentence which fails to take into account the provisional nature of provisional measures should be left without effect, and a temporary extension afforded to the sentence passed whose excess undermines the provisional aspect of their nature'. (*Fallos* 319:1492 (1996)). In the *Grupo Clarín* case, the Supreme Court established that in certain cases, a term of validity should be set for provisional measures so that those benefiting from them conforming to them and becoming disinterested in the progress of the process (*Fallos* 335:705 (2012)). The new draft bill of the CCPCN (Art. 158) establishes that the judge may set a term for the validity of provisional measures, taking into account the circumstances giving rise to them, which may be extended, allowing for the assessment of the conduct of the parties observed during the proceedings.

Generic provisional measures are any urgent measure that, according to the circumstances, is more suited than the latter to provisionally ensuring compliance with the sentence (Article 232, ACCPC).

In considering the object covered by provisional protection, we may distinguish between procedural (or formal) and material (or substantial) provisional measures. The former are limited to securing assets and/or temporary situations until the final sentence is issued (e.g., attachment, inhibition, etc.); while substantial or material measures are directed at expeditiously processing the rights of the person requesting them, given the damaging effects arising from the duration of the proceedings.[149] The idea is to avoid a judgment which is favourable but nonetheless ineffective due to its tardiness.

Conservative, innovative and positive measures can be distinguished by the effects they produce. Conservative measures seek to preserve the state of affairs existing at the time of issuance so that these are not modified during the time required to hand down the sentence (e.g., a measure to not innovate). Innovative ones, implicit in generic provisional powers (Article 230, ACCPC), tend to modify the state of affairs existing at the time of issuance, and substantially alter the situations in which the parties to the lawsuit find themselves, as it takes them back to an earlier state of affairs. Positive measures, like innovative ones, also seek to modify the state of affairs, but by taking things to a previously unknown situation. The last two categories translate into greater interference wielded by the judge in the sphere of the freedom of the defendants, prior to the issuance of the sentence.[150]

Depending on what it is trying to protect, the ACCPC legislates measures to secure property (e.g., attachment, sequestering, etc.) and measures to secure persons (e.g., provisional custody, Article 234, ACCPC).

B. Statutory Requirements

217. There are three requirements for provisional measures arising from the regulation of the national procedural system: (i) plausibility in law; (ii) danger in delay; (iii) injunction. In relation to the provisional measures requested and issued

149. In *Fallos* 334:1691 (2011), the Supreme Court held that 'a modern conception of the process demands an emphasis on the "efficacy" of the jurisdictional function and the instrumental nature of procedural norms, in the sense that their purpose is to protect those substantial rights whose protection is required'.

150. In the case of *Camacho Acosta* (*Fallos* 320:1633 (1997)) the Supreme Court held that:

> considering that an innovative precautionary measure is an exceptional decision because it alters the state of fact or law existing at the time of its issuance, and that by envisaging a favourable jurisdiction regarding the final ruling of the case, greater prudence is justified in appreciating the requirements to admit provisional protection.

(confr. *Fallos* 316:1833 and case P. 489 XXV, *Pérez Cuesta S.A.C.I. v. National States/* declarative action of unconstitutionality (prohibition to innovate) of 25 June 1996).

in the national or provincial contentious administrative proceedings, another requirement must be brought and proven: that the measure to be issued does not seriously affect the public interest.[151]

218. The favourable issue of a provisional measure does not depend on there being certainty as to what the law stipulates, but simply on mere plausibility. Consequently, the evidence provided must meet that standard and the judge's assessment must also adhere to it.

219. At the same time, it must be proven that there is a danger in further delay, providing grounds for interim relief, referring to the possibility of imminent injury or harm that could mean that the eventual recognition of the right invoked as the basis of the claim might come too late. The danger in the delay is the procedural interest invoked by the request for provisional measures. This need not always be proven, since in certain cases it is presumed by law (e.g., Article 212, paras. 2 and 3, ACCPC).

220. The injunction provides a guarantee for any damages suffered by the person receiving the effects of its execution, the idea being to preserve equality between the parties in the proceedings and counteract the unilateral nature of provisional proceedings. It should also guarantee the payment of the costs for this incidence, to be confirmed when the final judgment is pronounced, since it is premature to do so at the stage when the nature of the bond is being decided. The bond may be sworn, real or personal. The judge sets the quality and amount of the bond according to the greater or lesser plausibility of the law and the circumstances of the case. Guarantees provided by banking institutions or people of proven economic responsibility (Article 199, ACCPC) may be offered. A bond will not be required if the person or entity obtaining the measure: (i) is the Nation, a province, one of its departments, a municipality or a person who can prove they have the funds; (ii) acts with the benefit of litigating without expenses (Article 200, ACCPC).

C. Procedure

221. Provisional measures may be requested before the lawsuit is brought, as well as when, or after, this happens (Article 195, ACCPC) except in cases where the law requires the proceedings to have been initiated (e.g., the judicial administration of the company requires legal proceedings to be brought against a partner). The brief must express the right which the proceedings purport to ensure, the measure requested, the legal provision on which it is based, and compliance with the requirements corresponding, in particular, to the measure required (Article 195, ACCPC).

151. Articles 3 para. 3; 4 para. 1, 5, 13 inc. d, 14 inc. d), 15 inc. d) and amendments, Law 26,854 (2013); 22 inc. 1 section c) and amendments. In the province of Buenos Aires, *see* Law 12,008 (1997) and its amendments.

222. The competent court is the one handling the main proceedings (Article 6, paragraph 4, ACCPC). Courts must refrain from decreeing bonds when the knowledge of the case is not within their jurisdiction. However, if a judge orders an injunction when there is no jurisdiction, the measure will only be valid if it has been ordered in accordance with legal requirements, although this does not imply an extension of jurisdiction (Article 196, ACCPC). This rule adds that the judge ordering the measure must send the proceedings to the competent authority immediately after doing so.

223. In order to prove any provisional suppositions, and in accordance with the procedural line taken, the legal regime foresees that summary information may be offered with a view to obtaining provisional measures if accompanied by a document containing the questions asked of the witnesses and their answers, according to Articles 440, first part, 441 and 443, duly signed by them. The witnesses must be ratified when presenting said brief or in the first hearing (Article 197, ACCPC).

224. As the measure can be processed without the intervention of the other parties, procedural rules enable actions to remain reserved until the measures are executed. These are processed separately, and copies of the relevant actions of the principal are added where appropriate. The person who has to post a bond will only be informed of the actions when the measure is issued. If this does not happen, they must be notified in person or served with a writ within three days from the date when the provisional measure is taken. The party obtaining the measure will be responsible for any damages caused to the opponent by the delay in notification (Article 198, ACCPC).

225. The resolution giving rise or denying the provisional measure may be appealed by way by requesting a review. Subsidiary or direct appeal is also admissible. The possibility to lodge an appeal, if the measure is admitted, will be granted in return (Articles 198 and 485, paragraph 6, ACCPC).

D. Subsequent Contingencies

226. Due to the provisional nature of interim relief, and its inherent mutability, there are certain contingencies subsequent to the enactment of these measures that may arise, according to the length and validity of the relief granted.

1. Expiry

227. If a provisional measure is requested before a claim is brought, and is subsequently conceded, the ACCPC adopts an automatic expiry system that comes into effect if, within ten days following execution in the case of an enforceable obligation, a claim is not filed or mandatory pretrial mediation proceedings are not initiated. If the mediation procedure has already begun, this term will start to run again following twenty days from the date when the mediator issues the document with their signature certified by the MJyDH, showing that no agreement has been reached, or that the mediation was not carried out for any of the reasons authorized.

Costs and damages ensuing from an expired provisional measure will be borne by the person obtaining it. However, it cannot be proposed again for the same case prior to the proceedings being brought, as this can only happen once the proceedings are under way, as and when the assumptions for doing so are met (Article 207, ACCPC).

2. Modification

228. The ACCPC grants the creditor the power to request an extension, improvement or review of the provisional measure decreed for another party able to adequately satisfy the guarantee required. On the other hand, it grants the debtor the same power, enabling them to request substitution by a less burdensome measure as long as it also satisfies the interests of their counterpart. In this case, the resolution is issued after listening to both parties. Similarly, the judge has the powers to order a measure other than the one requested in order to avoid unnecessary harm (Article 204). However, these powers cannot be exercised when the measure has already been obeyed and notified, in which case it is up to the affected party to request the corresponding replacement.

3. Lifting

229. A party may request that a measure be lifted when they can show that the circumstances in which interim relief was granted have changed (Article 202, ACCPC).

This is a different assumption to review, because whereas in the latter, procedural activity focuses on questioning the existence of precautionary assumptions considered reliable in the resolution challenged in identical circumstances, in the case of the review, it must be shown that this situation has mutated.[152]

Likewise, the consequences of one situation and the other are diverse. A review may eventually imply the revocation of the measure, and with it the return to the *status quo ante*, meaning that the measure is no longer applicable. On the other hand, incidental proceedings to lift the measure could bring with them the extinction of the interim relief in the future, as the circumstances justifying it up until then have disappeared.

---

152. Although the decisions admitting or rejecting requests for provisional measures create a provisional legal status susceptible to review and modification at any stage of the trial, for this to happen, it is necessary for the assumptions defining their admission or rejection to have changed. Or for new elements of judgment to have been provided indicating the inconvenience of maintaining the sentence handed down and, where appropriate, authorize the measure ordered to be lifted (*Fallos* 327:2495 (2004)).

4. Liabilities

230. The national procedural system penalizes the excess use of provisional measures. These are cases where there is an abuse in the exercise of this power (Article 208, ACCPC).

As a rule, an objective condition and a subjective condition are required. The first refers to the fact that the provisional measure has been lifted (in a generic sense, comprehensive of expiry and revocation). The second implies that there has been a malicious, or at the least negligent, attitude on the part of the person obtaining the measure.[153]

However, the legislators exceptionally made provision for certain specific cases of liability where the points indicated above do not need to be proven. These are cases of automatic liability, where it appears to be objective: the lack of notification of the provisional measure conceded in timely fashion (Article 198, ACCPC), the expiry of the measure anticipated (Article 207, ACCPC), and the seizure of unattachable assets (Articles 219 and 220, ACCPC).

Conversely, certain situations of objective exoneration are also envisaged: against a rebellious debtor (Article 212 (1), ACCPC), against a debtor making an express or implied confession (Article 212 (2), ACCPC), or against an attachment based on a favourable judgment, even if this has been appealed (Article 212 (3), ACCPC).

E. Classification of Provisional Measures

231. The ACCPC (Article 232) and the numerous provincial codes defined in line with its criteria, authorize judges to grant all kinds of provisional measures that may be more appropriate (than those nominated) in the light of the protection envisaged, according to the criterion that seeks to avoid unnecessary harm .

1. Attachment

232. Attachment refers to the provisional measure aimed at securing and immobilizing one or more assets belonging to a person sued in a procedure of discovery or execution, in order to ensure the effectiveness of the sentence to be passed.

In procedural legislation, there are three types of attachment: (i) preventive (Article 209, ACCPC), (ii) executive and (iii) enforceable.

While the preventive attachment is a provisional measure, thus subject to the pertinent regime (characteristics, requirements of origin, effects, expiry), executive attachment must be agreed by the judge as the first measure when an execution is sought, by virtue of an executive order. An executive attachment may only be lifted when an asset cannot be attached, or in the event that any of the exceptions authorized by law as opposition to the execution of the sentence or executive proceedings (Articles 544 and 506, ACCPC) are successful.

153. *Fallos* 327:2746 (2004), in the case of *Exlogan S.A.*

Likewise, whereas a preventive attachment applies to cases seeking compliance with obligations to provide sums of money, and obligations consisting of handing over a specific item (Article 209, ACCPC), an executive attachment is used to ensure compliance with the obligation to provide a certain sum of money (Article 520, ACCPC), which is why it also requires amounts to be liquid (or easily payable) and enforceable. Unlike executive attachments, preventive ones must always be decreed under the responsibility and guarantee of the applicant (Article 199, ACCPC).

An enforceable attachment is ordered when the final judgment is executed. Both preventive and executive attachments may become enforceable once the right to do so is recognized through a sentence.

233. Certain assets are unattachable. The ACCPC mentions some of them in its Article 219. In addition, there are also several other assets declared unattachable by national laws. For instance, regarding remuneration, Law 14,443 (1958) rules that attachments must exclude wages, salaries, retirements and pensions not exceeding a certain amount, except for alimony, which must be set within a minimum permitting the subsistence of the alimony payer. For salaries, retirement payments and pensions exceeding that amount, attachments may be made for up to 20% of the monthly amount received. Statutes of limitations are of public order and therefore an attachment ordered on any unattachable assets may be countermanded ex officio or at the request of the debtor, their spouse or children, even if there is a court decision in favour of the attachment. Article 744 of the ACCC excludes from creditors' common guarantees those items such as clothing and furniture essential to the debtor, their spouse and children; the instruments necessary for the debtor to personally exercise their profession, craft or trade; the graves reserved for them, unless the claim concerns the costs of their sale, construction or repair; property affected by any religion recognized by the State; the rights of usufruct, use and habitation, as well as property easements, compensations corresponding to the debtor for moral and material damages derived from injuries to their psychophysical integrity; compensation for alimony corresponding to the spouse, partner and children with maintenance rights, in the event of homicide; and any other assets declared to be unattachable or excluded by other laws.

234. Attachment means that the attaching party has priority for recovery, however, this priority has no effect in the event of the debtor's bankruptcy or in the presence of a creditor with special privileges. Article 218 of the ACCPC provides that creditors obtaining the attachment of their debtor's assets when these are not affected by privileged credits, have the right to fully collect all credit, interests and costs, before other creditors, except in the case of bankruptcy. Subsequent attachments will only affect what is left after the credits referred to in earlier attachments have been repaid.[154]

154. Article 745 of the CCCN provides that a creditor who obtains the attachment of their debtor's assets has the right to collect their credit, interest and costs before other creditors. This priority may only be enforced against unsecured creditors in individual proceedings. If several creditors attach the

2. Sequestration

235. Sequestration refers to a provisional measure aimed at depriving a person of an asset which is the subject of litigation, or of a document required in order to bring a procedural claim.

Unlike the attachment, which can be applied to any property belonging to the debtor, sequestration only applies to certain things which are the subject of present or putative litigation (Article 221, ACCPC). Likewise, the things constituting its object cannot be used, since they usually remain in the hands of a third party.

3. Judicial Intervention

236. In general, judicial intervention refers to the provisional measure permitting a person appointed by the court as an auxiliary to intervene in the economic activity of a natural or legal person, to ensure forced execution or to prevent any alterations to the assets in question.

237. The purpose of the collection agent is to collect the cash required to comply with a previously decreed attachment, as a complement to it (as opposed to inhibition, which is, from this perspective, subsidiary). The function of the court auxiliary is limited exclusively to the collection of cash from the party attached as they have no involvement in the administration. The court determines the amount to be collected, which may not exceed 50% of gross income and must be deposited at the order of the court within the term determined (Article 223, ACCPC). The function of the informant is to provide news periodically on the status of the assets involved in the lawsuit, or in operations or activities, as established in the ruling designating this function (Article 224, ACCPC). A court-appointed auditor is provided for in Article 113 of the General Law of Companies (Law 19,550, Ordained Text 1984, with modifications) to replace the administrator of the corresponding entity, assuming management and oversight powers in temporary form.

4. General Property Inhibition

238. The general inhibition of assets is a provisional measure implying a prohibition on alienating or encumbering any recordable asset acquired or to be acquired. This measure is subsidiary to the attachment and is intended to come into effect when a debtor's assets are not known or do not cover the credit being claimed.

The person requesting the inhibition must state the name, surname and address of the debtor, as well as any other information that may identify the person inhibited, without prejudice to any other legal requirements.

---

same property belonging to the debtor, their ranking order is determined by the date when the measure was ordered. Subsequent attachments will only affect what is left after the credits referred to in earlier attachments have been paid.

The inhibition comes into effect on the date when it is filed. The attaching party, therefore, has priority to collect what they are owed before the person obtaining the general inhibition of goods, even if the latter had requested and been conceded the inhibition previously (Article 228, ACCPC).

An inhibition automatically expires five years after being recorded in the corresponding Registry by express legal provision, unless a party requests that it be re-registered before the expiry date by order of the court handling the proceedings. Expiry is lawful and requires no judicial declaration (Article 207, ACCPC).

5. Notice of Lis Pendens

239. Notice of lis pendens is the provisional measure that aims to guarantee the public nature of processes involving real estate. The property may be taxed and even sold, since the measure is limited to ensuring the publicity of the situation in dispute, but does not limit its availability.

The measure is appropriate when a claim is brought which could lead to the modification of an entry in the corresponding Registry and the right is plausible. If the claim is dismissed, the measure expires at the termination of the trial. If the court rules in favour of the claim, then the measure remains in place until the sentence has been met (Article 229, ACCPC).

6. Prohibition to Innovate and Contract

240. The prohibition to innovate is the provisional measure provided by the procedural regime aimed at preventing one of the parties from altering a state or situation while proceedings are under way, with the aim of rendering the provisions of the sentence useless or ineffective. Likewise, it extends to those cases where what is sought is to prevent the alteration of a previously existing factual state which the court orders be re-established after the proceedings have started.[155]

The requirements concerning provenance are the same as those for provisional measures in general: legal credibility, the danger of there being delays, and an injunction (the oath is insufficient). One particularity is that the procedure must have commenced, so that it cannot be petitioned in advance of the claim being brought (Articles 195 and 230, ACCPC).

241. The prohibition to contract is a provisional measure whereby the court may order the parties involved in proceedings where assets are in dispute to abstain from entering into the contract, and to make such a prohibition public.

155. A measure not to innovate is appropriate in the context of situations occurring prior to the claim being filed when the continuity and normal functions of interprovincial public communications service are at stake, and the situation existing at the time when the claim was brought involved the execution of provincial administrative acts subsequently challenged on credible bases prima facie, as contrary to provisions emanating from the federal government (*Fallos* 251:336).

This measure is usually ordered by the judge when the prohibition to contract certain goods arises by law, or contract, or to ensure the forced execution of the assets which are the object of the lawsuit. The measure singles out the object of the prohibition, and ensures that it is registered in the corresponding records and notified to the interested parties and third parties mentioned by the applicant. The measure will be left without effect if the person who obtained it does not bring their claim within five (5) days of it being ordered, and also if it can be proven to be inadmissible (Article 231, ACCPC).

7. Protection of Persons

242. The procedural regime provides for certain measures designed to protect the physical integrity or freedom of certain people, from the dangers to which they might be exposed. It thus authorizes disabled persons over 18 years of age to be placed under custody when they are abandoned or lack legal representation, or when they are prevented from exercising their functions; or they become involved in a lawsuit with their legal representatives where their conservatorship is in dispute.

F. Provisional Measures Against the State

243. In 2013, the law of provisional measures against the National State (Law 26,854) was enacted, establishing a differentiated system with respect to provisional claims brought against any action or omission on the part of the national State or its decentralized entities, or those requested by them (Article 1, Law 26,854). Hence, the ACCPC's rules on provisional matters described above are only applicable insofar as they are not incompatible with the requirements of Law 26,854 (Article 18). Likewise, in terms of *amparo*, the regime of provisional measures against the State is only partially applicable (Article 19).

Law 26,854 establishes specific suppositions for the origin of provisional protection, in some cases detailing the typical provisions pertaining to civil matters (e.g., in addition to requiring the demonstration of legal plausibility, they must also be able to demonstrate the illegitimacy of the material conduct attributed to the administration) and in others establishing the provisions to be made in this area of prosecution (e.g., not involving public interests).

Certain restrictions are also established that have been called into question: these include the one prohibiting the issue of provisional measures that affect, obstruct, compromise, distract from their destiny or in any way disturb the State's property or resources; one which prohibits provisional measures coinciding with the object of the main claim from being granted; and another establishing a term of validity for the provisional measure which is detached from the circumstances of the case, altering the rule maintaining provisional protection for as long as the conditions leading to its issue remain unchanged.

There are procedural aspects presenting certain peculiarities which favour the position of the National State when it is sued: (i) judges have a duty to declare their lack of jurisdiction, thus denying them the possibility of pronouncing on the provisional claim, except for exceptional cases – related to people in vulnerable situations or to certain rights of constitutional lineage (e.g., the environment, consumers) – in which case, the new judge must decide definitively on the origin of the injunction decreed by the previous one; (ii) if the unilateral nature of the provisional process is broken, the judge, prior to issuing a ruling, must require the defendant public authority to produce a report within a period of five days that accounts for the public interest compromised by the petition. This enables the defendant to make a statement regarding the admissibility and provenance of the measure requested and accompany this with the documentary evidence it deems pertinent; (iii) the rule regarding the effects of the appeal against the precautionary decision is reversed. The approach taken is that of the non-suspensive effect, except for the exceptional cases mentioned earlier.

§2. Default Proceedings

244. The ACCPC regulates the instance of the so-called rebellious party (Articles 5967) when the defendant, who has been notified of a lawsuit brought against them, decides not to present themselves in the period required to answer and notify their current domicile. It is also necessary in this instance for the claimant to request that the other party be declared in rebellion (Article 59, ACCPC).

Article 60 establishes that if the judge has any doubts when it comes to passing a sentence, the rebellious party figure is tantamount to a verbal admission of a fact, as affirmed by the claimant.

As said earlier (*see* paragraphs 145 and 186), when the defendant answers a lawsuit, according to Article 356, paragraph 1 of the ACCPC, they must recognize or deny, categorically, clearly and explicitly, each of the personal and essential facts given in the lawsuit, as well as the authenticity of any accompanying documents and the receipt of any writs addressed to them. Silence, evasive responses or the general and indeterminate denial of the facts, may be considered as the acknowledgement of the same.

However, Article 60 of the ACCPC says that rebelliousness constitutes a presumption that the acts attributed to the rebellious party are true. As this article only indicates a presumption to be taken into account by the judge, and according to Article 356 paragraph 1, this may be seen as an acknowledgment, it is customary in practice for the other party, despite the rebelliousness, to produce the evidence offered.

Article 61 of the ACCPC establishes that the judge can open evidentiary proceedings upon the request of one of the parties.

245. The rebellious party is notified subsequent to the judicial decisions under the terms of Article 133 of the ACCPC on the following Tuesday or Friday as appropriate, with the exception of the hearing called to cross-examine them on their version of the facts and the sentence (Articles 41 and 133, ACCPC). This will either be notified to their address or through edicts published in the official channels.

246. Article 63 of the ACCPC says that as from the time when the litigant is declared a rebellious party, the judge may order all the precautionary measures requested by the other party to ensure that the proceedings achieve their goal. If the rebellious party decides to present themselves at the proceedings, the precautionary measures continue to apply, unless they are able to justify their rebellion for reasons beyond their control (Article 65 of the ACCPC).

§3. Non-contentious Proceedings

247. When referring to the classification of proceedings, it has been pointed out, that depending on whether there is conflict between adverse parties or not, it is possible to distinguish between contentious and non-contentious proceedings (also called voluntary jurisdiction).

Voluntary proceedings are those where the subjects (whether petitioners or applicants) require the competent bodies to issue a pronouncement that constitutes, integrates, or gives effectiveness to a state or legal situation.

In its Book VII, the ACCPC regulates voluntary proceedings such as: authorization to contract marriage, guardianship and curatorship; copy and renewal of title deeds; authorization to appear at trial and exercise legal acts; examination of books by a business partner; and recognition of the acquisition and sale of merchandise.

Chapter 2. Review Proceedings

§1. General

I. The Right to Appeal

248. In its Article 18, the AC does not provide details on the scope of the right that it identifies as defence in court. However, Article 75 (22), incorporated following the 1994 constitutional reform, gave human rights treaties signed by Argentina constitutional hierarchy, broadening the scope of the right of access to justice. Article 14 (5) of the ICCPR and Article 8 (2) of the ACHR establish the guarantee ensuring that every person found guilty of a crime has the right to appeal the judgment before a higher court. Hence, it has been discussed whether the guarantee of a double instance has constitutional hierarchy, not only for criminal proceedings but also for civil ones.

The Supreme Court holds that the application of international standards establishing a guarantee of double instance is subject to there being a final judgment handed down against a 'person accused of a crime' or 'found guilty of a crime'. Therefore, judgments that convict or acquit a person accused of misdemeanours, contraventions or administrative infractions are outside its scope[156] and consequently lack constitutional hierarchy in civil proceedings.[157] This means that due legal process is not affected by the lack of double instance, 'except when the laws specifically establish this'.[158]

II. Concept, Classification, Requirements

249. The ACCPC dedicates Chapter IV of Title IV (general contingencies), of Book I (general provisions) to review proceedings, by separating them into ordinary and extraordinary review proceedings.

250. Ordinary review proceedings concern: (i) clarification, (ii) reversal, (iii) appeal, (iv) annulment, (v) complaint of appeal, and (vi) consultation. Extraordinary review proceedings are those which concern: (i) the inapplicability of the law, (ii) a federal extraordinary appeal, (iii) a complaint appeal for the denial of a federal extraordinary appeal, and (iv) a *per saltum* appeal.

251. There are certain requirements that are common to any type of review proceedings, which have to do with the role played by the party in the proceedings,[159] the existence of an interest in reversing the decision being contested, and whether it can be filed within the terms established by law.

156. *Fallos* 323:1787 (2000) and 325:2711 (2002).
157. *Fallos* 323:2357 (2000).
158. *Fallos* 329:1180 (2006).
159. When a third party is admitted to the proceedings, they have the right to appeal.

252. The procedure for each kind of appeal envisages the particular assumptions giving rise to it and the steps to be followed. Only a specifically foreseen appeal procedure may be used, and this cannot happen without first identifying the precise nature of the appeal being filed.

253. In proceedings involving several plaintiffs and defendants, an appeal only benefits the person filing it. For parties affected who do not file an appeal, in principle except for specific cases the decision becomes res judicata.[160]

254. The prohibition of *reformatio in peius,* derived from the maxim *tantum devolutum quantum apellatum*, indicating that the appellate judge has no more powers than those outlined by the appeal filed, is derived from the principle of consistency in force in civil matters. This pre-empts the possibility of objectively damaging or worsening the appellant's situation. Article 277 of the ACCPC only attributes jurisdiction to the Courts of Appeal on the basis of the appeals filed. In *Ozafrain v. The Central Bank of the Argentine Republic,*[161] the Supreme Court understood that 'the ruling placing the only appellants in a worse situation than that arising from the judgement under appeal, incurs in *reformatio in peius,* which constitutes a direct and immediate violation of the guarantee of defence in court and of property'.

§2. Ordinary Review Proceedings

I. Clarification

255. The judge may, ex officio (before notifying the sentence[162]) or at the request of a party, amend material errors, clarify obscure concepts or rectify an omission, provided that the amendment, clarification or rectification do not alter the substance of the decision.

As provided for in Articles 166 (2) and 272 of the ACCPC, the deadline for the parties to request clarification is three days in the first instance, and five days before the Court of Appeal.

Clarification is admissible as an appeal in the context of all judicial decisions. The reasons may be: (i) to correct material errors, meaning errors in the expression of the will rather than of the will itself; (ii) to explain obscure concepts, which refers to conceptual inaccuracies, as long as these do not alter the substance of the decision, and (iii) to rectify any omissions that may have been made.

When filing the clarification, the reasons justifying it must be stated. The deadline for presenting it is three days from the notification in the first instance, and five

160. In the case of *Alvarez v. Maldonado* (judgment of 12/27/2001) the BAPSCJ interpreted that, to the extent that each of the benefits provided for in the sentence had a certain independence, or when the content of the decision is joint or indivisible, the effect of the remedy can be extended to cover those who did not file an appeal against the judgment.

161. *Fallos* 319:1135 (1996).

162. Only purely numerical errors can be corrected after notification (Arts 166 (1 and 2) and 36 (6), ACCPC).

in the second instance and before the Supreme Court. It is resolved by the judge or court issuing the resolution, and its filing neither suspends nor interrupts the period for filing other appeals.

II. Revocation

256. Revocation or reinstatement involves filing a challenge aimed at getting the same judge who issued the appealed ruling to reconsider its content, modifying it in whole or in part (Article 238, ACCPC). It may only be brought against decisions to expedite proceedings (Article 160, ACCPC). It can also be brought before the Court of Appeal (Article 273, ACCPC) and the Supreme Court.

Revocation seeks to save time and avoid entering into any procedural activity that would require review by another judge, regarding matters of less procedural relevance and without there being any contradiction between the parties prior to this.

Resolutions issued by first instance clerks or legal deputies acting according to Article 38 of the ACCPC may also be replaced at the request of a party.

These must provide due justification and file within three days of the notification of the decision in question, except in the case of a decision ruled during a hearing, when it must be presented during the same. The judge will notify the opponent in the space of three days (or in the course of the hearing), unless reinstatement is brought against an order issued ex officio or at the request of the appellant, in which case it is not necessary for the opposing party to intervene (Article 240, ACCPC). If there are any controversial facts involved, the judge may open incidental proceedings allowing the parties to prove their allegations.

If the judge declares a revocation admissible and modifies the resolution in dispute, the opposing party may appeal it (Article 241, ACCPC). If the judge dismisses it, on the other hand, the order will remain final and enforceable, unless a supplementary appeal has been filed, in those cases where a court order causes damages which are impossible to repair in the final judgment (Article 242, ACCPC).

III. Appeal

257. An appeal is intended to get a body other than the one issuing the resolution to modify it either partly or wholly, and to rule both on the errors regarding the application of the law and those related to the appreciation of the facts and the evidence.

An appeal may be lodged against: (i) the final judgments; (ii) interlocutory judgments, and (iii) simple court orders causing damages that cannot be repaired by the final judgment. While in ordinary proceedings, the rule is the appeal (although there are court orders that cannot be appealed by express legal provision e.g., one admitting the intervention of a third party), in summary and executive proceedings, the principle of non-appeal governs. Hence, this remedy is only viable for specific cases (e.g., court orders resolving an injunction).

The Argentine system established a *suma gravamminis* to ensure that final judgments and other resolutions, whatever their nature, issued in proceedings where the amount under question is less than the amount set annually by the Argentine Supreme Court Agreement, may not be appealed.[163] For the purposes of determining the status of non-appeal, the amount applicable on the date when the claim or the counterclaim is filed will be the reference used. If, at the time of passing a sentence, a sum of less than 20% that was claimed by the parties is recognized, non-appealability will be determined in accordance with the capital recognized in the sentence. This provision does not apply to maintenance cases or those pursuing a party's eviction from property, nor to those cases where the application of procedural sanctions is under discussion. Nor does it apply to appeals filed against the award of fees or costs.

258. An appeal can only be brought by someone with a grievance resulting from the operative part of the ruling. A successful party cannot bring such an appeal, even when certain means of defence have been rejected. However, if the opposing party appeals, the higher court is empowered to handle all the issues submitted in first instance to the judge that could not be raised in the second instance, due to lack of interest. Therefore, the institution of adhesive or implicit appeal applies.[164] An eventual appeal is not allowed. However, a supplementary appeal for revocation is acceptable. An appeal is also regarded as inadmissible if the resolution being challenged is the consequence of another that was final. The principle of congruence in the appeal also applies, which means that the knowledge of the court of second instance is limited, not only by what constituted the *thema decidendum* in the instance of degree, but also by the measure of the grievance cited in the appeal which determined its jurisdiction.

259. The term for filing the appeal is five days in ordinary proceedings (Article 244, ACCPC). In summary proceedings, it is three days (Article 498, paragraph 3, ACCPC). In both cases, these are peremptory and individual deadlines, which run separately for each party as from the notification of the ruling in question.

260. The appeal is either filed in writing or made verbally, recorded by the court clerk or official, and merely involves the manifestation of the will to appeal. The grounds for the appeal must be presented after the judge decides to admit it, at the time established by law, depending on whether it is an appeal in plenary proceedings. If the rule about the need to provide grounds is violated after being granted, the appeal will be dismissed.

---

163. According to Art. 242 of the ACCPC (amended by Law 26,536 (2009)) final judgments and other resolutions, whatever their nature, passed in proceedings where the amount in question is less than the amount annually set by the Supreme Court, are unappealable. According to Supreme Court Agreement 41 (2019), the amount for the year 2020 was set at ARS 300,000. In the province of Buenos Aires, a minimum amount to appeal has not been established.

164. It has been pointed out in the Province of Buenos Aires, according to the interpretation of the BAP-SCJ, that the allegations or defences proposed by the winning party, unable to appeal because the result of the case was in their favour, may be submitted to the court of appeal if the ruling is revoked in that instance (Supreme Court Rules 56,034, judgment of 4 April 1995; Supreme Court Rules 52,049, judgment of 17 October 1995 and Supreme Court Rules 70,060, judgment of 18 April 2001).

The judge issuing the contested decision is the one who decides on the admissibility of the appeal. The concession can be granted in one of two ways: (i) in plenary proceedings, in the case of final judgments in ordinary proceedings or, (ii) in all other cases. The difference in the form of concession lies in the greater or lesser opening of the second instance. For this reason, the best denomination is held to be that of free appeal, and restricted or limited appeal. There are some procedural differences between these two forms of granting the appeal, since in the free appeal, the admittance of evidence is allowed in certain cases as is the allegation of new facts, which are not admitted in the related appeal. An appeal in plenary proceedings is based on the Appeal, while the appeal in relation to the appeal is based on the first instance. In an appeal in plenary proceedings the court ruling must respect the individual agreement and vote of the members, while in limited appeal cases, the joint vote of the judges of the Court of Appeal is sufficient.

261. If either party claims that the appeal should have been awarded in plenary proceedings, they may within three days request that the judge rectify the error. If the judge accepts the request, they must order the process to be sent to the Court of Appeal, in order for the appeal to be substantiated. If the judge rejects the request, the Court of Appeal, may ex officio, or at the request of a party made within the third day of the notification of the court order, grant the appeal in plenary proceedings (Article 276, ACCPC).

262. As for the actual filing of the appeal, it should be noted that the general principle is that this suspends the execution of the resolution contested, unless the law provides otherwise (Article 243, ACCPC).

263. The appeal is processed and resolved after it has been filed, unless the law establishes that it must be deferred pending the issue of the sentence, so as not to delay the course of the proceedings. These are situations where the legislator has prioritized the conclusion of the process in the first instance, with the consideration of the appeal left pending the moment when the appeal against the final judgment is granted.

IV. Nullity

264. An ordinary appeal to annul is a challenge which seeks to correct any structural defects inherent to the judicial resolution, when this fails to comply with the formal requirements prescribed by law (Articles 160 to 163, ACCPC). Both the errors preceding the judgment (channelled through incidental proceedings to annul, Article 169, ACCPC), as well as any flaws in the judgment peculiar to an appeal, remain beyond its scope of operation.

An ordinary appeal for annulment lacks autonomy in the national procedural regime, as it is understood to be inherently implicit in the appeal. Hence, the same admissibility requirements apply as for the latter. However, the appellant must refer in the memorandum or expression of grievances to any errors manifested in the judgment, otherwise they will be validated.

Nullity is a so-called positive appeal/remedy. In effect, Article 253 of the ACCPC provides that once the judgment is declared invalid, due to any inherent defects, the merits of the litigation are effectively resolved, so it cannot be forwarded to the Court of Appeal.

V. Complaint

265. Although the first instance judge issuing the decision in question carries out the first check to verify whether the appeal is admissible, it is the Court of Appeal that is assigned the last and final check to control the admissibility of the appeal. Hence, the ACCPC regulates the so-called complaint appeal, designed to question the decision of a lower-court judge regarding the dismissal of the appeal filed earlier. It is also appropriate to question the effective form taken by the appeal (whether it is suspensive, not suspensive, immediate or deferred).

The complaint, also called a direct or factual appeal, must be filed in a well-founded manner before the Court of Appeal, meeting certain criteria in order to be deemed admissible: (i) a single copy signed by the appellant's attorney which must be accompanied by the following: the brief giving rise to the resolution appealed and those corresponding to the substantiation, if this has taken place; (b) the decision appealed; (c) the document filing the appeal and, where appropriate, the revocation remedy if the appeal was filed in a subsidiary manner; (d) the court order dismissing the appeal; (ii) giving the date when: (a) the resolution appealed was notified; (b) the appeal was filed; (c) the dismissal of the appeal was notified. Once the complaint has been presented, the court will decide, without the need for substantiation, whether the appeal has been correctly dismissed or not. In the latter case, it will order that this be done accordingly. As long as the Court does not grant the appeal, the course of the proceedings will not be suspended (Article 259, ACCPC).

The same rules apply in the case of a complaint filed against the denial of an extraordinary appeal before the Supreme Court. In this case, the copies only need be presented when this court so requires.

VI. Consultation

266. The Argentine national regime provides, among the remedies available, for a so-called consultation (Article 253 b, ACCPC) in the case of the declaration of a person's incapacity. It is the duty of the magistrate of first instance to forward the file to the Court of Appeal for the purposes of safeguarding the defence of the person declared as disabled, establishing a system of double control over this situation.

§3. EXTRAORDINARY APPEALS

I. Remedy of Inapplicability of Law

267. Law 26,853 (2013) created various Courts of Cassation and suppressed the possibility of filing an appeal against the inapplicability of the law. This norm was repealed by Law 27,500 (2019), which once again modified the ACCPC in order to maintain the appeal against the inapplicability of the law granted against final judgments,[165] issued by a section of the Court of Appeal in contradiction to a decision ruled by another section of the Court of Appeal issued in the ten years preceding the date of the ruling appealed (Article 288, ACCPC). The decision about the remedy is taken by the Court of Appeal with all of its members present.

The main feature of plenary rulings is that the doctrine they establish is mandatory for the Court of Appeal and for the judges of first instance in the respective jurisdiction (Article 303, ACCPC).

268. The appeal must be filed within ten days of the sentence being notified, making clear the contradiction between the positions taken by the different Courts and the arguments justifying its award (Article 292, ACCPC).

II. Federal Extraordinary Appeal

A. Background

269. Deriving from the principle of constitutional supremacy (Article 31, AC), all the judges in Argentina exercise control over the constitutionality of the rules, avoiding applying those that are unconstitutional. There is therefore a diffuse judicial system of constitutional review where all judges are allowed to rule on the matter. The ability to decide on the constitutionality of a norm in the Argentine system is not limited to a single court.

270. Article 14 of Law 48 (1863) instituted the so-called federal extraordinary appeal, empowering the Supreme Court to safeguard constitutional supremacy and determine the intelligence of federal law.

271. The Supreme Court has understood that 'extraordinary review proceedings, denominated as such by case law and relevant doctrine, are those exceptionally permitted which allow the Court to ensure the primacy of the Constitution and determine the intelligence of the treaties, federal laws and commissions exercised on behalf of the national authority'.[166]

165. Judgments concluding the proceedings or making its continuation impossible are considered final (Art. 289, ACCPC).
166. *Fallos* 213:349 (1949).

Once a lawsuit has been filed before the provincial courts, a judgment is passed and the matter concluded in the provincial jurisdiction, while final judgments pronounced by the higher provincial courts may only be appealed before the Supreme Court when a federal issue has been configured in the lawsuit (Article 14, Law 48).

The essential assumption underlying the extraordinary competence of the Supreme Court arises from a federal question. Three criteria are foreseen in Article 14 of Law 48 to help identify the existence of a federal issue: (i) questioning the validity of a federal act and a decision counter to that validity; (ii) challenging a local act under for being repugnant to the AC, the laws and other federal norms, or the Treaties signed by the Nation and the favourable decision with regard to the local act; and (iii) the debate on the intelligence of a clause in the AC, a federal law or a Treaty signed by the Nation, and the existence of a decision contrary to the validity of the right based on this clause.

Law 48 itself, in its Article 15, took care to provide that the interpretation or application made by provincial courts of the codes of substantive law, such as the ACCC, may not give rise to the remedy given in Article 14 due to the fact that such codes are laws of Congress.

However, the aforementioned guidelines were expanded by way of interpretation by the Supreme Court, thus incorporating the possibility of ruling on questions of law and evidence by incorporating the notion of arbitrary judgment. At the beginning of the twentieth century, in *Rey v. Rocha,*[167] the Supreme Court referred to extraordinary cases of arbitrary judgments, devoid of any legal support and based solely on the will of the judges. Later, in *Storani de Boidanich v. Ansaldi,*[168] when analysing the principle of congruence, the Supreme Court held that as long as the final decision taken in first instance had incorporated rights to the appellants' assets, the Court's ruling could not then 'arbitrarily deprive' them of these.

Another interpretation made by the Supreme Court allowing it to admit cases which had not been not clearly foreseen in Article 14 of Law 48, is the matter of issues with serious institutional implications. This standard allows the Supreme Court to enter into the analysis of the case despite the omission of any requirement enshrined in the extraordinary federal review proceedings. In *Jorge Antonio,*[169] the Supreme Court, upon finding what, in its opinion, was a matter with serious institutional implications, understood that it could dispense with the need to take into account those requirements limiting the admissibility of an extraordinary federal appeal.

The third line of jurisprudence modifying Supreme Court jurisdiction concerns the *per saltum* appeal that permits its intervention, even though the decision appealed does not issue from the upper court in question.

This is an interpretive creation by the Supreme Court instrumented in the *Dromi* case,[170] where it held that in the event of federal issues displaying unequivocal and extraordinary circumstances of gravity, the requirement for the questioned decision to emanate from the superior court intervening in the case may be waived.

167. *Fallos* 112:384 (1909).
168. *Fallos* 184:137 (1939).
169. *Fallos* 248:189 (1960).
170. *Fallos* 313:863 (1990).

Law 26,790 altered Article 257 of the ACCPC,[171] and established that an extraordinary appeal may proceed regardless of the involvement of the higher court. This is for cases of federal jurisdiction where it is proven that the issue has serious institutional implications whose definitive and expeditious solution is necessary, and filing an appeal constitutes the only effective remedy for the protection of the federal law in question so as to avoid damages which cannot be repaired. Matters with serious institutional implications are those which arise in cases submitted to trial where the issues exceed the interest of the parties in the case, as they affect the public in general in such a way as to threaten the basic institutions of the republican system of government or compromise the principles and guarantees enshrined in the Argentine Constitution and the International Treaties incorporated therein. The Court may enable this instance with a restricted scope in exceptional cases. *Per saltum* extraordinary review proceedings only apply in the context of final judgments of first instance, comparable resolutions in terms of their effects, and those issued as injunctions. The Law expressly indicates that this kind of remedy does not apply in criminal cases.

Both in matters of arbitrariness and in terms of issues with serious institutional implications, the Supreme Court resorted to its powers as interpreter of the AC to run the limits set by the legislator regarding its competence.

272. Concerning the issue of which cases the Supreme Court decides to handle, Law 23,744 (1990)[172] established that it is empowered to use its discretion in dismissing an extraordinary appeal, due to lack of sufficient federal tort, or when the questions raised are insubstantial or lacking in importance (Article 280 of the ACCPC, according to the modification of Law 23,744). According to the background of Law 23,744 and its justification, this would allow one to infer that such a power would be used to restrict the admission of cases to the Supreme Court. However, the Supreme Court interpreted that the new wording given to Article 280 of the ACCPC broadened its discretionary powers to dismiss and admit those cases where it intervenes.

273. Regarding the development of extraordinary federal review proceedings, the Supreme Court issued a series of agreements incorporating two key initiatives whose use has, since their creation, been rather erratic and very limited. However, if used correctly, they could serve to improve the quality of the debates on major institutional issues. These involve public hearings to debate cases and accept submissions for amicus curiae. Supreme Court Rule 30 (2007), established a regime of public hearings, which may be: (a) informative, with the purpose of hearing and questioning the parties on aspects of the case to be decided; (b) conciliatory, aimed at urging the parties to find non-adversarial solutions; and (c) regulatory, with a view to taking the measures allowing the proceedings to move swiftly through the

---

171. Articles 257 bis and ter. were added.

172. The first objective of the law was to enlarge the majorities of the Supreme Court as a result of political issues explained in para. 4.

appropriate channels to achieve the best handling of the case. Supreme Court Agreement 28 (2004), 14 (2006) and 7 (2013), instituted a regime regulating the participation of amicus curiae in legal cases filed before it. In the last Supreme Court Agreement issued, several modifications were introduced to achieve an improvement in the intervention of these social stakeholders with a view to democratising and enriching the constitutional debate, as well as strengthening the legitimacy of jurisdictional decisions issued by the Supreme Court of Justice in matters of institutional significance.

B. Requirements

274. The requirements for bringing extraordinary federal review proceedings are given in the ACCPC (Article 256 et seq.), as well as in special laws and also arise from the criteria established by the Supreme Court in its sentences and Agreements.

For an extraordinary federal review proceedings to be admitted, the following conditions must be met: (i) the decision in question must emanate from a court of law; (ii) the existence of a judicial case is necessary; (iii) where a litigious issue has been resolved; (iv) that the resolution entails a lien being levied on the appellant; (iv) that the foregoing are in place at the time of the CSJN ruling; (v) that a final judgment is being challenged or that proceedings are prevented from continuing; (vii) that the decision emanates from the superior court handling the case; (viii) that the appellant's claim may be considered a federal matter; (ix) that this question is directly and immediately related to the outcome of the lawsuit; (x) the timely introduction and persistence of the federal issue throughout the different stages of the proceedings; (xi) the filing of the extraordinary federal review proceedings within a period of ten days; (xii) compliance with the requisite legal formalities; (xiii) that justification be self-sufficient, meaning that the remedy is sufficient for the appeal to be heard.

In its Rule 4,[173] the Supreme Court adopted the Regulations on filing extraordinary federal review proceedings, by invoking the attributions conferred on it by Article 10 of Law 4055 (1902), Article 21 of Decree-Law 1285/58 and Article 4 of Law 25,488 (2001). All these norms empower the Supreme Court to issue regulatory measures and any others it deems appropriate to ensure the best possible functioning of the justice system.

Furthermore, Rule 4 establishes regulations governing the filing of extraordinary federal review proceedings, which complement the provisions mentioned above:

1. Federal extraordinary review proceedings must be filed by means of a document of no more than forty (40) pages of twenty-six (26) lines, in a clearly legible font size (no less than 12 pt.). The same rules apply to the written reply to the notification foreseen in Article 257 of the Argentine Civil and Commercial Procedural Code.

173. *Fallos* 330:1314 (2007).

2. It must contain a cover page on a separate sheet of paper containing only the following data: a) the purpose of the presentation; b) the precise enunciation of the file's title page; c) the name of the person signing the document; if they are acting on behalf of third parties, of their clients, and of the legal counsel, if any; d) the domicile established by the applicant in the Federal Capital; e) the capacity in which the petitioner or their representative (as plaintiff, defendant, third party summoned, etc.) is intervening in the lawsuit; f) the specific decision against which the appeal is being filed; g) mention of the body, judge or court that issued the decision being appealed, as well as the identities of those who previously intervened in the lawsuit; h) the pronouncement notification date; i) clear and concise description of the issues raised as being of a federal nature, with a simple reference to the norms involved in such issues, and the Court's precedents on the subject, if any; as well as a summarized version of the statement on the point under debate that the appellant is seeking to obtain from the Court. No matter other than those mentioned in this paragraph will be considered; j) reference to the legal norms conferring jurisdiction on the Court to intervene in the case.
3. The next pages should present, in successive chapters and without incurring in unnecessary repetition: a) the demonstration that the decision appealed is from the superior court in the case, and that it is final or comparable to such, according to Court jurisprudence; b) a clear and precise account of all the relevant circumstances related to the issues being invoked as federal in nature, indicating the moment when these issues were first presented, how and when the appellant introduced their respective objection, and, where appropriate, how this was maintained subsequently; c) the demonstration that the pronouncement being challenged causes the appellant personal, concrete, and current harm, which is not derived from their legal action; d) the refutation of each and every one of the independent grounds supporting the decision appealed, in relation to the federal issues raised; e) the demonstration that there is a direct and immediate relationship between the federal regulations being invoked, and what was debated and resolved in the case, and that the decision which was contested is contrary to the right invoked by the appellant, based on said federal regulations.

In the event that the presentations do not meet the criteria for any of the remedies accepted for filing federal extraordinary review proceedings, or if these are deficient in any way, the Supreme Court will dismiss the request for review simply by mentioning the pertinent regulatory norm, unless, at its discretion, it understands that the breach does not constitute an insurmountable obstacle to the admissibility of the claim.

III. Complaint about Denial of Extraordinary Federal Review Proceedings

275. The complaint appeal effectively requests the Supreme Court to review the denial of the admission of the extraordinary federal review proceedings made by the court before which they were brought.

Article 285 of the ACCPC explains that a complaint brought against the denial of the extraordinary federal review process must be presented within a period of ten days, and be duly founded.

If the complaint concerns the denial of the extraordinary federal review proceedings, the Supreme Court may reject it simply by invoking Article 280 of the ACCPC.

As long as the Court does not admit the complaint, the course of the proceedings will not be suspended.

The admissibility of the appeal requires a deposit to be made, according to the amount established periodically by the Supreme Court Agreement.[174] This must be done when the complaint is filed.

If a deposit is not made, or is insufficient, the appellant will be informed that they have five days in which to make it up or otherwise the case will be declared void. If the complaint is declared admissible by the Supreme Court, the deposit will be returned to the interested party. If it is rejected, or the instance is declared to have expired, the appellant loses the deposit.

In Supreme Court Rule 4 (2007), mentioned in paragraph 271, the following requirements are established for filing a complaint appeal for denial of the extraordinary federal review proceedings:

4. The complaint appeal for denial of the extraordinary federal review proceedings must be filed in a document of no more than forty (10) pages of twenty-six (26) lines, in a clearly legible font size (no less than 12 pt.).
5. It must contain a cover page on a separate sheet containing only the data foreseen in Article 2, paras. a, b, c, d and e; and, also: f) the mention of the body, judge or court issuing the decision to deny the federal extraordinary appeal, as well as the names of those who previously intervened in the lawsuit; g) the pronouncement notification date; h) clarification as to whether the deadline foreseen in Article 158 of the ACCPC has been extended; i) where appropriate, proof that the appellant is exempt from making the deposit provided for in Article 286 of the ACCPC.
6. In the following pages, the appellant must refute, with concrete and reasoned arguments, each and every one of the independent grounds supporting the resolution denying the review proceedings in question. The brief is designed for this purpose only, and any other issues not raised in the extraordinary review proceedings may not be introduced.
7. When filing the complaint, this document must be accompanied by simple, clearly legible copies of: a) the decision challenged by the extraordinary federal review proceedings; (b) the document filing this last appeal; c) the

174. Agreement 40 (2019) set the amount of the deposit defined in Art. 286 of the ACCPC at ARS 100,000.

written reply to the notification foreseen in Article 257 of the ACCPC; d) the decision to deny the extraordinary federal review proceedings. Any defects in the grounds for their argument when filing the extraordinary appeal which the appellant might have incurred may not be compensated by the mere addition of the afore-mentioned copies.

If the complaint is declared admissible and the sentence is revoked, Article 16 of Law No. 48 (Article 285, ACCPC) will apply.

When the Supreme Court revokes the contested sentence through extraordinary federal review proceedings, it rules on the matter in dispute and returns the case for a retrial. It may also decide on the merits of the case, and may even order the execution of the sentence, especially if the case has already been returned once for the same reason (Article 16, Law 48, and Article 285 of the ACCPC).

Part V. Incidental Proceedings

Chapter 1. General Incidents

276. Any matter that has an accessory relationship with the main object of the lawsuit, arising during its development and not subject to a special procedure, will be dealt with in incidental proceedings. The ACCPC accepts this figure and the rules for resolving these matters in Articles 175 to 184. Among other provisions, the ACCPC refers to this general procedure, in the event that a public instrument is held to be false (Article 395), exequatur (Article 518) or determines the damages arising from the breach of an obligation to do something or not (Articles 513 and 514).

277. The judge handling the main proceedings is competent to hear incidental proceedings, a rule explained by the inherent connection between the two (Article 6, paragraph 1, ACCPC). Incidental proceedings may be filed with the brief and with the copy of the resolution and any other documentary evidence for the principal claim indicated by the parties and filed with and certified by the secretary (Article 177, ACCPC).

278. Anybody deciding to initiate incidental proceedings must state the legal grounds for these and offer all the evidence available (Article 178, ACCPC). When issues that may be dealt with simultaneously also threaten to paralyse the proceedings, they must be raised jointly in a single brief, provided that such joint processing is necessary. Failure to comply with this rule means that claims filed at a later date will be dismissed without further ado (Article 186, ACCPC).

279. If the incidental proceedings sought are manifestly inadmissible (among other assumptions, due to their being illegal, lacking legal grounds or interest, or because the person bringing them is not a party to the main case), the judge must reject them without further ado. This resolution may be appealed, but it stands firm until such time as the Court of Appeals issues a decision (Article 179, ACCPC).

280. In principle, in the case of a complementary or ancillary question, bringing incidental proceedings does not suspend the development of the main proceedings, except in those cases where the ACCPC expressly determines their suspension, or if the judge decides that doing so is indispensable in the light of the issue raised (e.g., a petition for annulment). A resolution in this case will be irrevocable (Article 176, ACCPC).

281. When incidental proceedings are admissible, the judge will substantiate these and notify the other party of their right to reply. This notification may either be communicated personally or served. Expedited summary proceedings are governed by the terms set by the judge, who will adopt the appropriate measures ex officio so that the incidental proceedings do not end up distorting the main ones (Articles 180 and 187, ACCPC).

If evidence has been offered which must be produced at a hearing, the judge will indicate a suitable date no more than ten days following either the answer to the notification or the deadline for doing so. To this end, the judge will summon any witnesses that the parties cannot oblige to appear and will adopt the measures necessary to treat the evidence that cannot be received at this hearing. If the evidence cannot be added before the hearing, it will only be taken into account if it is incorporated before the incidental proceedings are resolved, at whichever instance they are (Article 181, ACCPC). When it is materially impossible to produce the evidence at the hearing, this may be postponed or suspended – only once, for a period of no more than ten days (Article 182, ACCPC).

In the case of summary proceedings, there may be evidentiary limitations. This means that when expert evidence is offered, it must be by court-appointed experts, as bringing in external technical consultants is prohibited. In the case of testimonial evidence, no more than five witnesses may be proposed by each party. Likewise, witness statements may not be received outside the court's jurisdiction, regardless of their domicile (Article 183, ACCPC).

Taking into consideration reasons of economy and procedural expediency, any issues arising in the context of incidental proceedings without sufficient weight to constitute other independent proceedings will be decided in a single decision (Article 184, ACCPC).

Once the notification has been answered or has expired, if neither party has offered evidence or been ordered ex officio, or the evidence has been completed and received, where appropriate, the judge will issue a resolution (Article 185, ACCPC). The losing party must bear the costs, unless the judge decides otherwise. Furthermore, the judge will not substantiate any new incidental proceedings brought by the person convicted until they have paid the costs or deposited goods for the purposes of attachment. However, they may appeal against costs and fees imposed, with a deferred effect, unless one of the parties appeals the resolution resolving the incidental proceedings (Article 69, ACCPC).

Chapter 2. Incidental Procedures Governed by Specific Regulations

282. In this chapter we will only deal with incidental proceedings under special regulation in the ACCPC, which have not yet been dealt with elsewhere in this monograph. Please refer to the respective paragraphs for further information in relation to either writ of prohibition or plea, the benefit of litigating without expenses, annulment, the intervention of third parties, accumulation of proceedings and default.

§1. Challenge and Abstention

283. The challenge is based on the parties' ability to exclude the judge from hearing the case, when there are certain legal reasons capable of calling into question the impartiality of the judge's decisions. Abstention, on the other hand, is the prerogative or duty of the judge who may spontaneously inhibit themselves from hearing a case, when any of the circumstances foreseen by law occur.

Both institutions seek to safeguard the correct administration of justice and the impartiality of the judge.

Experts, mediators, clerks, or prosecutors can also be challenged or abstain themselves (Articles 39, 465, 466 et seq., ACCPC; Articles 13 and 14, Law 26,589).

I. Challenge With and Without Expression of Cause

284. The ACCPC accepts a challenge with or without an expression of cause. In the latter case, this power may only be exercised once in each case, and in the eventuality of joint action, only one of the plaintiffs or defendants may bring it (Article 15, ACCPC).

This is effectively a guarantee for the litigants, especially when it is difficult to prove the facts underpinning a legal cause for challenge. Challenge without due cause is prohibited in expedited summary proceedings, third-party proceedings, evictions and execution as it may affect the speed of the trials.

285. 285 Challenge without cause can only proceed against first and second instance judges (Article 14, ACCPC).

Regarding the former, a challenge without cause must be filed at the first procedural opportunity available to the party. This means that the plaintiff must bring it when filing the lawsuit, when requesting pretrial proceedings, a provisional measure, or during their first procedural presentation. The defendant must file a challenge at their first opportunity of intervening in the trial, either when answering the claim or when raising exceptions or attending a hearing. Failure to exercise the power to challenge at the first opportunity forfeits that right. Furthermore, the defendant also forfeits this right if they fail to exercise it in the course of their first procedural act (Article 14, ACCPC).

For Chamber judges, this power must be exercised the day after the first order issued is notified.

286. As for the procedure itself, once a challenge for cause without reason has been brought, the judge challenged must withdraw from the proceedings and forward, during the first business day following, the files to the next judge in line, without suspending the proceedings, deadlines, nor waiving compliance with the procedures already ordered. Consequently, a challenged judge cannot, under penalty of annulment, take part in the proceedings, except to examine the challenge and the party bringing it. However, they may hear those cases where the defendant's presentation follows the answer to the claim, where there is opposition to exceptions or a hearing aimed at annulling the proceedings, constituting a challenge without cause (Article 16, ACCPC). In this sense, depending on the result of the challenge, it may be determined whether or not it was opportune, and thus it may be considered reasonable to confer the power to rule on the merits of the challenge on the judge challenged themselves.

287. A challenge for cause is personal[175] and can be brought on any of the grounds established in Article 17 of the ACCPC. These include the following: (i) kinship by consanguinity to the fourth degree and second degree of affinity of the judge with any of the parties, their representatives or lawyers;[176] (ii) any interest in the lawsuit, or in another similar one, that the judge or their relatives may have to the degrees mentioned above, or partnership with any of the litigants, or attorneys, unless the company is anonymous. This interest must be immediate, direct and current;[177] (iii) the existence of any lawsuit pending with the challenger, not with the lawyers, which must be raised when the proceedings begin; (iv) if the judge is a creditor, debtor or guarantor of any of the parties, with the exception of official banks[178] and also, in principle, of the debts and current accounts held in private banks due to the use of the financial system; (v) if the judge is or has been the author of the complaint against the person bringing the challenge, or denounced or defended by them prior to the initiation of the lawsuit or under the terms of the law for the prosecution of magistrates, when the complaint is processed by the competent bodies; (vi) having been the defence judge of any of the litigants, or having issued an opinion or recommendations concerning the lawsuit, before or after it started. In such cases, the judge is understood to be biased, a circumstance justifying their removal from the case. However, the rule does not apply when the judge has issued an opinion as part of their theoretical or abstract work, or if they have previously resolved identical issues[179] or handled conciliatory actions; (vii) the judge has received significant benefits from one of the parties; (viii) the judge has a manifest friendship or enmity with any of the litigants, although, in the latter, the challenge will not proceed if any attacks or offences are made against the judge after they have begun to hear the matter.

175. Articles 124 and 125, RFNJ).
176. Articles 89, 529, 531, 533, 535 and 536, ACCC).
177. A challenge brought on the grounds that the judge intervened as a legislator when approving the law under discussion in the case, is not admissible (*Fallos* 326:131 (2003)).
178. *Fallos* 326:417 (2003).
179. *Fallos* 306:1644 (1984).

288. Regarding which persons are entitled to issue a challenge, and the appropriate procedural moment for doing so, the same rules apply as for a challenge without cause. This is so unless it is a supervening cause, in which case the challenger may bring it within five days of notification, and before the ruling is final (Article 18, ACCPC). The challenge must be solid, serious, clear and precise. In order to discourage totally unfounded claims, the ACCPC provides that once a challenge for cause has been dismissed, the costs and a fine of up to ARS 900,000 will be applied to whomsoever brought it, if it is found that there was malicious intent (Articles 29 and 45, ACCPC). Here, the intention to cause damage and the lack of grounds for the challenge filed must be proven.

289. A challenge for cause must be filed in writing before the judge being challenged, or the pertinent body (Chamber or Court), when it concerns one of its members. When a challenge is filed, the cause will be recorded, with an explanation of the facts and circumstances giving rise to it, as well as all the evidence provided to prove it. In this case, there may not be more than three witnesses (Articles 20 and 24, ACCPC).

If the judge challenged is from a Court of First Instance, the challenge is filed with the Chamber along with a report on the alleged causes and the main file. These are sent to the judge next in line, or to a surrogate, to continue with the proceedings, since the challenge does not suspend the main proceedings (Article 26).

The challenge is owed in limine when none of the causes foreseen are alleged, or are manifestly inadmissible,[180] or were submitted after the deadlines (Article 21, ACCPC). In principle, if the report submitted by the judge confirms the accuracy of the facts stated by the party, they will be removed from the case. However, the Chamber may dismiss it if it considers that it fails to reflect the causality anticipated. If the accusation is refuted, incidental proceedings will be opened for a trial period of ten days, after which the challenged judge will be given a hearing and the matter will be resolved (Articles 24, 25 and 27, ACCPC).

When a challenge is dismissed, a surrogate judge is notified so that they can forward the proceedings to the judge challenged. However, if declared admissible, the proceedings must be definitively settled by the surrogate judge, who will notify the challenged one, who may not hear it again, even if the cause giving rise to it later disappears (Article 28, ACCPC).

290. When the challenge is brought against a Chamber Judge or Supreme Court Justice, the collegiate body must issue a report and will proceed, depending on whether the facts are admitted or not, to deal with it separately or to substantiate the incidental proceedings. Here too, the body may, even when the facts are admitted, dismiss the challenge as inadmissible. The challenge will be resolved by the remaining competent judges, who may, if required, summon the court, according to the law and the RFNJ. When a challenge is filed, the judge or judges who have resolved the incidental proceedings will continue to hear the case.

180. *Fallos* 323:2466 (2000).

II. Abstention

291. Abstention refers to the power of the judges to withdraw themselves from duty ex officio when, in their opinion, any of the legal grounds present grave issues of decorum or delicacy requiring them to refrain from hearing the case. In the latter, a family relationship to other officials involved in the case in the course of their duties is not considered grounds for abstention.

As abstention is a personal power exercised by the judge, the parties may not oppose it or refute the grounds invoked. However, if the magistrate next in line believes that abstention is not applicable, incidental proceedings will be sent without further ado to the Court of Appeal, applying the rules explained in relation to the challenge for cause. Likewise, if it is shown that a judge who was prevented from hearing the case and who knowingly issued a ruling that is not a mere formality, they will be considered to be guilty of negligence under the law governing the prosecution of magistrates (Article 32, ACCPC).

Public prosecutors may not be challenged and, when there is a legitimate reason for their abstention, they must inform the judge or court and may recuse themselves from the case, being replaced by a surrogate (Article 33, ACCPC).

§2. Suspension of Proceedings

292. Judicial terms are peremptory and, in principle, non-extendable, for all those appearing in court, whatever their condition (Articles 155 and 159, ACCPC). The idea is to guarantee the proper exercise of the right to defence and the effective provision of justice within a reasonable period of time, as part of the guarantee of due process. Hence, the suspension of the proceedings and the extension[181] or abbreviation of the deadlines may only happen exceptionally and be of restrictive interpretation.

293. The proceedings may be suspended in a conventional manner, whether at the request of the interested party or by legal provision. In the first case, it must be the parties who agree to suspend the deadlines, specifying their reasons justifying the suspension. Proxies may not agree to a suspension over twenty days without showing the judge or court the agreement of their clients (Article 157, ACCPC). A request for the terms to be suspended is usually invoked when the parties are in the midst of negotiations. When only one of the parties requests the proceedings and deadlines to be suspended, the same steps must be taken. The reasons may be varied, the most common being force majeure or grave causes. The presentation of the request is notified to the judge who then decides what course of action to take.

294. Judges and courts are bound to declare the interruption or suspension of the terms when any of the circumstances indicated above make it impossible to carry out the proceedings. This also applies by virtue of a legal provision, such as the

181. Articles 158, 159, 342 et seq., ACCPC and Supreme Court Agreement 50 of 1986 (Judgments 308: 1523–1986).

death or disability of the party or proxy (Article 5.3 paragraphs 5 and 6, ACCPC), if they are harmful to any one in any way (Articles 1774 et seq., ACCC), third-party summons (Article 95, ACCPC), third-party domain (Article 99, ACCPC), among others.

§3. Substitution of Parties

I. Generalities

295. Procedural substitution operates when the law enables a person outside the substantive legal relationship under discussion to intervene as a legitimate party in proceedings. This may come about as a result of the death or supervening incapacity of one of the parties, eviction, a subrogation action, or the transfer of the object in dispute. The substitute claims judicial protection in their own name and interest, although by virtue of a right associated with a separate legal relationship, as this circumstance differentiates them from the representative, who lacks any personal interest in relation to the lawsuit, acting on behalf of a third party.

296. In the proceedings, a substitute enjoys all the rights, burdens and responsibilities in their capacity as party, with the exception of the likelihood of undertaking procedural acts implying, whether directly or indirectly, a certain influence over the rights of the party substituted, such as confession, withdrawal from the right, among others.

The defendant may oppose the claim made by the procedural substitute by bringing all the pertinent defences against it. In this context, the judgment handed down in the proceedings has the quality of res judicata for both parties, even though the party substituted has not been directly involved in the proceedings.

II. Certain Assumptions

297. In the event of the death or incapacity of one of the parties, once verified, the judge will suspend the proceedings and summon the heirs or their legal representative. They will also issue a warning against continuing the process in absentia or otherwise appoint an official defender. The heirs or those authorized to act on their behalf must join the proceedings in the state at which they are at (Articles 43, 53, paragraphs 5 et seq., ACCPC).

298. If the right in dispute is transferred during the course of the proceedings, whoever acquires it must, in order to act as the main party, obtain the agreement of the counterparty. Failing this, they may only act as an auxiliary of the party (Articles 44, 90, 9 and 97, ACCPC).

299. The so-called subrogation or oblique action is a typical case in point. Through it, creditors exercise the rights and take actions with regard to their debtors, with the exception of personal rights, in order to avoid neglect and with a view to satisfying their loans (Articles 739 and 741, ACCC).

The conditions of admissibility for this claim are that the creditor be able to demonstrate that are owed liquid and enforceable credit by the debtor, and that the debtor has been negligent in the exercise of their obligations, proof of their inactivity being sufficient for this purpose. This action is not admitted when the debtor is able to demonstrate solvency and economic capabilities. Prior judicial authorization is not necessary to exercise subrogation (Articles 111 ACCPC and 740, ACCC).

Once the subrogatory action has been brought, before the claim is transferred to the defendant, the ACCPC establishes a prior instance where the judge summons the debtor and gives them a period of ten days to formulate an opposition or file the relevant claim, in which case they will be considered as an actor. The opposition must be based on the fact that they have already filed a claim or on the manifest inadmissibility of the subrogation. In those cases when the debtor has previously exercised the action or decides to do so when intimidated, the creditor may intervene in the process as a simple concurring third party (Article 91 (1), ACCPC). If the debtor does not exercise any of the aforementioned prerogatives, they may also intervene at any time in the process jointly with the plaintiff, without this presentation having the effect of delaying or suspending the plaintiff's proceedings (Articles 112, 113 and 93, ACCPC). In all cases, the debtor may be called upon to respond in relation to the facts and documents in dispute. All exceptions proving the non-existence of credit, such as those arising from any actions taken by the debtor subsequent to the claim, are enforceable against the creditor, provided that they are not fraudulent (Article 742, ACCC).

The judgment will rule in favour of or against the debtor summoned, whether or not they have actually appeared in court (Article 114, ACCPC). Once the sentence has acquired the status of res judicata, the substitute may deepen implementation in order to secure effective compliance and have the corresponding assets transferred from the debtor's estate. They may receive up to the amount of the original credit granted, depending on the privileges and guarantees associated.

300. Other cases of procedural substitutes include the insurer who exercises the rights applicable to an insured party against a third party due to a claim up to the amount of the compensation paid (Article 80, Law 17,418). Or the transferor summoned for the purposes of eviction when the defendant as acquirer chooses to be excluded from the case (Articles 105 to 110, ACCPC).

Chapter 3. Other Issues Regarding the Conclusion of the Proceedings

301. The ACCPC states that the final judgment is the usual form of concluding the process. This means that any other actions producing the same or similar results qualify as abnormal modes of conclusion, even if some of these do not affect the substantive law which could assist the parties, making it possible to bring the claim anew in other proceedings.

302. Other case dispositions include consent, withdrawal, conciliation, transaction and lapse of a legal action. The first four constitute express manifestations of the will of the parties and suppose, with the exception of the withdrawal of the claim (proceedings), the settlement of the litigation and the impossibility of its being reissued. Likewise, each of these courses of action requires the judge's prior decision to admit or validate them. In the case of consent, this is a sentence, in the case of the others, an approving resolution.

Unlike the other means mentioned, the lapse of a legal action is based on the presumed will to abandon the proceedings expressed by the litigant who filed them in the first place. This, like the withdrawals of claims, in principle, does not prevent a new claim from being filed.

303. The rules about each of these means of concluding the process may be found both in the ACCPC and in other substantive measures regulating legal action in general and in particular, mainly and especially, the ACCC.

§1. Withdrawal

304. The ACCPC offers the possibility of withdrawing from both the claim and the right. Withdrawing the claim is the action by which the plaintiff or the parties, by mutual agreement, express their willingness to end the proceedings without a judgment being passed regarding the material right invoked as the basis thereof. This means that the same claim can be brought again in other proceedings, unless the statute of limitations has expired, since, according to Article 2547 of the ACCC, the interruption of the statute of limitations arising from the claim will be deemed not to have occurred if the plaintiff desists from it. This kind of withdrawal implies the end of the proceedings and the procedural actions performed during it have no effect, even though the evidence incorporated may be used in later proceedings (Article 304, ACCPC).

The withdrawal of the claim can be bilateral or unilateral. The first happens when the parties, by mutual agreement, at any point during the trial prior to the sentence, desist from the process by stating this in writing before the judge. The second occurs on the initiative of the plaintiff and requires the agreement of the defendant, according to whether or not the claim has been notified. In this sense, since the plaintiff can bring their claim again in another trial, once the lawsuit has been brought, the defendant may assert their interest in continuing the dispute in order to settle it definitively. Once the plaintiff has moved to desist, the judge will inform the defendant so that they can express their position with a view to securing their acceptance. In the case of opposition to this action, the withdrawal will be deemed ineffective and the proceedings will continue, unless the defendant has adopted a procedural attitude which is incompatible with the opposition sustained, such as a delaying exception that is to all intents and purposes the same as withdrawal. In any case, withdrawing from the claim is not deemed effective until it is accepted by the defendant (Article 306, ACCPC).

305. Desisting from a right refers to the action where the plaintiff renounces the material right they invoked as the basis of their claim, thus desisting from it and making it impossible to bring other proceedings for the same reason and cause (Article 305, ACCPC). In that sense, the effect of this kind of withdrawal is equivalent to that of res judicata, insofar as it is impossible to reissue the discussion concerning the existence of the material right. In this case, then, the defendant's agreement is not required, as the absence of interest is presumed due to the impossibility of the lawsuit being filed again in subsequent proceedings. This is the main difference between withdrawal and the right to withdraw (Articles 944, 946 and 947, ACCC). Desisting from the right can be revoked until such time as it is judicially ruled (Article 306).

306. Those who are party, and legitimized and procedurally capable, may desist from the claim or the right. When acting in conventional representation, those wishing to withdraw from the right without bringing charges must be entrusted with special powers. At all events, judges usually require that these powers include details of any existing express prerogatives for withdrawing, whether from the claim or from the right (Articles 120, 121, 122, 358, 375 and 692, ACCC).

307. It cannot be presumed that a party will withdraw from the claim or a right, so such a move must be made expressly and its interpretation is restrictive. It may be total or partial, as would occur in the case of the joinder of claims.

308. Once the withdrawal of the claim or the right has been presented, the judge will examine it to establish its compliance with legal requirements and will resolve the extinguishment of the proceedings and/or the right, imposing costs as appropriate and ensuring the fees of the professionals involved, and filing the proceedings. Withdrawal of the right is not binding on the judge, who may decide not to approve it if it concerns personal rights.

The costs will be borne by the person who withdraws, unless otherwise agreed by the parties. If the right is abandoned, due to changes in legislation or jurisprudence subsequent to the claim being filed, and this can be carried out without undue delay, the costs are distributed in the order caused (Article 73, ACCPC).

§2. AGREEMENT

309. The defendant can agree with the claim brought against them: the agreement is the statement whereby they recognize that the claim filed by the plaintiff is well founded and admits not only the facts on which it is based but also all legal allegations.

The agreement, as an act of recognition, has a direct effect on the relationship with material law which is the subject of the proceedings.

310. An agreement can be struck at any stage of the proceedings prior to the sentence (Article 307, ACCPC). As regards form, it may not be subject to any condition or reservation, and must be categorical and precise, leaving no room for doubt. It may be express when the defendant clearly acknowledges the claim brought against them, or otherwise tacit or implied by the procedural conduct adopted with respect to the claims raised by the defendant.

311. Once the agreement is made, the judge must also pass judgment in accordance with the law, since the recognition by itself lacks any decisive force. In this sense, the judge may dismiss the agreement and order proceedings to continue, when what is intended, accepted or provided for, would compromise public order (e.g., when the object of the agreement may not be disposed of by the parties). The sentence must comply with the formalities of any interlocutory decision. When the agreement is partial, it may be argued that it is inappropriate to issue a judgment immediately regarding the claim in question, and that it must be deferred until the conclusion of the proceedings. In the case of voluntary joint litigation, the acceptance by one of the joinder parties authorizes a judgment to be passed, while the case continues as regards the remaining parties. In the case of necessary joint litigation, the agreement formulated by a joinder party has no effect for as long as nobody else agrees, due to the indivisibility of the claim, although they are exempted from the burdens inherent to the subsequent development of the litigation and, eventually, from the costs arising from those proceedings where they were not involved.

312. Since the agreement is tantamount to defeat, the costs must be borne by the defendant. However, this principle gives way when the defendant in due course recognizes the plaintiff's claims as well founded, and agrees to satisfy them, unless they have incurred in default, or if the claim arises through their own fault. The principle also fails to apply if agreement is reached within five days of being notified of any titles and instruments presented in delayed form. In all cases, for such an exception to proceed, the agreement must be real, unconditional, timely, total and effective. Likewise, if the background to the proceedings indicates that the defendant did not provide any reason justifying the bringing of the lawsuit and gave their agreement within the term required to answer the claim, thus fulfilling their obligation, the costs will be borne by the plaintiff (Article 70, ACCPC). For a more detailed analysis of this point, please refer to the paragraphs mentioned above.

313. The ACCC contains specific dispositions concerning the way in which the parties agree about their rights. It establishes that the transaction is a bilateral legal act where the parties make reciprocal concessions and extinguish litigious or doubtful obligations, which is a way of extinguishing both the obligations and the proceedings (Article 1641, ACCC). It can be done through the presentation in court, by one or both parties, of the agreement signed jointly by them; or it may take the form of signing the hearing minutes before the judge. The transaction will not be considered concluded until the parties have agreed before the judge to the respective agreement, and they may withdraw from it at any time prior to this moment (Article 1643, ACCC).

Once the transaction of the litigious rights has been carried out through any of the aforementioned forms, the judge examines the requirements and conditions demanded by the law to validate the transaction, to see if they concur. These include the capacity, personality and possibilities of compromising the rights according to the different prohibitions intrinsic to public order. If there are no objections, the judge approves it; otherwise, the proceedings continue. Recently approved codification has however led to the transaction producing the effects of res judicata, without the need for judicial approval (Articles 308, ACCPC and 1642, 1644, 1645 and 1647, ACCC). At all events, the provision may not be applied in collective proceedings, given the nature of the issues involved and the interests at stake. Moreover, Article 54 of the consumer defence law (Law 24,240, as modified by Law 26,351) (LDC) expressly establishes the need for the conciliatory agreement or transaction reached in this type of proceeding to be authorized via a court order.

314. In principle, issues affecting the State in its capacity as a public authority may not be submitted to the ruling of arbitrators, to the exclusion of the judges, unlike those related to private matters.[182]

315. The transaction extinguishes the rights and obligations waived by the parties and assumes the authority of res judicata over them (Article 1642, ACCC). This is the result of the presentation of the brief in court, or if the transaction is celebrated before the judge, without prejudice to its being judicially authorized. In the absence of an authoritative resolution, the proceedings are not annulled, and the transaction cannot be executed by means of enforcing the judgment.

§3. Conciliation

316. The main feature of conciliation is the judge's intervention. The parties may, through the process of conciliation, decide upon a withdrawal, a transaction, an agreement, or a combination of all of these, including features common to all. Hence, conciliation is considered an agreement between the parties, where they make up their differences before the judge, who approves it via a resolution to the effect of res judicata.

182. Articles 1649, 1651 et seq., ACCC.

317. The judge has the power at any time to order the parties to make a personal appearance in an attempt to reach conciliation (Article 36, paragraph 2, ACCPC). This configures a judicial prerogative whose exercise depends on the likelihood of the case being resolved through an agreement, which can be exercised at any time during the development of the proceedings. Notwithstanding this, the ACCPC provides for certain cases where this procedure is mandatory. In this way, as much as in preliminary hearings as in trials for divorce, personal separation, annulment of marriage and maintenance, the judge will try to reconcile the parties during the course of the hearings held for this purpose (Articles 360, paragraph 1, 34, paragraph 1, paragraph 2, 639 and 640, ACCPC). Both the sanction of nullity in the case of the judge's absence in the preliminary hearing and the fine imposed on whomsoever is supposed to provide maintenance in the event of default are indicative of the importance placed upon conciliation as a form of resolving the litigation as well as the interests and concerns vested in it by the legislator.

318. Once the conciliation agreement has been concluded by the parties before the judge, the latter will verify their capabilities or the scope of the mandates, the disposition of the rights at stake and, if there are no objections, will issue a ruling and award costs, regulating the fees of the professionals involved in the absence of agreement. As it is the judge who is driving the conciliation, each of the aforementioned requirements will have been evaluated prior to approval, speeding up this process. In the case of the preliminary hearing, the parties may propose conciliatory formulas, and thus the content of the conciliation and the approval issued by the judge are recorded in the hearing minutes. Failure to reach an agreement is also detailed in the minutes but without substantiation, as the intervening parties are not questioned about what happened (Articles 360 and 360 b., ACCPC). The judge may dismiss a conciliatory agreement when its terms are manifestly abusive or illegal. Conciliatory agreements approved have the status of res judicata for the parties, and may be carried out through the procedure used to execute sentences.

§4. Lapse of a Legal Action

319. The lapse of an instance is a way of concluding the proceedings that operates when the plaintiff shows no interest in moving the case forward during the legally established time frame and conditions. The party bringing action takes on the burden of driving the proceedings through their different stages, a burden that is justified by the time and money spent by both defendant and State on maintaining a judicial instance open for an indefinite amount of time.

Grounds for a lapse lie within the presumption of disinterest of the instance, supposing a prolonged period of procedural inactivity and the need to put an end to the organ's duties. It represents an attempt to endow the administration of justice and its commitment to public interest with rationality, effectiveness and efficiency, thus avoiding the indeterminate duration of the lawsuits.

320. The assumptions required for a lapse to operate are: (i) the existence of open principal or incidental proceedings. These are understood to refer to the entire set of procedural acts occurring after a claim has been filed (even if the resolution providing for its notification has itself not yet been notified), or after a request for incidental proceedings or an appeal have been filed. It covers the period until the resolution or sentence is issued (Article 310, ACCPC); (ii) the existence of procedural inactivity, assuming the total paralysis of the judicial proceedings due to the absence of appropriate action by one of the parties driving the proceedings. This means that an expiry cannot be invoked when proceedings are pending resolution, or, when the delay in issuing this resolution is attributable to the court, if the prosecution of the proceedings depends on a certain action required of the secretary or the first official by the ACCPC or Superintendency regulations (Article 313, paragraph 3, ACCPC). This inactivity must continue during the period set by the ACCPC. Any action by the parties or the court which helps to drive the proceedings thus interrupts the lapse process, leaving the period expired without effect, and a new one must be drawn up from there. Thus, an impulse by one of the joint litigants affects the others (Article 312, ACCPC); and (iii) the duration of the periods established in Article 310 of the ACCPC, which are calculated from the last action taken by the parties, or the last resolution or action taken by the judge, secretary or first official, aimed at driving the proceedings. Deadlines vary depending on the type of instance, process or incidental proceedings, applying the term in which the prescription operates if less than these. These run through non-working days,[183] with the exception of those corresponding to judicial bank holidays; those for which the Supreme Court has decreed the suspension of terms, or of the term during which the process has been paralysed or suspended for reasons of force majeure or circumstances beyond the control of the parties (e.g., the loss of the file); the agreement by the parties or by order of the judge, unless the resumption of the proceedings is subject to procedural acts to be carried out by the party responsible for driving the proceedings (Article 311, ACCPC).

321. Expiry can be declared in any kind of proceeding, except in labour cases (where activity is led by the judge), judgment enforcement proceedings (except for unrelated incidents), probate, and voluntary proceedings in general, with the exception of any incidents created, and when the sentence is requested, unless there is ex officio evidence dependent on the parties (Article 313, ACCPC).

A declaration can be made ex officio or be petitioned by a party. It may operate against any person party to the trial, except disabled persons, or those absent and lacking legal representation in the proceedings (Article 314, ACCPC), a rule that is in line with what is established in relation to the statute of limitations set by the ACCC (Articles 2543, paragraph c) and 2550).

In the first case, a lapse does not operate by right alone, as it is the judge who, after verifying that the conditions described above have been fulfilled, and before any of the parties drives the procedure, takes an ex officio decision about it (Article 316, ACCPC).

In the second case, the request can be made in the first instance by the defendant, in the incidental proceedings, by the counterpart of whoever brought it, and at the

183. *Fallos* 319:907 (1996).

appeal stage, by the respondent (which will imply, if both parties appealed, the withdrawal of the appeal filed by the petitioner if the lapse is successful). The request must be made before the applicant gives their consent, to either the court or the party, for action to be taken following the expiry of the legal deadline, and be substantiated by the counterparty under penalty of annulment (Article 315, ACCPC).

Unlike the nationwide regime, the CPCBA establishes the possibility that, once a lapse is raised at the request of a party, or ex officio, the interested party is requested to express, within five days, their intention of continuing with the trial and prove useful activity allowing the proceedings to continue, under warning of decreeing the lapse in the case of non-compliance. If the lapse is raised again, it may be resolved without any warning (Articles 315 and 316, BAPCCPC).

322. The declaration of the expiry of the main proceedings may imply the extinction of the material right invoked to support the claim. This is because, once the court's desertion has been declared, the interruption of the statute of limitations applicable to the claim is considered not to have happened (Article 2547, ACCC). Conversely, the declaration of the expiry of the counterclaim and incidental proceedings does not affect the main instance.

Once the expiry has been declared, and the statute of limitations no longer applies, a new action can be brought and may even use the evidence produced in earlier proceedings now expired. Expiry in a second or extraordinary instance endows the resolution appealed with the force of res judicata (Article 318, ACCPC). Likewise, the ACCPC establishes that only the decision accepting the request for revocation in the first instance may be appealed. In the remaining instances, a decision is only subject to reinstatement if decreed ex officio (Article 317, ACCPC).

Once the judgment for a lapse is signed, any interim measures brought will be ordered to be lifted and the costs awarded to the plaintiff, unless the expiry includes the counterclaim, in which case they will be awarded in the order caused. Costs include the expenses incurred in the expiry incidental proceedings as well as in the main proceedings. In incidents and appeals, the costs must be paid by those who brought them (Articles 73, 74 and 315, ACCPC).

323. Attorneys-in-fact, as well as lawyers, administrators or legal representatives, may be held liable for damages arising from the declaration of expiry in the event that such liability is proven (Article 314, ACCPC).

Part VI. Legal Assistance and Costs

Chapter 1. General

324. The validity of the guarantee of continuous and effective judicial protection places the State before its duty to ensure that all those under its jurisdiction enjoy due access to justice (Articles 1.1 and 25, ACHR). This positive obligation of the State to remove economic obstacles preventing access to the courts in order to ensure the effective right to be heard is a particularly relevant aspect, as ordinarily, the structural and, in particular, economic inequality of the parties, leads to unequal possibilities of defending their rights.

Both the ICHR and the Inter-American Commission of Human Rights[184] have emphasized the obligation of the State to provide free legal services to persons lacking resources, thus protecting their right to effective judicial protection.

In its Advisory Opinion 11 (1990),[185] the ICHR highlighted that:

> if a person seeking the protection of the law to enforce the rights guaranteed by the American Convention, finds that their economic position (in this case, their indigence) prevents them from doing so because they cannot afford the necessary legal assistance (…) they are effectively discriminated against because of their economic standing, being placed in conditions of inequality before the law.

Thus, the legal protection of persons, without discrimination, in situations of vulnerability was considered a duty of the State.

---

184. *See Report on Poverty and Human Rights in the Americas*, OEA/Ser.L/V/II.164, http://www.oas.org/en/iachr/reports/pdfs/Poverty-HumanRights2017.pdf which held that:

> States must design a comprehensive and coordinated policy - backed up with adequate public funding – to ensure that persons living in poverty and extreme poverty have full access to adequate judicial protection. They must establish instances and judicial remedies that are adequate and effective in rural, marginalized and economically disadvantaged areas, in order to ensure full access to effective judicial protection. They must also increase the number of state counsel available. They must remove the sociocultural discriminatory patterns that hinder full access to justice. (p. 177)

185. https://www.corteidh.or.cr/docs/opiniones/seriea_11_ing.pdf.

325. Free legal assistance is a necessary yet insufficient condition for protection to be effective. This was stated in the aforementioned Advisory Opinion 11 (1990), where the ICHR expressly recognized that the absence of free legal assistance may not be the only economic obstacle to accessing justice, pointing out that the costs of the proceedings are also a factor to be considered at this point.

In *Cantos*, the ICHR observed that the States should seek to not put obstacles in the way of citizens who turn to judges or courts to ensure their rights are determined or protected, as 'any domestic law or measure that imposes costs or in any other way obstructs individuals' access to the courts and that is not warranted by what is reasonably needed for the administration of justice must be regarded as contrary to Article 8(1) of the Convention'.[186]

326. The Plenary Assembly of the XIV Edition of the Ibero-American Judicial Summit held on 4–6 April 2008, in the city of Brasilia (Federative Republic of Brazil), adopted the Brasilia Rules on Access to Justice of the People in Vulnerable Conditions. This decision affirmed the commitment to an inclusive model of justice, open to all sectors of society and especially sensitive to the needs of the most disadvantaged or vulnerable (Points 12 and 13). The rules are intended to guarantee the conditions of effective access to justice for people in a vulnerable condition, without any discrimination, encompassing the set of policies, measures, facilities and supports allowing such individuals to fully enjoy the services of the legal system. The Supreme Court, in its Agreement 5 (2009), adhered to these rules, considering them to be a valuable tool in an aspect deserving of particular attention in terms of access to justice.[187]

---

186. *See* judgment of 28 November 2002, https://www.corteidh.or.cr/docs/canes/articulos/seriec_97_ing.pdf (§ fifty). In this case, the Regional Court decided that the amount that the Argentine courts required of the petitioner as court fees, were in violation of the rights enshrined in Arts 8 and 25 of the ACHR, considering that they had been denied access to the benefit of litigating without costs.

187. *See* Supreme Court Agreement 5 (2009) in https://www.csjn.gov.ar/sentencias-acordadas-y-resoluciones/acordadas-de-la-corte-suprema.

Chapter 2. Costs

§1. Concept and Basis for the Imposition of Costs

327. The necessary expenses directly arising from the substantiation of the trial itself, and those made in the interests of pre-empting the conflict by complying with obligations, including mandatory pretrial mediation, make up the costs (including court fees, legal fees, sending briefs). It follows that the concept excludes unnecessary or superfluous expenditures and those that are not a direct consequence of it (Article 77, ACCPC).

328. During the development of the lawsuit, each of the parties pays the expenses related to their actions, since it is only when the judge issues a sentence that it is decided who will be ultimately responsible for paying the costs generated (Article 163, paragraph 8, ACCPC).

The ACCPC, like all provincial ordinances, follows a system based on the objective criterion of defeat, which means that as a rule, costs are awarded to the party defeated in the litigation (Article 68, ACCPC).

This sanction is not based on the subjective aspects of the behaviour of the person who has to pay, but on a measure derived from the objective fact of defeat with a view to safeguarding the assets of the person forced to bring a lawsuit to protect their rights.

However, the objective principle of defeat as the basis for the imposition of the sentence on costs is not absolute, since the procedural code itself provides for certain exceptions, some imposed by law and others left to judicial discretion. In those cases, the exemption from paying costs does not imply an absolute release: although the party defeated in court does not have to cover the expenses incurred by the winner, they must cover their own and half of those incurred in common.

329. The ACCPC also adopts the informal taxation system, thanks to which, even in the event that the order to pay has not been requested by the parties, it must determine them at the time of sentencing (Article 163 paras. 8 and 68, ACCPC).

§2. Legal Regime

330. The general principle is enshrined in Article 68 of the ACCPC, which states that the party defeated in the trial must pay all the expenses incurred by the winner, even if the latter has not requested it. However, it then provides – as an exception to this rule – that the judge may totally or partially exempt the unsuccessful litigant from this responsibility, provided that such a decision is based on merit, and expressed in the pronouncement, under pain of nullity. Generally, the reasons for this have to do with specific situations rendering the application of the general principle unfair (e.g., the existence of plausible reasons to litigate, the complexity of the issue, or the existence of case law on the matter).

There are also reasons specifically provided by the legislator which envisage exceptions to the principle of the imposition of costs on the loser.

I. Costs Borne by the Successful Party

331. One of the exceptions contemplated is where costs are borne by the winner. The ACCPC explains that this occurs: (i) when the background to the case shows that the defendant did not provide any reason for the trial being brought, having acquitted themselves within the terms required to answer the claim, and fulfilling their obligation (Article 70); and (ii) when it incurs in *plus petitio*, which happens if the other party were to have agreed to the limit of the amount of the claim established in the judgment (Article 72).

II. Costs for Order

332. In certain cases, the ACCPC directs each litigant to bear the expenses incurred by their actions and also pay for half of those that are common. This happens, according to the national procedural regime: (i) when the defendant recognizes that their adversary's claims are well founded and agrees to satisfy them, unless they have incurred in default or because the claim arose because of something they did; (ii) when they agree within five days of being apprised of any titles and instruments which were presented late. For the procedure of exemption from paying costs to proceed, the agreement must be genuine, unconditional, timely, total and effective (Article 70); (iii) in cases of transaction and conciliation, with respect to those entering into the settlement, since the general rules will apply to the rest (Article 73); (iv) when desisting is due exclusively to changes in legislation or case law and will be carried out without undue delay. However, in all these cases, the parties can agree on something different, as anything agreed to the contrary is fully valid (Article 73); and (v) if the plaintiff acquiesces to an indication which runs counter to their claim (Article 76).

III. Other Cases Contemplated

333. Outside of the assumptions detailed, the ACCPC has anticipated some special situations.

A. *Partial and Mutual Deadline*

334. These are cases where the outcome of the process is partially favourable to both parties, which could occur particularly in the event of the accumulation of claims, as some could be accepted and others rejected. The ACCPC indicates that, in these cases, the costs of the proceedings will be compensated or distributed prudently by the judge in line with the success of each litigant (Article 71).

B. Joinder

335. In the cases of proceedings involving several parties, the costs are shared out among the litigants, unless the nature of the obligation means that what is appropriate is the joint sentence. However, when the interests they each represent in the trial are very different, the judge may award costs in proportion to these interests (Article 75, ACCPC).

C. Lapse of a Legal Action

336. When the instance lapses, the person sentenced to pay the costs is the plaintiff, since they were the ones responsible for bringing the proceedings (Article 73, ACCPC).

D. Nullity of Proceedings

337. If the proceedings are annulled for reasons attributable to one of the parties, the costs arising from the act or omission giving rise to this annulment must be borne by them (Article 74, ACCPC).

E. Incidental Proceedings

338. With incidental proceedings, the principle of defeat according to Article 68 of the ACCPC applies to the fact-finding process. On this point, it is relevant to note that, except in the case of incidental proceedings brought in the course of hearings, the code prohibits new incidental proceedings being brought by whoever was ordered to pay costs in a previous case, for as long as they fail to pay the amount due or have it attached.

§3. Scope of the Award to Pay Costs

339. The scope of the order to pay court and legal costs arises from the concept indicated in paragraph 460. This refers to the necessary expenses directly arising from the substantiation of the trial itself, and those made in the interests of preempting the conflict by complying with obligations, including mandatory pretrial mediation (such as court fees, legal fees, sending briefs). Along the same lines, any superfluous or useless expenses are not subject to reimbursement.

Expenses corresponding to requests which have been denied are charged to whoever incurred or gave rise to them, even if the sentence is favourable in the main (Article 77, ACCPC).

The judge, for their part, may prudently reduce expenses, in the event of their being excessive.

340. Regarding the amount of the expenses making up the trial costs, in Law 24,432 (1994), Argentine legislators incorporated a specific provision to Article 505 of the Civil Code, which was maintained in the ACCC (Article 730). The provision limits the costs of the first or only instance (including professional fees) to 25% of the amount of the judgment, award or transaction ending the dispute.

If the costs awarded, practised in accordance with tariff regulations or local customs, exceed this percentage, the judge must proceed to share out the amounts among the beneficiaries. The calculation of the percentage indicated does not take into account the fees charged by the professionals representing, sponsoring or assisting the party sentenced to pay the costs.

Chapter 3. Benefit of Litigating Without Expenses and Related Figures

§1. Benefit of Litigating Without Fees

341. The lack of financial means to meet trial-related expenses is the main obstacle generally encountered by defendants. In order to comply with the positive obligation imposed by the ACHR (Article 2) and the AC (Article 75 paragraph 23), the State must designate certain tools to guarantee the validity of real, continuous and effective judicial protection, ensuring that the parties in litigation are truly in equality of conditions (Article 16, AC) and can enforce their constitutional right to defence in court (Article 18, AC).[188]

342. The benefit of litigating without expenses is a mechanism provided by procedural law which enables those without sufficient resources to cover court fees to access justice without having to pay the costs for as long as their economic condition fails to improve. The Argentine system does not make this conditional on the petitioner certifying that they lack any economic support, hence the ACCPC indicates that people without resources may apply either before filing the claim or at any stage during the process, for the benefit of litigating without expenses, and they are not required to show their income levels in order to qualify, regardless of the origin of their resources (Article 78, ACCPC).

343. The plaintiff may apply for the benefit of litigating without expenses prior to filing the lawsuit, at the same time, or after the trial has commenced. In the latter, a time limit is established on the possibility of doing so. In fact, in proceedings where the facts and evidence are controversial, the law stipulates that the application for litigating without expenses may only be requested until such time as the preliminary hearing is held. With trials that are purely legal in nature and do not require evidence to be shown, the request may only be made until such time as the status of the trial is declared. The only exception is afforded to cases where supervening circumstances may be verified to justify the subsequent award of the benefit, logically subject to its allegation and proof.

344. Procedural law requires the petitioner to formulate their request before the judge hearing the main proceedings, with the mention of certain points as follows: (i) the facts on which it is based; (ii) the need to claim or defend judicially either the plaintiff's own rights or those of their spouse or underage children; and (iii) the indication of the proceedings about to commence or which must be intervened. The plaintiff must, in the same brief, offer evidence to demonstrate the impossibility of obtaining a remedy, accompanying the questioning of the witnesses and their statement under oath, or promise to tell the truth in answer to questions made under the

188. The Supreme Court has said that such a benefit is supported by two precepts of constitutional roots: the guarantee of defence and equality before the law (Arts 16 and 18, AC). This effectively ensures the provision of justice services, not in formal terms but on the basis of a criterion adapted to the economic situation of the contenders. *Fallos* 322:148 (1999).

general provisions of the law, and respecting the form of the questions provided for witness evidence in general. The judge will order, without further ado, the necessary steps to be taken to ensure that the evidence offered is produced as soon as possible and will summon the opposing litigant and the body charged with determining and collecting court fees, which may provide oversight (requesting witnesses to be summoned to corroborate their statement) and offer other evidence. The award of the benefit is decided in the light of the judicial appreciation of the evidence produced in each specific case, as the alleged objectives must be met.[189]

A fine will be levied if the facts alleged as the basis for the petition for the benefit of litigation without expenses are found to be false (Article 80, ACCPC).

Once the evidence is produced, the petitioner, the other party, and the body which determines and collects court fees will be notified for a period of five calendar days, after which the judge will either dismiss or resolve the benefit whether in whole or in part.

345. While the petition is being resolved, the parties are exempt from any expenses arising from the incidental proceedings brought for these purposes, and accordingly do not have to pay any of the pertinent taxes or stamp duty, unless it is denied. The main proceedings are not suspended – unless this action is required in the new claim brought – so any expenses incurred there must be met until such time as the benefit is granted.

The resolution to grant or dismiss the benefit has provisional effects and may be modified following allegations of a change in circumstances enabling it. The ACCPC thus indicates that if the petition is denied, the party involved may offer other evidence and request a new resolution. Similarly, if a benefit is granted, it may be left without effect at the request of the interested party, when it can be shown that the person in whose favour it was issued no longer has the right to the benefit.

346. Once the benefit is granted, it applies retroactively up to the time when the claim regarding court and other fees was made, when these have not been met or expired, which depends on when the claim was brought. The party obtaining such a benefit will be totally or partially exempt from paying costs until such time as their financial situation improves. If they win the lawsuit, they must cover the expenses incurred in their defence (which may be official or private) up to the maximum of one-third of the amount they receive by way of compensation. Consequently, the professionals intervening in their defence may demand the payment of their fees from the party awarded costs, and from whomsoever obtained the benefit according to the limitations indicated in this article (Articles 84 and 85, ACCPC).

Subjectively, the benefit is granted according to whoever is the defendant in the proceedings in question, although there is a possibility that it could be extended against another person in the same trial, following their summons to appear (Article 86, ACCPC).

---

189. The Supreme Court has repeatedly said that benefit of litigating without expenses is granted subsequent to prudent judicial appreciation, as long as the evidence added by the incidental proceedings meets all the requirements necessary to enlighten the judge concerning the credibility of the alleged conditions of poverty (*Fallos* 311:1372 (1988), 315:276 and 1025 (1992)).

§2. SOME RELATED FIGURES

347. Beyond the figure of the benefit of litigating without expenses, the legislator has found it necessary to establish certain specific statutes of limitation in some matters, taking into account the special nature of the issues involved. This is a technique of differentiated procedural protection aimed at levelling generic inequalities in the substantial relationships involved in the proceedings.

348. In this sense, the Consumer Defence Law establishes that any legal actions brought to defend interests of collective influence have the benefit of free justice.

Regarding individual actions, the last section of Article 53 of the Consumer Defence Law states that legal actions brought in accordance with this law enjoy the benefit of free justice, empowering the defendant to bring ancillary proceedings, in which case the benefit ceases. The benefit must be interpreted in a broad sense, within the scope awarded in Articles 83 and 84 of the ACCPC, including both the payment of taxes and stamp duty as well as court and legal expenses.

349. Article 20 of the Labour Contract Law 20,744 (1976) (LCL) establishes the benefit of gratuity in the judicial or administrative procedures that the worker, or his successors in title, must initiate against the employer. The worker or their rights-holders shall enjoy the benefit of litigating without costs as regards any legal or administrative proceedings arising from the application of this law, professional statutes or collective labour agreements. In addition, the worker's home may be included as an asset for the purposes of paying costs.

The benefit of litigating without costs enshrined in Article 20 of the LCL is limited to enabling the worker to enjoy access to justice by dispensing them from paying the corresponding taxes and stamp duties, and safeguarding their home from repossession. However, this is not enough to exempt them from paying costs, as they may only have provisional access to this provision when they request the benefit of litigating without expenses, supported by the arguments detailed above.

There are similar provisions at provincial level. For example, in the province of Buenos Aires, Law 12,200 (1998) provides, within the framework of public law, for cost-free actions at administrative and judicial headquarters, including labour and social security claims, whatever the type of employment relationship and the jurisdiction where they are brought. The law also specifies that in court, workers and beneficiaries of the pension system automatically have access to the full benefit of litigating without expenses, by right, thus ensuring they are exempt from paying court and legal fees.

Part VII. Evidence

Chapter 1. Burden of Proof

§1. General Principle

350. The rules regarding the burden of proof are intended to determine how best to split up the activity required to prove the facts contested between the parties. These are guidelines indicating to the parties who is required to prove what. At the same time, they serve to inform the judge which party should bear the consequences arising from the absence of evidence and act as an element to support conviction in the event of insufficient evidence.

As a general principle, each party bears the burden of proof regarding the facts or statements which they intend to produce a given legal effect (Article 377, ACCPC). Whoever invokes a fact to establish their claim or defence is obliged to prove it.

351. If a particular party is unable to prove a certain hypothesis regarding the facts and the opposing party appears reluctant to collaborate with respect to its clarification, it is possible to attribute to the latter the negative consequences of the state of uncertainty.

In Argentina, doctrine on the so-called dynamic burdens of proof has been widely used and is frequently employed by lawyers and judges, as this figure proposes that the judge has room to interpret the effective possibilities of each party providing proof in a broad way.[190] The principle to which we refer here prevents one of the parties from obtaining benefits resulting from the probative difficulty in which their opponent finds themselves.

352. The Supreme Court has developed a line of precedents that relaxes the rule on burden of proof established in procedural codes. In *Pinheiro v. Instituto de Servicios Sociales para el Personal Ferroviario,*[191] it considered that the disappearance of relevant evidence under the counterpart's custody could not benefit the latter. The criterion applied was based on both parties' duty to collaborate in clarifying the main facts.

---

190. Regarding the doctrine of 'dynamic burdens of proof', *see* J. Peyrano, J. Chiappini, 'Lineamientos de las cargas probatorias dinámicas', *El Derecho* 107–1005 (1984), J. Peyrano, 'Doctrina de las cargas probatorias dinámicas', *La Ley* 1993-B-1034, J. Peyrano,''Fuerza expansiva de la doctrina de las cargas probatorias dinámicas', *La Ley* 1999-B-1027, among other works by the same author.
191. *Fallos* 320:2715 (1997).

In *Galli de Mazzucchi v. Correo,*[192] the Supreme Court understood that the rules of the burden of proof must be interpreted according to the nature and characteristics of the conflict submitted before the judge, to give primacy to the truth and avoid excessive formal rigour undermining the clarification of the facts.

353. The ACCC established that the principle of flexibility of proof should be used in family proceedings and that the burden of proof falls on the party in the best conditions to prove it (Article 710). In the matter of compensation for damages, the ACCC provided that the judge may allocate the burden of proof of guilt, or of having acted with due diligence, to either party in consideration of who is in the best position to provide it. If the judge considers it pertinent, they may inform the parties that they intend to apply such a criterion in order to allow the litigants to offer and produce any elements of conviction they deem necessary for the purposes of their defence (Article 1735).[193]

354. The Procedural Codes of La Pampa (1993, Article 360), Formosa (2002, Article 374), San Juan (2008, Article 340), Santa Cruz (2016, Article 355), Chaco (2017, Article 355) and Mendoza (2017, Article 166), considered the possibility of making the burden of proof more flexible.

The new ACPC bill regulates the institution (Article 214), as it provides that – depending on the particularities of the case – the judge may, ex officio or at the request of a party, require the party in a better situation to contribute evidence to prove a certain fact. Among other circumstances, the presumption of being in a better position may arise due to the party's proximity to the evidence, or because they have the object of proof in their possession, or there are special technical circumstances. This could also be because they intervened directly in the events giving rise to the litigation or simply because the other party is unable to do so. The party responsible for the burden of proof (reversing the onus probandi) is guaranteed a sufficient period of time to produce the evidence.

§2. Powers of the Judge in Matters of Evidence

355. The ACCPC assigns the judge the function of directing the proceedings, and therein grants them the powers required to do so effectively. This includes the

192. *Fallos* 324:115 (2001).

193. The CCCN establishes that contracts may be proven by all suitable means with a view to reaching a reasonable conviction according to the rules of sound criticism, and in accordance with the procedural laws, except any legal provision foreseeing a special means (Art. 1019). Contracts which require formality for evidentiary purposes may however be proven by other means. Any instrument produced by other party, the predecessor in title, or another interested party which makes the contract's existence credible, is considered a principle of instrumental evidence (Art. 1020). As for causal factors, exculpatory and chance relationships, the burden of proof corresponds to the person who alleges these (Arts 1734 and 1736). The burden of proof of external causes, or showing it is impossible to comply, falls on the person who invokes it (Art. 1736). Damages must be demonstrated by whoever invokes these, unless the law imputes or presumes these, or they clearly arise from the facts themselves (Art. 1744).

possibility that the judges – concurrently with the burden on the parties and respecting their right to defence – may provide evidence on their own initiative to clarify the facts in dispute (Article 36 (2) ACCPC).

Evidentiary powers attributed to judges do not however imply a derogation of the dispositive principle, as the burden of proof is still on the parties together with the proposition of the facts or statements of conflict. Furthermore, the powers conferred on the judge do not authorize them to incorporate evidence about facts not provided by the parties. Thus, these powers in principle may not be exercised as a way of substituting the omission or negligence of the parties, since they have the right to control their exercise and produce evidence to the contrary.

§3. Presumptions

356. Presumptions are the consequences that the law or the judge derives from a known fact in order to affirm another unknown. As such, they involve a process of reasoning based on clues which apply the rules of logic and experience to reach a specific conclusion regarding the existence of the fact to be proved.

357. Presumptions may be legal or simple. Legal ones include *iuris tantum* or *iure et de iure* presumptions, according to whether or not they admit proof to the contrary. Both release the beneficiary from the burden of proof. Simple or judicial presumptions are those made by the judge based on logical and reasonable rules of evaluation and procedure of the proof of cause. To this end, the facts or indications underlying the reasoning must be duly verified and be various, serious, precise and consistent (Article 163 (5), ACCPC).

358. The conduct of the parties during the process may constitute an element of conviction for the judge, corroborating the evidence provided, in that it is tantamount to a clue. This means taking into consideration the specific circumstances of the case, the attitude assumed by the defendants and their duty to cooperate (Article 163 (5), ACCPC).

§4. Weighing of the Evidence

359. The ACCPC has adopted the rules for logical and reasonable rules of evaluation and procedure as a system for weighing evidence. This expression was taken from the Spanish Civil Procedure Law of 1855, which had as a precedent the indications given in Articles 147 and 148 of the Royal Council Regulation of 1846. This system enables the judges to form their own convictions regarding the evidence in court freely, according to the rules of experience and logic. Thus, they do not need to express their evaluation of all the evidence produced in the sentence but only refer to those elements which are essential and decisive to decide on the case

(Article 386, ACCPC). For this purpose, they must take into consideration the following: which are the alleged, controversial and conducive facts, the evidence provided, its value, relevance, whether it is misleading or not, and a joint analysis as well as any existing presumptions and the rules for the allocation of the burden of proof.

§5. Evidentiary Principles

360. The principles making up the evidentiary system are: (i) evidentiary unit, which requires the joint and coherent consideration of the evidence; (ii) acquisition of evidence for the proceedings, regardless of which party has provided it; (iii) the need for proof, in order to demonstrate the underlying facts of the claim; (iv) freedom of evidence, both in the sources and in the means of proof, subject to the limitations of public order; (v) application of scientific rules and experience in the acquisition of evidence and its assessment; *favor probationes,* in relation to the admissibility and interpretation of evidence; (vii) open to the public, except for exceptional reasons of reserve; and (viii) veracity, involving an attempt to investigate the 'truth' in the proceedings. Other principles such as collaboration, immediacy and good faith also affect the evidentiary subsystem.

Chapter 2. Offer and Admissibility of Evidence

§1. General Background

361. In the ACCPC, the areas governing evidentiary activity can be divided into four moments: (i) the offer of evidence, (ii) admissibility, (iii) the production of evidence, and (iv) its assessment when passing judgment.

362. The ACCPC establishes that the initial documents should be accompanied by documentary evidence, or an indication of its whereabouts and all other supporting evidence offered, excluding exceptions to the law. In some provinces, the type of hearing held determines when the proof should be presented. In this sense, in 'ordinary' proceedings, documentary evidence is attached to the initial documents, or its location is specified, leaving the remaining evidence to be offered at the stage of admission of proof. In summary and expedited summary proceedings, on the other hand, the documentary evidence must be provided in the initial brief, as well as the offer to provide any remaining evidence.

363. The ACCPC requires the following kinds of facts to be substantiated when: (i) they are controversial. All facts that have either not been denied or have been recognized by the counterpart do not require proof; (ii) they are conducive, inasmuch as they are relevant to the resolution of the conflict; (iii) they are legally bound to be proven as they constitute the presumptions of the rules invoked when bringing the claim; and (iv) they are not relieved of doing so based on the kind of fact (e.g., those which are obvious, evident and protected by legal presumptions), by virtue of legal provisions, or due to special circumstances (e.g., dynamic evidentiary charges).

364. In accordance with Article 2595 of the ACCC, when foreign law is applicable, the judge establishes its content and must interpret it in the same way as the judges of the State to which that right belongs, without prejudice to the fact that the parties may allege and prove the existence of the law invoked. If the content of foreign law cannot be established, then Argentine law applies. In principle, foreign law is considered a fact in the internal order.

The ACCPC (Article 3773) provides that when a foreign right is invoked as the basis of a claim, it must be proven, without prejudice to the fact that the judge may – if it has not been proven – investigate its existence and apply it to the legal relationship in dispute.

Articles 1 and 2 of the Additional Protocol to the Treaty of International Procedural Law of Montevideo of 1889 provide that the law of signatory countries does not need to be the object of proof, as long as the judge refers to it correctly.

§2. Sources and Means of Proof: Concepts

365. Sources are all those elements providing different aspects of proof concerning the facts in controversy in the proceedings. The means of proof are the forms, channels, instruments or modes through which knowledge, data or information can be obtained from sources for the proceedings.

The ACCPC and the provincial codes accept a broad criterion to enable the widest possible access to sources of knowledge. Any means of proof can be offered, as long as it does not undermine morality, public order, the personal freedom of the litigants or third parties, and as long as their use for the case is not prohibited,[194] and they are not used to substitute one means for another expressly provided. The kind of evidence regulated in the ACCPC includes documentary, informative, confessional, testimonial, expert and judicial recognition.

§3. Admissibility and Relevance

366. The procedural norms referring to the place, time and form of evidentiary activity come under provincial authority. However, as regards intrinsic admissibility, these powers must respect the statute of limitations enshrined in substantive laws.

367. If some type of evidentiary source is at risk of being adulterated, lost, or is at risk of being difficult to obtain at a later stage (e.g., a witness who is very old or seriously ill), the ACCPC recognizes the possibility of producing it in advance (paragraph 184).

368. The evidence provided by the parties must be admissible, pertinent or conducive to the resolution of the litigation and, therefore, admissible for the judge to form a conviction, will be valid.

The notion of admissibility of evidence is linked to its substantial or formal legality. Thus, proof is admissible when its use is not prohibited by law and has been offered in the timeframe, manner and form prescribed by the ACCPC. For example, illegal evidence or that excluded by substantive[195] or procedural norms is inadmissible. The ACCPC establishes that evidence can only be produced regarding those facts articulated by the parties in their respective briefs, as those that are manifestly inappropriate, superfluous or imply delaying tactics will not be admitted (Article 364, ACCPC).

Relevance is about analysing whether the chosen means of proof is suitable for extracting the knowledge sought from the evidentiary source in question (logical relationship). If the evidence is not relevant, it is declared inadmissible. Evidence is taken to be conducive when it matches the facts in dispute in the proceedings and thus serves to clarify them.

194. Article 378, ACCPC. This means that a statement obtained through torture cannot be used as evidence, unless it is used against the person accused of practising it as evidence that such a statement has been made (Arts 15 of the United Nations Convention against Torture and Other Cruel, Inhuman or Degrading Treatment or Punishment, and 10 of the Inter-American Convention to Prevent and Punish Torture).

195. For example, cases involving State or professional secrets (Arts 51, 153–157, 222 et seq., Criminal Code).

The utility of the evidence refers to whether it helps the judge to form a conviction concerning the truth of the statements made by the parties. It is carried out by the judge when passing a sentence.

369. Proof must be rendered according to the means expressly provided by law. When a 'novel, unforeseen or hitherto unrepresented' means not included among those detailed in the ACCPC is provided, it must be checked by comparing it to the provisions of other similar means or, failing that, in the manner established by the judge. Hence, it is inadmissible to exchange, substitute, or expand a means of evidence using another corresponding method according to the law, the source or the nature of the facts. When evidence is offered, each of the conditions or preparation required by each means of evidence must also be met, under penalty of inadmissibility.

370. Resolutions about the production, denial and substantiation of evidence are final. The interested party may propose them again at the appeal stage, when the file is sent on the occasion of the appeal brought against the final judgment (Article 379, ACCPC).

Chapter 3. Incorporation of Evidence

§1. General Background

371. The timeframe for producing evidence is set by the judge and may not exceed forty days, although extending it beyond this term has no consequences. The timeframe is calculated as from the date of the preliminary hearing (Articles 367 and 370, ACCPC).

§2. Negligence and Expiry of Evidence

372. If evidence is not supplied within the deadlines set, the ACCPC provides for this to be declared negligent or having expired.

There is negligence when, due to omission or attributable error, the interested party causes an unjustified delay in producing the evidence (Article 384, ACCPC). However, when the delay is not attributable to the party offering the evidence, or when the evidence has been offered by both litigants,[196] it is not classed as negligence.

Charges of negligence must be raised by the interested party and handled as incidental proceedings, a request which suspends the production of the evidence in question. In cases where evidence is produced and added before the expiry of the term set to answer the incidental proceedings brought, requests for negligence will be dismissed, without prejudice to imposing the costs on the party that failed to produce evidence as required. Evidence for which there is a declaration of negligence may be produced before the court when appealing the sentence.

373. Evidence expires automatically, without there needing to be a request by the other party, and responds to an objective criterion: the breach of certain duties that the law requires from the person presenting it. Thus, failure to comply with these leads to the loss of the validity of evidence, even if the probationary period has not expired.

§3. Documentary Evidence

374. This refers to both written instruments (documents signed by their authors) and to any other objects (plans, maps, photographs, videos, etc.) of a representative nature. Both substantive and procedural legislation primarily regulate matters concerning the instruments. Nevertheless, the rules contained in the ACCPC enable the other documents mentioned to be produced, with the necessary adjustments.

375. Documentary evidence must be offered and accompanied with the respective initial claims or objections. In the case of documents not in the possession of

196. *Fallos* 246:38 (1960); 247:720 (1961), for instance.

the party, which by their nature are difficult to acquire or require complementary evidence to be undertaken, their mention is sufficient, with reference to their content and ensure that they can be produced when necessary.

Both the parties and any third parties in possession of essential documents for the solution of the dispute have the obligation to exhibit them or say where the originals may be found. The judge may order these documents to be exhibited but if the party refuses to present them and there are other elements of judgment whose existence and content are manifestly plausible, this constitutes a presumption that such documents do not exist. Third parties may object only when the document is their exclusive property and its exhibition may cause harm (Articles 387, 388 and 389, ACCPC).

376. Public instruments are those granted by a public official or notary within the limits of their competence and in accordance with the formalities prescribed by law. The ACCC explains that public instruments are public deeds, their copies and testimonies, the instruments issued by public officials and notaries under the conditions mentioned above, and state-issued securities (national or provincial government or of the City of Buenos Aires) in accordance with the laws that authorize its emission. For a public instrument to be considered valid, a public official is required, within the framework of their competence, to act and sign it as well as the parties and, where appropriate, their representatives. When the instrument does not meet the fundamental standards of due process, it may be validated as a private instrument if signed by the parties (Articles 290, 291, 292, 294 and 299-312, ACCC).

377. Private instruments are those that do not meet the aforementioned requirements and may be produced by the parties or third parties. These documents may be formulated in the way deemed most convenient. Any amendments affecting the essential parts of the act implemented must be signed by the parties; otherwise, the judge will determine to what extent this affects the instrument's standing as evidence. It must be signed by the parties to be considered valid (Articles 313 and 316, ACCPC).

378. Public instruments are presumed to be authentic and have probative value by themselves without the need for recognition. Private ones do not have such value until the authenticity of the signature appearing in them can be proven, either through its author's express or tacit recognition, or through other forms of verification (Articles 390, 391, 393 and 394 ACCPC).

379. As for content, a public instrument testifies to the existence of the act, the date, the place and the facts which a public official declares were fulfilled by or before them and of the declarations of the celebrant about any conventions directly related to the main object of the act. Facts are presumed to be authentic until declared false in civil or criminal proceedings. Complaints as to its accuracy represent an attempt to have the instrument declared invalid, either because it has been materially adulterated or because the facts affirmed as being fulfilled before the public official are inaccurate. In civil law, this can be raised autonomously or as part of incidental proceedings, within ongoing proceedings (Article 395, ACCPC). Authenticated facts are presumed to be so until evidence to the contrary is produced (Articles 296, 299 and 312, ACCPC).

380. Regarding private instruments, recognition of the signature implies recognition of content, which pre-empts the possibility of it being challenged by whoever recognizes, except when there are flaws in the act of recognition. Regarding third parties, the evidentiary effectiveness of these instruments applies as from the moment their date is established. This can be proven by any means and must be explicitly acknowledged by the judge (Article 317, ACCC).

Correspondence can be presented as evidence by its recipient, although if it is confidential it may only be used with the consent of the sender. On the other hand, third parties must require the consent of both sender and recipient in case it is confidential (Article 318, ACCC).

Accounting records, whether compulsory or voluntary, correctly kept according to prescribed requirements, also constitute documentary evidence for court purposes (Articles 320, 322 and 330, ACCPC).

The ACCC foresees that the probative value of private instruments must be explicitly acknowledged by the judge, who must weigh up issues such as the congruence between what happened and what was told, the precision and technical clarity of the text, common practices, any prior relationships and the reliability of the supports used and technical procedures applied (Article 319, ACCPC). Unrecognized private documents may serve to provide clues for the purposes of making certain presumptions.

§4. Witnesses

381. Witnesses are natural persons who are not involved in the proceedings and are different from the parties, able to testify about their sensory perceptions and experiences of past events. When such an account is only possible as a result of the possession of technical knowledge, an expert witness is required, to whom the rules of both types of evidence will be applicable.

The limitations on admissibility are exceptional and must be legally established. For instance, the birth, marriage or death of a person cannot be proven by witnesses. Nor can contracts for instrumental use or formal contract be proven exclusively by witnesses, unless it is impossible to obtain proof in writing or due to the beginning of execution (Articles 1019 and 1020, ACCPC).

382. When the law prohibits the testimony of certain witnesses, either generally or under certain circumstances, they are referred to as excluded. This exclusion can operate in any lawsuit, against or in favour of certain people or with respect to certain acts. For example, the law prohibits calling witnesses under the age of 14, or accounts by direct relatives or spouses, even if legally separated, except in the case of signature recognition. The judge must dismiss ex officio and without the need for justification, inadmissible testimonial evidence, while the parties retain the power to object if this is unduly ordered (Articles 426, 427 and 428, ACCPC).

383. Testimonial evidence may be offered with the parties' respective opening briefs or objections, without prejudice to the judge's power to require, ex officio, witness statements from those persons mentioned by the parties in their briefs or whose knowledge of the main facts arises from other evidence being offered.

Each party must draw up a list of the witnesses that they wish to be called, specifying identification details and the contested facts their statement concerns. These requirements allow the other party to challenge them, in the case of excluded witnesses, or cross-examine them properly at the hearing. Only those errors, which make identification and the consequent power of control over them impossible, justify ruling that the evidence is inadmissible. When such information is not known, all that is required is to indicate the data necessary to individualize it. The number of witnesses proposed cannot exceed eight per party. The judge may ex officio or at the request of a party call other witnesses only if strictly necessary and useful for the resolution of the proceedings (Articles 333, 429, 430 and 452, ACCPC).

The party offering testimonial evidence is responsible for examining the witness, according to which the witness will give a statement at the respective hearing. Examinations may not refer to more than one fact, nor suggest an answer, nor be offensive. They must be formulated in an interrogative way, clearly and specifically and without technical references, unless the questions are addressed to experts (Articles 429 and 443, ACCPC).

384. Once the admissibility of the evidence has been declared, the judge sets the place, day and time when the hearing will be held, at which all the proposed witnesses must give testimonial statements. Witnesses are required to appear to testify. Non-compliance entails various penalties of a procedural and criminal nature. These include the possibility of obliging them to appear by public force or by imposing fines. The ACCPC exempts certain officials from the obligation to appear and delegates their definition to the Supreme Court. Such witnesses must give a written statement, respecting the same formalities as the other witnesses and within the terms set by the court.

Witnesses are summoned by the court, except when the party proposing them assumes the burden of ensuring they appear at the hearing. Normally, the statement is given at the courthouse, unless the effectiveness of the testimony is enhanced by the recognition of a site or the witness is prevented from appearing there (Articles 426, 433, 434, 453 and 454, ACCPC).

385. Witness evidence expires when the party offering it: (i) did not attend the hearing and failed to examine the witness; (ii) did not send the summons and thus the witness did not appear; (iii) did not request the compulsory measures in the event of the witness's unjustified absence at the first hearing; and (iv) does not request a new hearing within the fifth day following the second hearing which failed for reasons not attributable to them (Articles 432 and 437, ACCPC).

386. Testimonial hearings should be taken by the judge. However, the ACCPC expressly enables these hearings to be delegated to secretaries and legal officials (Articles 38 (5) and 360 (5), ACCPC). In practice, this task is generally carried out by the latter.

Before testifying, witnesses must take an oath to tell the truth. The court official will inform them of the criminal consequences that false or incomplete statements may entail. A preliminary examination is held to verify the identity of the witness if there are any reasons why they should not be admitted, and to assess, at the appropriate procedural moment, the reliability of their testimony.

Whoever is taking the hearing may freely examine the witnesses about their knowledge of the contested facts, respecting the substance of the examinations proposed. Both parties have the right to examine the witness during the hearing. Questions may be modified or dismissed ex officio by the judge when manifestly useless. The judge may also dispense with continuing to examine the witness when questions proposed or answers given show that the exercise serves no purpose (Articles 438, 439, 440 and 441, ACCPC).

The witnesses must answer about what they perceived, without being able to rely on any support, unless this is authorized by the judge due to the nature of the question. They may refuse to answer when this implies the confession of a crime, compromises their honour or reveals a professional, military or other kinds of secret. They cannot be interrupted in their statement and must always provide a reason for what they say.

387. In the event of serious evidence of false testimony or another crime, the judge may order the arrest of the alleged culprits by placing them at the disposal of the competent judge and sending them a copy of the corresponding proceedings. In its Articles 243 and 275, the Penal Code classifies the breach of the obligation to appear and tell the truth as crimes (Articles 442, 444, 445, 447, 448, and 449, ACCPC).

388. The parties may question the adequacy of the testimonies in their arguments. At the time of sentencing, the judge must weigh, in accordance with logical and reasonable rules of evaluation and procedure, whether these apply, analysing the circumstances and reasons corroborating or undermining the force of the statements (Article 456, ACCPC).

§5. Party Examination

389. Testimony in court involves a statement made spontaneously by a party or one prompted regarding the truth of past events, related to their personal actions or knowledge, which are unfavourable to them and favourable to the other party.

The recognition of the statements or facts that are the subject of controversy shows the party that there is a need to produce other evidence in this regard (Article 404, ACCPC).

390. Such testimony may be judicial or extrajudicial, depending on whether or not it is given in court. Extrajudicial testimony made before the other party is valid and binding in court, provided that it can be proven. If a confession is made to a third party, this only constitutes a mere assumption (Article 425, ACCPC).

A confession may also be express or tacit, depending on whether there is a definite and categorical acknowledgement of the respective facts, or it is inferred from certain attitudes assumed by the confessor (e.g., evasive answers). In principle, an express confession is binding for the judge and irrevocable for the party while a tacit one is capable of being refuted by means of evidence to the contrary.

391. The interrogatories are drawn up from the list of questions presented by the other party. This consists of a set of statements drawn up in an assertive, clear and concrete manner, relating to a single controversial fact linked to the personal actions of the litigant summoned to answer interrogatories. The judge has the power to modify, ex officio and without recourse, the order or terms of the questions as long as this does not alter their meaning. The judge may also eliminate superfluous questions and interrogate the parties freely, who may also ask reciprocal questions in order to clarify inaccuracies in the content of the positions or answers (Articles 410, 411, 413 and 415, ACCPC).

392. Legal persons may oppose the choice of the litigant summoned to answer interrogatories made by the counterpart, provided that they are able to allege that the representative selected did not personally intervene or have any direct knowledge of the facts, and propose a substitute, recording the reasoning of the hearing. When there are no objections, and/or the proposed person ignores the facts, the party will be considered to have confessed (Article 406, ACCPC). In the case of state public persons or those with state participation, a statement must be requested by means of an official letter from the competent body (Article 407, ACCPC).

Joint litigants may not interrogate litigants who are in the same position, unless they invoke different rights.

393. The notification of the interrogatory hearing is made under the warning that, if the witness fails to appear without just cause, they will be considered to have confessed (Articles 409, 417, 418, 419, 420 and 421, ACCPC). A witness must take an oath or promise to tell the truth. The current regime does not contain any provisions regarding perjury. However, if the party tells falsehoods when answering under oath, the judge at the time of sentencing may take into account these circumstances and sanction their conduct as reckless or malicious, or use this as evidence to admit the claim (Articles 45 and 163 (5), ACCPC).

Witnesses must answer without resorting to advice or supports of any kind, except in the case of specific data or special circumstances, with the judge's authorization. In this case, they must attend the hearing with these elements.

The answers must be affirmative or negative and should add any explanations as considered necessary. If the witness states that they do not remember a fact, this could be taken as a confession, when circumstances make such an answer unlikely. The litigant summoned to answer interrogatories may refuse to answer when they consider that the positions do not meet the required conditions, or when they are irrelevant as they fail to deal with the contested facts. In the first case, the judge will decide immediately whether to admit, reject or reformulate the position. In the second case, a record must be made, and resolution may be postponed until the time when the sentence is passed. If the judge rejects the proposal, it may be considered as a confession (Articles 404, 412, 413, 414 and 417, ACCPC).

394. When a plaintiff does not appear at the hearing without due cause or fails to provide the list of questions and the litigant summoned to answer interrogatories is present, the testimonial evidence will be declared to have expired (Article 410, ACCPC).

395. The ACCPC attributes a qualification to express judicial confession as full evidence. However, its weight decreases when the statement made is openly opposed to the evidence of reliable instruments of a previous date added to the file or to the claim filed in the process. In case of doubt, a confession must be interpreted in favour of the person who makes it (Articles 423 and 424, ACCPC). Judicial or extrajudicial confession may be revoked when it has been given by mistake, or fraud, violence and other vices are involved which could void consent. These flaws must be specifically alleged and proved in the corresponding manner and opportunity, in line with the rules established for nullities.

396. The new ACCPC bill substitutes confessional evidence for the free questioning of the parties (Articles 263 to 247). Interrogation is carried out under the duty to tell the truth. It is taken ex officio by the judge when they consider this to be pertinent. Its effects and scope are similar to the interrogation of witnesses, as it constitutes full evidence against the person making the statement, even in the case of the respondent's failure to answer. In other words, it prevents respondents from refusing to testify without harmful consequences (Article 240, new ACCPC bill).

§6. Expert Evidence

397. Expert evidence refers to activities performed by certain people with special knowledge in some area of science, art, industry or a specialized technical discipline, in order to clarify the contested facts during the proceedings when these require specific technical knowledge to explain them, beyond the strictly legal knowledge of the judge. Experts are assistants of the Administration of Justice with special knowledge in certain areas (Article 457, ACCPC).

398. When the discipline or profession is regulated, the expert must have a qualification or academic title in the area and be a member of the respective professional association. To be appointed as an expert in a case, they must be registered on the list of official experts of the Justice system and not have had any disqualifications or suspensions. If the discipline is not regulated or does not exist where the proceedings are taking place, an expert with the right kind of qualification, or any person able to prove their knowledge in the matter may be appointed (Article 464, ACCPC). Academic, scientific or technical institutions, whether public or private, may also be appointed in this capacity or consulted for said purposes (Article 476, ACCPC).

399. In most disputes, expert evidence is offered voluntarily by the parties. However, there are some cases where the law requires it, such as when age needs to be determined in the absence of other evidence (Article 99, ACCC).

400. In all proceedings, an expert examination may only be carried out by a single expert appointed ex officio, except when agreed by the parties (Article 462, ACCPC) or in other cases established by law where more than one may be appointed (e.g., in proceedings concerning civil incapacity). If there are three experts, the judge will be responsible for instructing them how to give their opinions (Article 458, ACCPC).

401. Expert evidence must be offered by the parties in their opening briefs, specifying the area of expertise required and the specific points to be covered. The counterpart has the possibility of expressing their disinterest in the respective evidence, or examining the proposed points of expertise, or suggesting others (Article 459, ACCPC).

402. The judge appoints the expert at the preliminary hearing, who is drawn from those on the list, unless there is an agreement between the parties. The judge also sets the areas of expertise to be covered and the deadline for answering. Experts are not public officials, hence they can refuse to accept an appointment. However, repeated and unjustified refusals may result in their being dropped from the list of experts. When they accept the task, an expert may require the judge to establish a sum of money as an advance for expenses, counted as part of their eventual fees. The party offering evidence must deposit the fixed sum under the condition of this being declared void (Articles 463, 469 and 470, ACCPC).

403. The parties may challenge the expert with just cause for the same reasons as the judges, due to lack of competence or qualification in the matter. The expert appointed by mutual agreement may be challenged for supervening causes (Articles 465-468, ACCPC).

404. The evaluation must be performed by the designated expert, and the technical consultants, the parties and their lawyers may bear witness to the process and formulate the observations they deem pertinent. The opinion must cover the points requiring expertise, with details on the technical operations developed for this purpose and the scientific principles on which it was founded. The technical consultants involved must also provide similar information. The parties may make observations to the opinion and request clarification. The judge has the power to order another expert evaluation to be performed, or to improve or broaden the one carried out, by either the same expert or another one. They may also order the execution of complementary measures such as plans, examinations or reconstructions (Articles 472-474, ACCPC).

405. Expert opinions will be evaluated by the judge in accordance with logical and reasonable rules of evaluation and procedure, taking into account the competence of the expert, the scientific or technical principles on which these opinions are based, the observations made by the technical consultants or lawyers, whether the conclusions drawn agree, and other elements of conviction offered. The analysis of these elements may justify the judge's departure from the opinion in question, either for technical reasons or because they have reached other conclusions based on a comparison with other legal elements (Article 477, ACCPC).

406. The parties have the power to appoint a technical consultant, who must be a person versed in the appropriate area, for instance, science, art, technical issues or a particular discipline. The consultant acts as a technical advocate for the party that proposed them, advising and assisting them in everything related to the scope of their knowledge. Consultants can be appointed and replaced by a party on its own, unless there are other joint litigants who do not agree, in which case the judge will unseat one of those proposed (Article 459, ACCPC).

407. Experts and technical consultants have the right to collect their fees for the work performed, which will be ordered by the judges according to the tariffs governing each profession, in line with the nature, complexity, quality and time taken to do the work. As these are expenses incurred by the proceedings, they make up court costs (Articles 461 and 478, ACCPC).

§7. Informative Evidence

408. The report on evidence ensures that the data listed in the records or files belonging to third parties or the parties themselves, which could be useful to prove the contested facts in the case, can be contributed to the proceedings, provided that this data is not based on the parties' own personal knowledge.

409. Reports requested from public offices, registered notaries, private entities or simple individuals must be about the specific, clearly specified facts contested in the proceedings and may involve requests for the referral of files, testimonies or certificates related to the trial. Reports aimed collecting material to expand or replace another means of evidence are not allowed (Articles 396 and 397, ACCPC).

410. The person who receives the request is obliged to provide proof of receipt, answer the request, or otherwise send the materials requested directly to the judge. They may only refuse to answer if this involves the prior reserve or secrecy. The judge will resolve any objections, weighing for this purpose the justifications given. In the event of unjustified delay in the referral, the judge may apply progressive penalties. The parties may question the reports produced when they are incomplete or do not answer to the facts listed in the subject of the request, and draw up further requests for this purpose (Articles 375, 398, 400 and 401, ACCPC).

411. The deadline of applicability of the evidence expires when the public office or private entity requested fails to send it in the timeframe set and the party that requested it does not ask the judge to reiterate the request within a five-day period (Article 402, ACCPC).

§8. JUDICIAL INSPECTION

412. Judicial inspection is the examination conducted by the judge hearing the case, concerning things, places or people, with a view to identifying their characteristics, qualities or conditions and forming a direct impression.

413. Gathering data about things, places or people, may involve carrying out certain representative procedures, such as scientific examinations or the reconstruction of the facts, to better clarify the facts contested and the way in which they have occurred. To this end, the judge may summon experts and witnesses to this process, organizing scientific examinations and receiving any witness statements or explanations deemed necessary. The judge must also let the parties know that they may invite their technical consultants to this procedure (Articles 471, 473 and 475, ACCPC).

Inspection must be carried out personally by the intervening judge with all the attendant guarantees of publicity and control required and may undertake the procedure in any part of the country if necessary. The parties, their representatives, lawyers and consultants, and each one of the intervening parties may make all the observations they consider pertinent during the development of the process, which must be recorded in the minutes (Articles 382 and 480, ACCPC).

414. This means of evidence can be ordered ex officio or at the request of a party, although it is the judge's prerogative whether to allow or concede it. Its use is limited and exceptional. If the judge admits the procedure as evidence, they must outline its objective and define location, date and time.

Part VIII. Particular Proceedings

Chapter 1. General Background

415. Book IV of the ACCPC is dedicated to regulating what it calls particular proceedings. These are proceedings governed by specific rules linked to the particularities of the type of conflict they aim to resolve, but which refer to the provisions established for plenary proceedings.

Chapter 2. Processes to Determine Fitness for Trial

416. *416*.The ACCPC uses terminology that differs from the advances made in Argentine legislation regarding constraints on personal civil capacity or fitness. It contains three chapters, the first two referring to the declaration of insanity and deaf-muteness, and the third to special conditions for civil disqualification. The provisions of the ACCPC must be interpreted taking into consideration that: (i) through Law 26,378 (2008), the RA ratified the Convention on the Rights of Persons with Disabilities and its optional protocol, approved by a resolution of the UN General Assembly dated 13 December 2006; (ii) Law 26,657 (2010) was enacted on mental health; and (iii) the ACCC contains substantive and procedural norms regarding restrictions of capacity.

417. Law 26,378 guarantees that people with mental illness living in Argentina have both the right to the protection of mental health and the full enjoyment of human rights as recognized in international human rights instruments with constitutional hierarchy (Article 1). In addition, it establishes that addictions must be addressed as an integral part of mental health policies (Article 4), and that the existence of a mental health diagnosis does not under any circumstance tip the balance in favour of the presumption of risk of harm or disability, as this may only be deduced from the interdisciplinary evaluation of each particular situation at a given moment (Article 5).

418. The ACCC establishes the following general rules regarding the restriction of the exercise of legal capacity: (i) a person's general capacity to exercise their will is presumed, even when admitted to a healthcare establishment; (ii) limitations on capacity are of an exceptional nature and always imposed for the benefit of the individual; (iii) State intervention is always interdisciplinary in nature, both in its treatment and in legal proceedings; (iv) the person has the right to receive information through whatever means and technologies necessary to ensure their understanding; (v) the person has the right to participate in legal proceedings with due assistance, which must be provided by the State if they lack the means; and (vi) the focus should be on achieving the least restrictive therapeutic alternatives regarding their rights and freedoms (Article 32).

In accordance with the principles explained above, and in line with the provisions enshrined in the Convention on the Rights of Persons with Disabilities, the supports designated must be in favour of the person's autonomy and seek to secure decisions responding to the preferences of the person protected. Only by exception, when the person is absolutely unable to relate to their environment and express their will in any suitable way, medium or format, and when the support system is ineffective, may the judge declare disability and appoint a curator (Article 32, ACCC).

419. Article 33 of the ACCC establishes that active standing is the responsibility of the interested party, of a spouse who is not de facto separated, and the partner, as long as cohabitation has not ceased, of relatives to the fourth degree; if by affinity, to the second degree and the Public Ministry.

A competent judge is one whose professional radius of action encompasses the domicile of the person whose capacity is under examination, or the place where they are being treated, with the goal of ensuring the greatest immediacy possible and thus guaranteeing effective judicial protection with respect to the interested party (Article 36, ACCC).

420. The ACCPC requires two medical certificates. If these cannot be obtained, it authorizes the judge to request the opinion of two forensic doctors to be issued within forty-eight hours (Article 624, ACCPC). However, the ACCC establishes that, during the process, the judge must order the necessary measures to guarantee the personal and patrimonial rights of the person. The judgment regarding a person's incapacity must determine which acts require the assistance of one or more supports, and which need the representation of a curator. The judge may also designate support networks and people deploying specific functions depending on the case (Article 34, ACCC). From another perspective, the ACCC empowers the judicial body to embargo goods and property and take any measures it deems appropriate to ensure that movable property and securities cannot be touched when 'insanity is clear'. This is an extreme situation which should be limited to those cases where the person is absolutely unable to interact with their environment and express their will in any suitable way, medium or format, and the support system is ineffective (Article 32 *in fine* ACCC).

421. The judge must be in direct contact with the interested party during the proceedings and interview them personally before issuing any resolution, ensuring accessibility and reasonable adjustments to the proceedings according to their situation. The Public Ministry and at least one lawyer providing assistance to the interested party must be present at the hearings (Article 35, ACCC).

Article 626 of the ACCPC stipulates that, after hearing the Counsel for Minors and the Disabled, the judge will decide on the appointment of a provisional curator, meaning a registered attorney.

The ACCPC envisages the possibility of ordering a person to be admitted to hospital in the case of 'a person suffering from insanity who poses a danger to themselves or third parties', a rule that must be interpreted in accordance with Article 32 (f) of the ACCC which establishes the need to select the least restrictive therapeutic alternatives regarding rights and freedoms.

422. The ACCC provides that hospitalization without a person's consent, whether or not their capacity is restricted, may only happen if all the necessary measures provided in the special legislation and the rules established therein are met, in particular: (i) hospitalization must arise from an evaluation performed by an interdisciplinary team in accordance with the provisions of Article 37, with reasons for this decision and justified by the absence of an effective alternative which is less restrictive of their freedom; (ii) that there is a certain and imminent risk of significant damage to the protected person or to third parties; (iii) that this is a therapeutic option of a restrictive nature and should only be contemplated for the shortest time possible and must be supervised periodically; (iv) there must be a guarantee of due process, immediate judicial control and the right to defence through legal assistance; and (v) the decision ordering hospitalization must specify its purpose, duration and how often it is to be reviewed.

423. The ACCPC establishes the content to be included in the interdisciplinary opinion, specifying that this should refer to (i) the diagnosis; (ii) the approximate date when the disease manifested itself; (iii) the prognosis; (iv) the regime recommended to ensure the protection and assistance of person presumed to be suffering from insanity; and (v) the need for hospitalization. Following the production of the interdisciplinary report, which the ACCC states is indispensable, and other evidence, the parties will be notified and summoned to a hearing with the Counsel for Minors and the Disabled.

424. For its part, the ACCC (Article 37) gives indications as to the content of the decision, establishing that the decision must contemplate the following aspects related to the person in whose interest the proceedings are being held: (i) their diagnosis and its outlook; (ii) the date when the situation became apparent; (iii) any existing personal, family and social resources; and (iv) a regime to protect, assist and help the person enjoy the greatest autonomy possible.

The decision should define the scope of the restrictions envisaged and specify which actions and functions are prohibited, ensuring that their personal autonomy is as little affected as possible. Likewise, one or more support persons or curators must be appointed in accordance with the provisions of Article 32 of the ACCC, indicating which acts may be performed on behalf of the person with a disability and how this is to be done.

The decision must be registered with the Registry of Civil Status and Capacity of Persons and must be recorded as a marginal note on the birth certificate to ensure it is binding upon third parties. Once the restrictions have been lifted, the registration is immediately struck out.

This decision may be appealed within five days by the plaintiff, the person whose capacity is being restricted, the provisional curator and the Counsel for Minors and the Disabled. If no appeal is presented, the ruling is submitted for consultation so that the Court of Appeals may, after hearing from the Counsel for Minors and the Disabled, resolve without the need for further substantiation regarding the legality of the decision.

The costs will be borne by the complainant if the judge considers the error in which they incurred when formulating the complaint inexcusable, or if there was malicious intent involved. The expenses and fees charged to the person presumed insane may not exceed 10% in total of the value of their assets.

425. The ACCPC establishes that a person declared insane or who is disabled may request that they be allowed full use of their capabilities. For these purposes, the judge designates three psychiatrists or legal experts to examine the person, and, following the procedures indicated for the declaration of dementia, may or not permit them to do so.

The ACCC points out that the review of the declarative decision may take place at any time, at the request of the interested party. In the case envisaged in Article 32 (declaration of incapacity), the sentence must be reviewed by the judge within a three-year period taking into account any new interdisciplinary opinions and including a personal hearing with the interested party. The Public Ministry must ensure the judicial review process is fulfilled effectively, and urge, where appropriate, that it be held if the judge has not carried it out within the period established therein.

426. The Civil Code repealed by the ACCC, which entered into force in 2015, subjected the declaration of disability due to deaf-muteness to the rules applicable to people with mental illnesses. The ACCPC stipulates that 'the provisions referring to the process of incapacity govern the declaration of incapacity of a deaf-mute person who is unable to make themselves understood in writing and, where appropriate, declare the cessation of such an incapacity'. This figure has in practice not been applied, as the ACCC has not regulated it in accordance with the new standard.

427. Law 22,434 added Article 637 bis to the ACCPC, establishing the option of disqualification, which currently only applies to people whose profligate lifestyle may expose their spouse, partner, or any underage or disabled children to the loss of their estate.

Chapter 3. Maintenance and *Expensae Litis*

§1. Maintenance

428. The purpose of maintenance or child support proceedings is to satisfy a claim based on the obligation to provide support deriving from a parental or marital relationship or one of coexistence, as established by the ACCC (Articles 537, 538, 541 and 498, et seq.).

In accordance with the provisions enshrined in the ACCC, the petition for maintenance is handled through the shortest proceedings established by local law and cannot be added to another claim (Article 543). Hence, the scheme used is summary proceedings.

The ACCPC stipulates that the party filing a claim for maintenance must, in their brief (i) explain by virtue of which role they are making the claim; (ii) indicate, albeit approximately, the economic position of the person who should be providing maintenance; (iii) provide all the documentation in their possession supporting their position; and (iv) offer evidence. If a party offers a statement, the counterpart must testify at the first hearing (Article 638). According to the ACCC, a relative requesting maintenance must prove that they lack sufficient financial means and cannot acquire these through work, whatever the reasons for ending up in this state (Article 545). The code also specifies that the defendant has the burden of proving that there is another person who is similarly or more closely related who is able to provide maintenance, so that they can either avoid the responsibility or share it with another. If several parties are being sued for this purpose at once, then the defendant may summon all or some of the others to court, so that the judgment be applied to them all (Article 546).

429. Regarding the procedure, the ACCPC establishes that the judge, besides immediately taking any evidentiary measures requested, shall summon a hearing to take place within a ten-day period as from the date the claim is filed, at which the parties must appear personally as well as a representative from the Department for the Protection of the Rights of Minors, if applicable. The judge must at this point ensure that the parties reach a direct agreement, and may thus approve it forthwith, ending the trial (Article 639).

If the person from whom maintenance is required does not appear at the hearing without just cause, the judge: (i) will order them to be fined in favour of the other party; and (ii) will set a new hearing within five days, notifying the date and time, under warning that the amount of the maintenance will be ruled in accordance with the claims made by the plaintiff and the conclusions drawn by the judge from the file (Article 640). If it is the plaintiff who fails to appear at the hearing, the judge will call a new hearing, in the same manner and term provided for in the previous article, under the warning of dismissing the claim if they are not present (Article 641). The ACCPC authorizes both plaintiff and defendant to be absent with justification on a single occasion. If the economic limitations continue, they must be represented by a proxy, under warning of the aforementioned sanctions.

During the hearing, the defendant must demonstrate the lack of legitimacy of the person seeking maintenance, as well as their own financial situation or that of the plaintiff. To do so they have only two options: to submit instrumental evidence or to request reports whose completion cannot be allowed to delay the period set for the judge to issue a ruling.

430. When ruling, the judge will assess the evidence to determine the amount of the maintenance, or refuse it, if applicable. The judge will issue a sentence within five days, without the need for a request from the parties. Once the claim is admitted, the judge sets the amount they consider to be fair and order it to be paid monthly in advance, from the date of the mediation (Article 644, ACCPC).

The ACCC establishes that maintenance is due from the day when the claim is filed, or when the defendant is challenged, using trustworthy means, provided that the claim is presented within six months of the challenge. As for maintenance accruing during the trial itself, the judge will set supplementary allowances in accordance with the provisions governing the unattachment of wages, retirement payments and pensions, which must be paid independently (Article 548).

The ACCPC establishes that the payor's lack of activity at procedural level may create the presumption, subject to proof to the contrary, that they have no need of support, and, according to the circumstances of the case, may determine the expiry of their right to collect the payments in arrears referring to the corresponding period of inactivity (Article 645).

A judgment denying maintenance may be appealed with suspensive effect, whereas a judgment in its favour means that support must be paid until such time as the Court of Appeal issues a pronouncement on the matter (Article 647).

§2. *Expensea Litis*

431. Expensea litis refers to the amount that a supported person has the right to require from the payee in order to cover the expenses of a specific court proceeding (e.g., divorce). The claim is processed in accordance with the rules governing the maintenance trial (Article 651, ACCPC).

Chapter 4. Accountability for Commercial Transactions

432. These proceedings are linked to the obligation weighing on those performing administrative acts in favour of a third party, and their purpose is to obtain a report on the steps taken, specifying the ensuring financial status.

433. According to the ACCPC, the claim can be brought by the administrator or spontaneously by the person obliged to render accounts. In the first case, the claim concerning the obligation to render accounts is subject to the rules governing plenary proceedings. It is notified with the warning that if the defendant fails to answer it, or admits the obligation but does not render account within the term determined by the judge, the claim presented by the plaintiff will be approved, as regards everything that the defendant fails to show to be inaccurate (Article 652). The code also establishes that incidental proceedings may apply as long as (i) there is a judicial sentence ordering a party to render accounts; or when (ii) the obligation to render them arises from a recognized public or private instrument, or has been admitted by the obligor when required in the pretrial proceedings (Article 653).

The ACCPC empowers the judge to set the deadlines for notification and production of evidence, taking into account the complexity of the accounts and documents provided.

The corresponding documentation must be provided together with the balance of transactions, although the judge may consider that those items for which it is not customary to ask for receipts and are reasonable and credible are justifiable (Article 655). The plaintiff may claim the payment of the balances recognized by the defendant, without waiting for the final resolution on the accounts and without it being understood that these have been accepted (Article 657, ACCPC).

Spontaneous accountability must be promoted with the deposit slip for the amount of the debit balance, which will be transferred to the interested party, for the term set by the judge, under the warning of being considered as compliant if they are not challenged when answering. The procedure established for the request for accountability is applied, as appropriate.

Chapter 5. Measurement and Demarcation

434. In its fifth chapter, the ACCPC regulates processes for measurement and demarcation. The second supposes the existence of the first, as by means of measurement one can check the surface area of a property and establish its limits (Article 658).

435. The plaintiff must: (i) state their name, surname and current address; (ii) establish their legal domicile; (iii) provide the title deeds to the property; (iv) indicate the name, surname and address of their neighbours, or otherwise state that they do not have this information; and (v) appoint a surveyor to carry out the operation. If the claimant does not meet these requirements (Article 660, ACCPC), the judge may simply dismiss the claim ex officio without informing the defendant.

Once the request has been presented with all the requisite information, the judge must order a survey to be carried out by a land surveyor appointed by the applicant, ordering edicts to be published for three days, summoning those with any interests affected by the survey. The edicts must give the location of the property, the name of the applicant, the address and name of the courtroom, and the place, day and time for the exercise. The request for a measurement must also be made known to the Topographic Survey Directory (Article 661).

This includes the duties to be performed by the surveyor and aims to ensure that the expert will, after complying with all due requirements, take measurements in the place, day and time indicated, in the presence of the interested parties or their representatives. Once the survey has been completed, a record must be drawn up with the details of the operation and the name of the boundaries witnessed. If there is any disagreement, the reasons for these must be given, with the citation summons being presented to the court and a report on the surveyor's activities to the Topographic Survey Directory with duplicate copies of the record and the measurement plan. The surveyor is responsible for any damages caused by unjustified delay (Article 662).

The Topographic Survey Directory may request the judge to provide the file with the title deeds. It must send one of the copies of the record, the plan and a report of the technical value of the operation carried out within thirty days of receiving the formal records or the file requested from the judge. If the Topographic Survey Directory has no observations concerning the measurement and there is no opposition from the measurement nor any opposition concerning boundaries, the judge will approve it and send the documents requested by the interested parties.

When such observations or oppositions are based on purely technical grounds, the interested parties will be notified in the terms set by the judge. Once the notifications have been answered or the term to do so has expired, the judge will resolve whether or not to approve the measurement or order the pertinent rectifications, if any.

436. As for demarcation, the ACCPC provides that this may be performed by means of an agreement or by judicial process. If this involves an agreement, the public deeds containing the demarcation made by the parties must be presented to the judge, with all the corresponding background documentation. After the Topographic Survey Directory has intervened, the demarcation will be approved, if applicable (Article 673).

As for judicial demarcation, the ACCPC provides that any claim be dealt with according to the norms governing ordinary court cases. If the defendant does not object to the demarcation being carried out, the judge will appoint an expert surveyor ex officio to carry out the measurement. The norms governing the measurement process are applied, as appropriate.

Chapter 6. Division of Ownership

437. These measures allow parties to conclude joint ownership. Specifically, they allow an immaterial right over the undivided portion belonging to the joint owner to be materialized into a portion equivalent to the interest in relation to whatever is the object of joint ownership.

The claim is treated in ordinary court proceedings, and the judgment, in addition to general requirements, must contain the express decision, where possible, on the form of the division, according to the nature of the subject in question. If this is not established in the judgment, once it is executed, the parties will be summoned to a hearing for the appointment of a real estate appraiser or auctioneer, as appropriate, and to agree on the form of the division (Articles 676 and 677, ACCPC).

The ACCPC (Article 678) also regulates the division of assets carried out extra judicially. It stipulates that the judge, after the corresponding ratifications, and the necessary summons, will resolve on the case either approving or dismissing it, without any recourse.

Chapter 7. Injunctions and Possessory Action

438. Those injunctions regulated by the ACCPC may be brought on the occasion of the disturbance or stripping of the ownership or possession of a movable or immovable piece of property, or on the occasion of new building works affecting a piece of property. The purpose of these injunctions is to obtain a judicial decision protecting or restoring ownership.

The ACCC expressly contemplates that possessory actions are aimed at protecting both possessions and ownership. In its Article 2238, the ACCC establishes that possessory actions according to disturbance or disempowerment, are intended to maintain or recover the object over which there is a power relationship. They are granted following material acts, whether these have taken place or are about to take place, executed with the intention of taking possession, against the will of the holder or owner.

Article 2246 of the ACCC provides that possessory actions be processed through the most abbreviated hearing proceedings established by procedural law, or as determined by the judge, according to the circumstances of the case.

Chapter 8. Eviction

439. Eviction refers to the procedural route available to recover the use and enjoyment of property which is being occupied by someone without the title deeds allowing them to retain it. A claim for eviction can be brought by the owners of the property in question, and any others with rights over it, against tenants, subtenants, tenants in a precarious financial situation, intruders and any other occupant charged with its restitution (Article 680, ACCPC). Hence, if the defendant alleges and is able to prove that they are the owner, this legal route is inadmissible and redress must be sought by means of the appropriate possessory action.

440. The ACCPC authorizes a preliminary request for protection in cases where the grounds invoked for the eviction are non-payment or the expiry of the contract. In these cases, immediate evacuation of the premises may be obtained according to the procedures provided for in Article 680 bis, subject to a guarantee. If it is proven that the plaintiff obtained this measure by hiding facts or documents proving a leasehold relationship or the payment of rent, in addition to forfeiting the guarantee, a fine will be imposed in favour of the other party.

441. Both in the claim and in the response, the parties must state whether or not there are subtenants or third-party occupants (Article 681). The ACCPC establishes that if the plaintiff is not in possession of this information, they may refer to the notification procedure, the response to the claim, or both.

Notice may be served (Articles 683 and 684) at the property whose eviction is required. The judicial officer in charge of the notification will try to locate the property by asking the neighbours if they cannot identify the premises in question. Likewise, if they have sufficient information, they will request the occupants of the property to identify themselves and explain their relationship with the defendant (Article 684). If notice is served in an apartment building and the unit has not been specified in the documents, the judicial officer must ask the building supervisor or neighbours whether the defendant lives in the building before serving them notice with due identification Otherwise, they must return the notice with a note informing the result of their efforts.

When notice is served on someone in the property in question, the judicial officer must: (a) inform each of the subtenants or occupants present of the existence of the lawsuit at the time, even if no charges have been brought against them, warning them that the judgment will have an effect on all of them and that they may exercise the rights that they deem correspond to them within the period established to answer the claim; (b) ask those present to identify themselves and inform the judge whether they and others are tenants or subtenants according to their statements; or (c) require, if necessary, assistance from public forces of law and order, search homes and demand that identity documents or others be produced as necessary.

442. The eviction proceeds if the defendants took possession or occupied the property with a lawful title, ten days after the notification of the judgment, if the eviction judgment is based on the expiry of a term, rent payments in arrears or the termination of the contract due to abusive use or any other cause attributable to the tenant. In all other cases, within ninety days of notification of the judgment, unless a special law establishes different terms (Article 686, ACCPC).

443. Only documentary, party declaration and expert evidence is admitted in eviction proceedings instituted for non-payment of rent or due to the expiry of the contract term. A judgment passed in the framework of eviction proceedings may applied to all those occupying the property, even if they were not mentioned when notice was served, or were not present at the trial (Article 687).

Chapter 9. Other Special Proceedings

§1. *Amparo* Proceedings (Constitutional Remedy or Redress)

444. Amparo proceedings (constitutional remedy or redress) were incorporated into the Constitution in the 1994 reform process (Article 43) where they are defined as a rapid procedure designed to counteract any act or omission undertaken by public authorities or individuals, that currently or imminently harms, restricts, alters or threatens, either arbitrarily or with manifest illegality, any rights and guarantees recognized.

However, Law 16,986 (1966) explains that these represent the way of requesting protection against any act or omission on the part of a public authority that, currently or imminently, harms, restricts, alters or threatens, either arbitrarily or with manifest illegality, the rights or guarantees explicitly or implicitly recognized by the AC, with the exception of individual freedoms protected by habeas corpus.

Regarding acts or omissions undertaken by private subjects, the rules of the summary procedures apply (Article 321, ACCPC).

445. Amparo is not admitted in the following cases: (a) when there are other judicial or administrative remedies protecting the constitutional right or guarantee in question; (b) the act contested was undertaken by an organ of the judicial power or thanks to the express application of the National Defence Law 16,970 (1966); c) legal intervention directly or indirectly compromises the regularity, continuity and effectiveness of the provision of a public service, or the development of the State's essential activities; (d) a broader debate is required to determine whether the act is valid or not, or the proof or declaration of the unconstitutionality of laws, decrees or ordinances; or, (e) if the claim was not filed within fifteen business days from the date the act was performed or should have occurred.

Depending on the wording of the constitutional norm, the existence of administrative proceedings should not obstruct their admission, nor the need to declare the unconstitutionality of the norms, given that there are constitutional mechanisms which allow judges to declare the unconstitutionality of the norm on which the harmful act or omission is founded.

The competent judge is the judge of first instance with jurisdiction in the location where the act takes place, or has or may have effect. The law on the matter provides that the relevant rules be observed concerning jurisdiction by reason of the subject matter, unless they give rise to reasonable doubt in this regard, in which case the judge must accept jurisdiction of the case (Article 4, Law 16,986).

446. Any person or legal entity who considers themselves to be affected according to the aforementioned presumptions that the norm establishes in Article 1, may, either by themselves or via representatives, be permitted to take action. Legal action may also be brought, under the same conditions, by associations that, without being legal entities, are able to prove that they are not going against the public good by displaying their statutes.

447. The claim must be submitted in writing indicating: (i) the name, surname and real and legal addresses of the plaintiff; (ii) the identity, inasmuch as is possible, of the author of the act or omission; (iii) a detailed account of the context that produced or is in the process of producing the infringement of the right or constitutional guarantee; and (iv) the request or claim itself, in clear and precise terms. All instrumental evidence available must be attached or sent separately if unavailable, indicating the place where it is kept, and indicating any other means of proof the plaintiff intends to use.

Once the admissibility of the claim has been decreed, the judge will require the corresponding authority to produce a detailed report on the background and grounds for the measure being challenged, which must be sent within a reasonable period of time set by the judge. If the step to request a report is omitted, this is cause for annulling the proceedings.

448. The defendant must comply with the burden of offering evidence when answering the report, in the manner established for the plaintiff. Once the report has been produced, or it has not been provided by the deadline for doing so, and there is no evidence on the part of the plaintiff to be examined, a well-founded judgment will be issued within forty-eight hours, granting or dismissing the protection.

The measure provides that if evidence has been offered, the judge must order it to be produced immediately, calling a hearing to be held within three days. If neither the plaintiff nor their representative appear at the hearing, they will be considered to have withdrawn their complaint, and the proceedings will be filed and costs imposed. If it is the defendant who fails to attend, any evidence provided by the plaintiff will be received, and the judge will proceed to pass a ruling.

Within three days of receiving the report referred to in Article 8, or after the trial hearing has been held, the judge will issue a ruling.

449. The ruling admitting the action must contain: (i) the name of the authority against whose resolution, act or omission the *amparo* is granted; (ii) the precise determination of the conduct to be complied with, with the necessary specifications for its proper execution; and (iii) the term for compliance with the resolution.

The law only enables appeals to be lodged against the final sentence, rejection in limine and those resolutions providing measures not to innovate or suspending the effects of the act contested. The appeal must be filed within forty-eight hours of the notification of the resolution contested, and must be dismissed or granted within forty-eight hours. If granted, the file will be sent to the respective Court of Appeal within twenty-four hours. If dismissed, the plaintiff must file an appeal within twenty-four hours of the notification of dismissal, and a judgment must be issued within three days.

The final judgment ensures that the *amparo* is considered res judicata and any actions to be taken or appeals to be filed are up to the parties.

§2. COLLECTIVE REDRESS

450. The Argentine Constitution has since 1994 recognized the existence of collective advocacy rights and endows a range of different social and political actors with the procedural legitimacy required to protect them (Article 43, AC). However, Congress has not passed a law that regulates collective redress.

Although there are certain rules for the protection of collective rights such as the General Environmental Law 25,675 and the Consumer Defence Law 24,240 they contain procedural provisions that do not regulate all the particular aspects of the issue.

Given such an inexplicable legislative omission, the Supreme Court has adopted an important role in establishing rules to allow this type of discussion to be developed in an orderly fashion, not only through its jurisdictional functions, establishing different principles and rules within the framework of the judicial cases submitted for its decision, but also by issuing Supreme Court Rules. It has through jurisprudential means established numerous rules and principles governing class action, setting clear guidelines related to the publicity of litigation, and the intervention of third parties, both to guarantee a better, more informed and generalized participation and to establish predictable rules creating appropriate standards for the management of this type of conflict.

Part IX. Enforcement of Judgments

Chapter 1. Enforcement of Judgments at National Level

§1. General Considerations

451. Article 8 of the ACHR establishes the right to effective judicial protection, both during the stages leading to a judgment being passed and in those foreseen for the effective realization of what has been decided. A judgment, as a state legal act, has coercive capacity and is an unavoidable step required before achieving the protection of rights, which is specified when the decision is made effective.

The IHCR ruled against the RA for violating Article 8 of the ACHR in *Furlan*[197] (2012). The ICHR decision offers an insight into the dysfunctional nature of the Argentine procedural model and the difficulties faced by victims when attempting to get the State to comply with judicial rulings issued locally. The facts of the case are related to the ten years that Furlan had to wait until obtaining a final judgment, which is an obvious violation of the guarantee of reasonable time provided for in Article 8 of the ACHR on the right to a fair trial. After the ruling was issued, the Argentine State argued that the debt had been consolidated due to the country's economic crisis. Another three years passed before Furlan was able to obtain repair, whose value was 80% less than the amount recognized by the judgment. In paragraph 219 of its decision, the ICHR expressly understood that the execution of the judgment ordering Furlan to be compensated was not properly carried out and therefore violated Article 8 of the ACHR. It made clear that execution is a crucial part of the guarantee of due process as enshrined in Article 8 of the ACHR.

§2. Enforcement of Judgments Handed Down by National and Federal Judges

I. Debtor Defences

452. The provisions of the ACCPC concerning the enforcement of judgments establish a stage whereby a judgment debtor may present a limited number of defences before they have to sell their attached assets. If the judgment debtor does not resort to the defence options provided for in the ACCPC, or if these are rejected

197. Judgment of 31 August 2012. At: https://www.corteidh.or.cr/docs/canes/articulos/seriec_246_ing.pdf.

by the judge, at the request of the party benefiting from the conviction, the judge may order the former's assets to be sold. If this involves the obligation to perform certain deeds, in the event of non-compliance, the payment of a sum of money may be established to compensate the party bringing the enforcement proceedings (Articles 513, 514 and 515, ACCPC). The judgment may be partially enforced, even if an appeal has been filed against it, for the amounts corresponding to the part of the sentence that has become final (Article 499, ACCPC).

453. The presumptions for execution are: (i) that the judgment is final. This happens following the consent of the party convicted. Consent may be understood to be an express manifestation as such, or the failure to lodge the appeal available in a timely manner; and (ii) that the deadline for compliance with the order has expired. The term begins to run as soon as the judgment is final. When the term for compliance with a judgment has expired, and no remedies have been sought (Article 499, ACCPC), ordering a certain amount to be paid, the settlement of the amount to be paid by the party against whom enforcement is sought must be approved, if this is not clear from the judgment (Article 502, ACCPC). The judgment debtor may however object to the settlement and even appeal it (Article 503, ACCPC).

454. The judge involved in the proceedings also has jurisdiction over the enforcement stage. However, this particular rule regarding jurisdiction may vary according to the location of the assets to be auctioned, or the obligations to be fulfilled, for reasons of convenience with respect to their fulfilment (Article 501, ACCPC).

455. A judgment involving paying certain sums of money is usually the most frequent. Furthermore, its importance lies in the fact that it underpins all the others, as any other kind of judgment can potentially be translated into the payment of a sum of money.

One of the requirements of any judgment is the order for these sums to be liquid and fixed. A judgment for a due or liquidated sum means that its existence and amount is certain and determined or, where appropriate, when the debt in question can be easily and promptly paid. This happens when the amount owed is expressed numerically or, failing that, when the judgment sets the parameters for its calculation in such a way that it can be easily translated into a simple arithmetic operation (Article 502, ACCPC).

If a judgment orders the payment of one amount while another is subject to settlement, the creditor may pursue the payment of the first without having to wait for the approval of the settlement making the second amount due. This makes it possible to avoid unnecessary delays, which could provide the debtor with the possibility to dispose of their assets to the detriment of their creditor (Article 502, ACCPC).

If there is a sum due, whether this is enshrined in the judgment, which may be inferred by means of a simple arithmetic operation, or is the result of the approved settlement, at the request of a party, the debtor may be ordered to pay in order to avoid the attachment of their assets. When this injunction is not met, the debtor's assets may be attached for the corresponding amount (Articles 502, 503 and 504 in fine, ACCPC).

II. Attachment of Debtor's Assets

456. Attachment is an essential aspect of enforcement proceedings, intended to satisfy the creditor's rights through the dispossession and economic transformation or auction of the debtor's assets.

In order to avoid unnecessary damage to the debtor or in response to other objective circumstances, the judge may set limits on the attachment, or substitute the goods offered. These powers must however be exercised prudently.

457. According to Article 242 of the CCCN, all the debtor's assets are involved in the fulfilment of their obligations and constitute a common guarantee for their creditors, with the exception of any declared unattachable or unenforceable in this code or by special laws. Article 743 of the CCCN provides that the debtor's present and future assets constitute a common guarantee for their creditors. The creditor may demand that the debtor's assets be auctioned off, but only to the extent necessary to satisfy their credit. All the creditors may have these assets executed on an equal footing, unless there is a legal reason for preference.

A creditor obtaining the attachment of assets from their debtor has the right to collect their credit, with interest and costs, over other creditors. This priority may only be enforced against unsecured creditors in individual proceedings. If several creditors apply to have the same property of the debtor attached, their rank and order are determined by the date when the attachment was ordered. Subsequent attachments may only affect the surplus remaining after earlier loans requiring attachments have been repaid (Article 745, CCCN).

458. Article 744 of the CCCN lists those assets which may not be attached. These include: (i) the clothes and furniture required for the debtor's essential use, that of their spouse or partner and children; (ii) the instruments necessary for the personal exercise of the debtor's profession, craft or trade; (iii) their graves, unless what is being claimed is their sale, the price of their construction or repair; (iv) property involved in any religion recognized by the State; (v) the rights of usufruct, use and habitation, as well as property easements, (vi) any indemnities corresponding to the debtor for non-pecuniary damages and material damages deriving from harm to their psychophysical integrity; (vii) compensation for maintenance corresponding to their spouse, partner and children with maintenance rights, in the event of homicide; and (viii) other assets declared unattachable or excluded by other laws. According to Articles 244 et seq. of the CCCN, the property inhabited may be included in the family asset regime to preserve it from the creditor action after registration.

III. Execution Order

459. Once the term for compliance with a judgment ordering the payment of a certain amount has expired, and the opposing party has no resources left to bring (Article 499, ACCPC), the judge will proceed to approve the settlement of the amount to be paid by the debtor, when this is not apparent from the judgment itself (Article 502, ACCPC). The person convicted may object to the settlement and even appeal it (Article 503, ACCPC).

Once the amount to be paid by the person convicted has been determined, the judge may, at the request of the creditor, order the attachment of the debtor's assets and require them to sell up (Article 505 ACCPC).

The notice of sale is served by substituted service or equivalent means, except in cases of default.

460. The debtor has a period of five days to file a claim based on false execution, its statute of limitations, make a payment, release from debt, waiting or remission. Only the aforementioned exceptions are admissible, although in terms of case law, in order to enable the fair settlement of the dispute and the due exercise of the right of defence, a broad interpretation is given. The claim of invalid judgment may only be brought in the case of the adulteration or material falsification, total or partial, of the judgment to be enforced. Regarding the motion to dismiss based on the statute of limitations, the term is five years (Article 2560, CCCN), which is calculated from the date when the judgment is final. Payment must be total, prior, timely, undoubted, documented, accepted, and its transfer possible in material and legal terms. For that reason, if after having defaulted, the debtor makes an attempt to pay by depositing the amount claimed, and such a payment is resisted by the creditor, no payment exemption can be justified. Compensation is admitted as case law within this defence, since it is a way of extinguishing obligations, which produces the same legal effects as payment. Release (as a deduction of the amount of the debt), waiting (extension of the term by the debtor) and remission (waiver or forgiveness of the debt) can only arise in the context of certain behaviours or attitudes on the part of the creditor following the judgment. These, once they have been formally accredited, alter the total, partial or temporary enforceability of the ruling. Lis pendens may be filed whenever there is another procedure pending between the same parties by virtue of the same cause for the same object.

Any exceptions must be founded on circumstances pursuant to the pronouncement of the judgment, as previous events are included (even if not previously raised) within the debate developed in the hearing passed as res judicata. They can only be accredited using the records of the proceedings and the documents produced by the creditor, which must be offered and provided when raising an exception. No other means of proof may be admitted, although in certain cases, as long as the summary nature of the proceedings is not undermined, the rigour of this rule may be relaxed. For example, if, in order to verify whether a payment has been made, it is necessary to admit evidence in order to send a notification to a bank or appraise a document. If the pertinent documentary evidence is not attached, the judge will reject the exception without substantiation, and this decision will be irrevocable (Articles 505507, ACCPC).

461. When the debtor does not raise an exception, the resolution ordering the execution to be carried out is final.

When defences are raised, the judge must give the other party the opportunity to answer them and after the response decide what course of action to take. One option is to order the execution proceedings to continue, either dismissing or accepting the defences brought and consequently lifting the embargo on the goods concerned. This resolution may be appealed. If the party appealing is the creditor, then the rejection of the execution will be suspended, and any acts of a mandatory nature continued. However, if the person lodging the appeal is the debtor, the process to monetize their assets will be suspended, unless the creditor is able to provide a guarantee against the damages liable to arise from an auction performed on the basis of a resolution subsequently revoked by the appeal (Articles 508 and 509, ACCPC).

462. When the judgment does not detail the parameters allowing the sum to be easily calculated through a simple arithmetic operation, a settlement must be drawn up.

The settlement is a filing which determines the amounts to be paid subject to the bases and guidelines included in the judgment to be enforced. The settlement must give clear and precise details, including deadlines, the indices to be used and coefficients obtained as well as any other guidelines provided for in the executive order (Articles 165 and 503, ACCPC). When the settlement process becomes complex, expert arbitrators or amiable compositeurs may be called in (Article 516, ACCPC).

The creditor is charged with filing the settlement. If they do not do so within ten days from when the sentence becomes enforceable, it may be filed by the debtor. In either case, the opposing party may intervene. Any objections will be processed as incidental proceedings, which will enable, if necessary, the possibility of producing evidence to that effect in that area.

The judge may dismiss the settlement when the indices and coefficients used and obtained have not been made explicit. If there are no objections, or if these have been dismissed, the judge will approve the settlement.

In *Francisco Cerro v. the Central Bank,*[198] the Supreme Court agreed to review the approval of a settlement, arguing that settlements leading to manifestly unreasonable results, regardless of economic reality, are questionable.

463. Once the settlement is admitted, at the request of a party, an attachment is ordered and the rules governing the execution of the obligations to pay certain sums of money are followed.

464. When the party bound by the sentence does not satisfy their obligations as recognized in the judgment within the period established, the plaintiff may either request a third party to do so at the cost of the debtor or request compensation for the damages incurred by the non-execution. Similarly, when someone violates their obligation not to engage in certain behaviour, the creditor has the right to request

198. *Fallos* 319:2300 (1996).

that the things or situation be restored to the state prior to the violation of the obligation not to do so, at the expense of the debtor, or to receive compensation for the damages caused (Article 514, ACCPC). In both cases, the decision is up to the creditor.

465. In order to induce the debtor to personally comply with the sentence, given that they cannot be physically compelled to do so, the judge may impose mandatory sanctions (Article 37, ACCPC). Although such restrictive application measures are exceptional, they are usually far reaching to ensure that compliance with judicial decisions does not depend exclusively on the will of the person bound to do so.

466. Once the party has exercised their option, the judge may order either the destruction or completion of works by a third party at the cost of the debtor or the payment of the damages. In the latter case, when the operations are simple or the judgment sets the amount to be applied in the case of non-execution, the settlement will be approved in accordance with previously specified rules. In the other cases, especially when these are more complex, summary proceedings are recommended. The decision about the procedure is irrevocable (Articles 513 and 514, ACCPC).

467. The judgment notarizing the deed must contain the warning that if the person obliged to sign the title transfer deed does not do so within the period established, the judge will sign it on their behalf, at the debtor's expense (Article 512, ACCPC).

The creditor must certify that there are no obligations in their charge and identify the notary public agreed between the parties or otherwise propose one to be appointed. The judge signs on behalf of the debtor, in their name and at their expense.

468. When the judgment mandates that something be delivered, and this is not carried out within the legal term, and other necessary measures for execution have been met, the judge will issue an order to dispossess the debtor of the object being held (Article 515, ACCPC).

If the debtor cannot be dispossessed of the object of litigation because this is either physically or legally impossible, the norm stipulates that its value in pecuniary terms may be paid in money plus damages, if these can be proven. The amounts of the value of the object in question, and any eventual damages are enshrined in a settlement or by means of summary proceedings at the judge's discretion, a judgment which is irrevocable.

If the settlement is complex, slow and difficult to justify or requires special knowledge, the judge may call upon expert arbiters or amiable compositeurs to determine it (Article 516, ACCPC) for the effects of enforcing the judgment, which may not be appealed.

The parties must give their consent when amiable compositeurs are involved, and these must act in accordance with the guidelines set. Likewise, the decision requiring the matter to be resolved by the arbitrators must also detail the guidelines governing their actions. There are certain cases when such a degree of complexity is likely or common, such as when it involves the liquidation of a company. In these cases, the judge has to choose between ordinary, summary or incidental proceedings, taking into account the particular characteristics and size of the assets, the magnitude of the company, and the relationships and interests of the parties in dispute. Whatever the judge's decision about the proceedings to be followed, it is not appealable.

§3. Enforcing Judgments Against the State

469. Due to the economic crises affecting Argentina on a cyclical basis, there are innumerable barriers limiting the rights of those who bring financial claims against it. In order to enforce judgments in their favour, creditors have to respect certain terms and conditions that end up deferring enforceability and making it difficult to achieve.

Law 3952 (1900) on lawsuits against the RA in Article 7 provides that judicial convictions against the Nation are limited to declaring the existence of the right, meaning that they constitute the recognition of the right sought. In *Pietranera,*[199] the Supreme Court understood that Article 7 of Law 3952 does not imply a form of authorization allowing the State not to comply with judicial sentences. This would mean placing it above and beyond legal obligations, when it is precisely the State which must ensure their observance. The SC added that once the conviction has been signed and the term for voluntary compliance has elapsed, it may enjoin the organ accused to state when it intends to comply with the sentence, under warning that, if there is no response or the period indicated is unreasonable, this will be set by the court. Once the term of the injunction has expired without any response or if the State fails to comply, the judge is empowered to enforce the judgment.

The RA has defaulted on its external debt five times throughout its history: 1827, 1890, 1982, 2001 and 2019. To this should be added the so-called Bonex Plan of 1989, which also meant a restructuring of public obligations. Law 25,344 (2002) pertaining to the economic-financial emergency of the national State and the consolidation of debts was in force until 2018.

It is common for the State, when obliged to comply with a judgment, to request extensions for doing so, invoking the impossibility of compliance as public interests are at stake.

If the issue involves judgments obliging it to pay sums of money not included in a debt consolidation regime, once the judgment is firm, the creditor must first settle the accounts. After these are approved and signed, the creditors will be in a position to request payment and can require the judge to order the pertinent summons to be issued to the defendant state body. If the expenditure is not authorized, the necessary provisions must be made to include it in the general budget for the following fiscal year. When the budget for the financial year when the sentence is to be met lacks sufficient credit, the executive must make the necessary provisions to include it as an expense in the following year's budget. The obligations are paid in order of seniority according to the notification date, until the resources assigned by the National Congress have been exhausted. Hence, the National State can take some

199. *Fallos* 265.291 (1966).

three years before paying the credit which is the subject of the judgment. Direct execution is only appropriate if the State does not meet its obligation and this period has elapsed.

In *Giovagnoli*,[200] the Supreme Court held that Law 24,624 (1995) whose Article 19 established the non-attachment of public sector assets intended to cover budgetary expenditures, thus protecting their free availability should be interpreted in such a way as to be commensurate with the principles and guarantees enshrined in the AC and the rest of the legal system. The SC pointed out that a mechanical and generalized approach cannot be taken since it would infringe the rights of individuals in a position to execute sentences in accordance with these last two rules, which, incidentally, is inconsistent with the intention of the legislator. Thus, it interpreted that Article 19 was adopted to ensure that rational guidelines were followed when fulfilling the obligations incumbent upon the State, preventing the administration from being placed, through the rule of a peremptory judicial mandate, in the situation of not being able to satisfy the requirement, because it lacks the funds provided by the budget for this purpose. Hence, it does not follow that the State is beyond the legal order that it is obliged to protect, or that it is exempt from complying with court decisions. According to the Supreme Court, the creditor may execute the sentence requiring a sum of money to be paid when (i) the executive, despite having been notified of the final settlement, did not request the National Congress to include it in the following year's fiscal budget and the regular period of sessions where the budget law containing the respective credit should have been discussed has closed, or (ii) when the expenditure is included in the general budget of the National Administration. The Supreme Court also argued that the lack of budgetary allocation for paying the credit recognized in court must be proven by whoever calls for Article 19 of Law 24,624 to be applied.

It should also be noted that Law 26,854 (2013) introduced a special regime for interim measures in those cases where the executive is a party or is involved in some way. This regime establishes a set of strict requirements and guidelines limiting the effectiveness of injunctions that could potentially be brought against the National State in order to ensure the effective compliance with the sentence sought.

---

200. *Fallos* 322:2132 (1999).

Chapter 2. Recognition and Enforcement of Foreign Judgments

§1. Multilateral and Bilateral Treaties

470. Judgments passed by foreign courts may be enforced according to the provisions of the treaties signed with the country in question. Law 22,921 (1983) enshrined the provisions of the Inter-American Convention on Extraterritorial Validity of Foreign Judgments and Arbitral Awards and the Inter-American Convention on Execution of Preventive Measures, signed in Montevideo on 8 May 1979, at the second of the Inter-American Specialized Conferences on Private International Law[201] of the Organization of American States. Within MERCOSUR, the Protocol for Jurisdictional Co-operation and Assistance in Civil, Commercial, Labour and Administrative Matters, signed on 27 June 1992, was enshrined in Law 24,578 (1995), whose Articles 18 to 24 detail norms regarding the enforcement of judgments and arbitration awards.

Likewise, Law 25,935 (2004) enshrines the Agreement for Jurisdictional Co-operation and Assistance in Civil, Commercial, Labour and Administrative Matters signed between the Mercosur states and the Republics of Bolivia and Chile, in Buenos Aires on 5 July 2002. It contains rules on the enforcement of judgments and awards in its Chapter V.[202] The RA signed the following bilateral cooperation and legal assistance treaties containing rules on the execution of sentences: (i) with China (Law 26,672 (2011)); (ii), with Tunisia (Law 26,667 (2011)); (iii) with the Russian Federation (Law 25,595 (2002)); (iv) with France (Law 24,107 (1992)); and (v) with Italy (Law 23,720 (1989)).

Likewise, Article 68 section 2 of the ACHR provides that the part of the ICHR ruling ordering compensation may be enforced in the respective country according to the internal procedures applicable to the enforcement of judgments against the State, without any type of exequatur or summary proceeding.

§2. Exequatur

471. For a foreign judgment to obtain exequatur and be enforced in the RA, it must comply with the provisions of Article 517 of the ACCPC, which establishes the following requirements: (i) that a judgment with res judicata authority in the State where it has been pronounced is issued by a competent court according to the Argentine norms of international jurisdiction, and is the consequence of the exercise of a personal action, or of a real action on personal property, if it has been transferred to the Republic during or after the court proceedings held abroad; (ii) that the defendant against whom the judgment is to be enforced was personally summoned

201. The status of the ratifications of these conventions may be consulted at http://www.oas.org/es/sla/ddi/docs/derecho_internacional_privado_resumen_estado_firmas_ratificaciones.pdf.

202. The status of the ratifications of these treaties may be consulted at https://www.mercosur.int/documentos-y-normativa/tratados/.

and their defence guaranteed; (iii) that the judgment meets the necessary requirements to be considered as such in the place where it was issued as well as the conditions of authenticity required by national law;[203] (iv) that the judgment does not affect the principles of public order enshrined in Argentine law; and (v) that the sentence is not incompatible with another pronounced, previously or simultaneously, by an Argentine court.

The competent court for enforcing a foreign judgment is the corresponding Court of First Instance, depending on the matter which is the subject of the foreign judgment (Article 518, ACCPC).

472. The request is made before this magistrate, accompanied by (i) the testimony of the foreign judgment (duly legalized and translated); and (ii) the testimony of the actions proving that the judgment is final and all other requirements have been met. If the execution of the foreign judgment is ordered, this must be done in accordance with the procedures for the execution of judgments passed by Argentine courts. It must be made clear whether the judgment orders the payment of a liquid or illiquid amount or is about doing or not doing, giving or not giving something (Article 518, ACCPC).

A resolution recognizing the judgment as enforceable may be appealed by the aggrieved party.

If the judge validates the judgment as an order, the relevant guidelines for the enforcement of judgments must be followed for the enforcement process.

473. Regarding arbitration decisions, Argentine Law 23,619 (1988) enshrines the Convention on the Recognition and Enforcement of Foreign Arbitral Awards, commonly known as the New York Convention of 1958. In *Deutsche Rückversicherung AG v. Caja Nacional de Ahorro y Seguro,*[204] the Supreme Court held that Article III of the 1958 Convention on the Recognition and Enforcement of Foreign Arbitral Awards provides that the Contracting States shall not impose conditions appreciably more rigorous than those applicable to the recognition or enforcement of national arbitration awards. Consequently, if a national judgment is issued in violation of debt consolidation rules, the solution is not the nullity of the ruling issued under said conditions, but its adaptation to that legal regime. In the case of a foreign arbitral award, enforcement must be carried out in accordance with the provisions for public order making up the debt consolidation regime. However, any omission in the application of that regime by the arbitral tribunal may not inexorably prevent its recognition and execution.

In the case of foreign arbitral awards, in addition to the aforementioned requirements, Article 519 bis of the ACCPC orders the following: (i) that the extension of jurisdiction in favour of the foreign arbitral tribunal is valid, meaning that it deals exclusively with matters regarding international assets, not those cases where

203. Argentine Law 23,458 ratifies the 1961 Hague Convention abolishing the requirement to legalize foreign public documents for all State parties, establishing the apostille provided therein as the only formality. If the judgment is issued by a State not a party, it will be necessary to request the intervention of the Argentine Consulate in the location where the judgment or award which needs to be converted into an enforceable ruling was issued.

204. *Fallos* 342:1524 (2019).

Argentine courts have exclusive jurisdiction or where a prorogation is prohibited by law (519 bis, paragraph 1, ACCPC) and (ii) that the issues be subject to arbitration according to Argentine law (519 bis subsection 2°, ACCPC). The norm establishes that any questions that could be the object of a transaction are arbitrable. Once these measures have been met, a request must be made for the execution of the foreign arbitral award before the corresponding judge of first instance through the exequatur procedure.

In addition to these requirements, the enforcement of foreign court awards requires proof that the extension of jurisdiction is admitted and does not affect the exclusive international jurisdiction of the Argentine courts or lead to a legal prohibition, and that the issues making up the arbitration agreement are not excluded from the arbitration procedure (Articles 519 bis and 737, ACCPC).

474. A foreign judgment may be usefully asserted in proceedings to establish a res judicata exception or as evidence. In those cases, it must also be proven that the judgment meets the requirements established in Article 517 of the ACCPC.

Chapter 3. Documentary Proceedings

475. In order to collect monetary debts, the ACCPC incorporated a limited number of defences into a document as part of summary proceedings called execution proceedings. In the event that whoever is defeated in the execution proceedings has access to defences that they have been unable to raise so far, as they were not included on the ACCPC's list, they may request a subsequent hearing once the judgments imposed in the proceedings have been complied with (Article 553).

476. Once the lawsuit has been filed, accompanied by the document claiming payment of a debt, the judge, after analysing the document, issues a resolution ordering a judicial officer to go to the defendant's domicile to collect the payment, attach any assets available, and summon them to enter a plea within a period of five days (Articles 531 and 542, ACCPC).

The ACCPC establishes the essential elements or presumptions that a document must meet in order to be considered as an automatically enforceable document. It states that executive proceedings may be followed, provided that by virtue of a document entailing enforcement, the lawsuit does in fact involve an enforceable obligation to pay liquid amounts of money or those that may be easily settled (Article 520, ACCPC).

The elements making up the automatically enforceable document include the existence of a money debt, instrumented on the basis of a legal act, or recorded in a representative instrument, which is liquid or may be easily settled, enforceable (that is, not subject to any specific term), and is not governed by any condition or provision manifested as required by law.

Article 523 of the ACCPC lists some of these document forms, but adds that others, that are enforceable by law without being subject to a special procedure, also share these characteristics. The documents mentioned in Article 523 of the ACCPC are as follows: (i) public instruments; (ii) legally recognized private instruments or those whose signature has been certified by a notary public; (iii) the recognition of liquid and enforceable debt as rendered before a competent judge; (iv) the approved or recognized account; (v) a bill of exchange, credit invoice, voucher or promissory note, cheques, and proof of the balance in the bank's checking account; (vi) credit due from real estate rentals or leasing; and (vii) the credit for common expenses (Article 524, ACCPC).

Additionally, there are executive proceedings (Article 525, ACCPC), considered to be an expeditious means of making or completing documentation that does not in itself contain all the elements required to enforce execution. Through executive proceedings, certain aspects pertaining to the documentation may be corrected by the creditor, who may request: (i) that documents not requiring enforcing be recognized; (ii) that for a lease enforcement, the defendant should state whether they are a tenant or leaseholder and, if so, display the latest receipt of payment. If the required party categorically denies that they are a tenant and their condition as such cannot be speedily proven in irrefutable fashion, the executive proceedings will not continue and the payment of the credit will be claimed through ordinary proceedings. If, during this process, the status of tenant is proven, the judgment will include the imposition of a fine in favour of the other party, equivalent to 30% of the amount of the debt; and (iii) that the judge designate the deadline for making the payment, if this is not specified in the document establishing the obligation, or if the debtor is authorized to do so when they can, or when they have the means to do so.

477. Article 544 of the ACCPC establishes the only exceptions that the defendant can raise as: (i) incompetence; (ii) lack of legal status of the creditor, debtor or their representatives, due to their lack of civil capacity to stand trial or because they lack sufficient representation; (iii) lis pendens under way in another competent court; (iv) false or defective documentation used to request enforcement. The charge of falsehood may only be brought when the document has been tampered with. Defectiveness only concerns the extrinsic forms of the documentation but do not question the legitimacy of the cause. The express recognition of the signature does not prevent the judge from admitting the exception of falsehood based on the adulteration of the document, although such exceptions are inadmissible if the existence of the debt has not been denied; (v) statute of limitations; (vi) documented payment, whether total or partial; (vii) compensation of credit in liquid form resulting from a document that entails enforcement; (viii) downsizing, postponement, remission, novation, transaction, conciliation or documented agreement; or (ix) res judicata.

478. The debtor may also, within a period of five days, request that enforcement be declared invalid. This may only be based on the following: (i) if the payment notice was not legally undertaken, as and when, in the act of requesting the declaration of nullity, the debtor deposited the sum set in the legal order, or raised exceptions; (ii) the rules established for summary proceedings are not complied with, for as long as the debtor is unaware of the obligation, denies the authenticity of the signature, their status as tenant, or the fulfilment of the condition or provision requested. A petition for annulment is inadmissible if the debtor does not mention the objections raised that they have been unable to bring, in terms of showing the serious nature of their request.

479. In principle, defences aimed at examining the cause of the obligation are inadmissible. However, despite the limited nature of the defences that a defendant may raise in summary proceedings, in *Burman*[205], where the family home of a retiree with scarce economic resources was at stake, the Supreme Court argued that the limiting nature of summary proceedings cannot entail manifest excess ritual, as this is incompatible with the right of defence. This would happen if the debtors were deprived of the possibility of alleging, in a foreclosure, any modifications to the collection proceedings and other legal remedies conducive to mitigating its effects, without any other basis than the dogmatic statement that such arguments do not refer to extrinsic forms or to the basic presumptions of summary proceedings. These are judged ineffective in terms of excluding the analysis of issues related to the

205. *Fallos* 305:226 (1983).

theory of unforeseen contingencies and the regular exercise of rights. A similar criterion was followed in *Municipality of the City of Buenos Aires v. Hospital Alemán*,[206] where it was held that an extraordinary federal appeal may be exceptionally admitted in an enforcement judgment when it is clear that there is no enforceable debt. This was based on the assumption that otherwise, the situation would end up giving way to excessive formal rigour with the ensuing serious impairment of constitutional guarantees.

480. Defences and evidence offered must be made known to the other party bringing the executive proceedings who has a period of five days to answer and offer evidence (Article 547, ACCPC).

481. After the evidence offered by the parties has been produced, the judge will issue an order of judicial sale, when the goods attached will be auctioned and sold off. If the defendant litigated without a valid reason, or obstructed the normal course of the proceedings with manifestly inappropriate articulations, or otherwise unjustifiably delayed proceedings, a fine is imposed in favour of the executor, amounting to between 5% and 30% of the debt, according to the degree of procedural misconduct and its delaying effects on proceedings (Articles 550 and 551, ACCPC).

482. The order of judicial sale may be appealed: (i) when the judge dismisses any exceptions without substantiation; (ii) when the exceptions have been processed as being of pure law; (iii) when evidence has been given regarding objections and defences; or (iv) when the evidence covers points beyond the natural scope of the proceedings, or causes irreparable damage to the subsequent ordinary trial.

The model of summary proceedings followed by the ACCPC is structured around a subpoena to raise defences. This summons is understood as an invitation for all possible defences to be raised, and far from being a speedier way to comply with obligations, it in fact constitutes a much lengthier process over time.

483. The new ACCPC bill incorporates order payment procedures, whose purpose was to entrust the presumed debtor with the initiative to start proceedings to discuss the legitimacy of the debt being claimed. Article 445 identifies the cases where a petition for order payment procedures may be filed and establishes that these may be selected by whoever intends to: (i) pay an obligation implemented through the securities foreseen by the CCCN and through special laws; (ii) pay a monetary obligation of any amount, liquid or easily settled, determined, expired and enforceable which has not been implemented in an automatically enforceable document; (iii) fulfil an enforceable obligation to give quantities of things or securities, or to give certain, determined personal things; (iv) evict someone from real estate property due to non-payment, following the expiry of the contractual term or when the obligation to return the property can be enforced; (v) grant a public deed; (vi) transfer motor vehicles; (vii) cancel a pledge or mortgage; or (viii) divide up a co-ownership.

---

206. *Fallos* 320:58 (1997). Reiterated in the *Faget de Adzija* case published in *Fallos* 320:2176 (1997).

The proceedings begin with a petition to order payment procedures, in which the obligation claimed must be identified. If the issue involves the payment of a pecuniary obligation, the capital and interest rate(s) must be indicated, detailing the period covered and the penalties incurred as well as a brief description of the circumstances invoked as the basis of the obligation being claimed if this is not a security, and the documentary evidence that the party intends to use. In the request to order payment procedures, the plaintiff must declare that the information provided is true. Any deliberate falsehood or misrepresentation may lead to a fine being imposed in favour of the opposing party of between 10% and 30% of the intended value (Article 446, new ACCPC bill).

The judge will carry out a formal admissibility check of the request for order payment procedures. This involves evaluating whether the request is properly founded, and whether the documentary evidence is sufficient to conclude that, after a preliminary examination, compliance with the obligations claimed may be ruled, by means of an order for payment (Article 447, new ACCPC bill).

According to Article 448 of the new ACCPC bill, the payment order must record that it was issued based on the information provided by the petitioner, without prior accreditation, and that whatever is laid down therein will give rise to a legally enforceable document unless opposition is raised within the same proceedings. The judge will order the defendant to choose within ten days whether they will: (i) comply with the order for payment procedures and prove as much during the proceedings, when this is an out-of-court process, in which case they do not have to pay court fees; or (ii) file an opposition claim, invoking the facts and rights against the origin of the plaintiff's claim and adding the proof that they intend to use. If an opposition claim is filed against the judgment ordering payment, the judge will order it to be processed according to the rules of the hearing or special proceedings, taking into account the circumstances of the case, unless the order for payment proceedings concern a security, in which case Articles 449 to 453 apply. Filing an opposition claim suspends the enforceability of the judgment for payment.

Chapter 4. Judicial Sale of Assets

484. The ACCPC regulates the different phases of the sale of goods (Articles 563 to 593). This process is controlled by the judge who appoints a legal auctioneer to sell the goods at a public auction.

If the vendor causes any unnecessary delay in the execution of the sentence, the judge will impose a fine that can vary between 10% and 30% of the amount of the sentence.

485. Electronic auction procedures have been incorporated into the Procedural Codes of the Provinces of Mendoza (Articles 278 et seq., 2017) and Chaco (Articles 563 et seq., 2017). In the provinces of Buenos Aires,[207] Cordoba,[208] Entre Rios[209] and San Luis, the judicial power has established procedures for the electronic auction of goods.

486. Law 24,441 (1994) allows for judicial foreclosure to take place out of court. Articles 52 to 67 deal with the procedure, which is only available in cases where the parties have agreed to issue a collateral mortgage note. Thus, after making an extrajudicial summons for the amount owed to be paid, the creditor may present the collateral mortgage note or coupons required, if these had been in circulation, before the competent judge to request that the state of occupation and the delivery of the provisional tenure of the property be checked. These are procedures carried out in the presence of a notary public designated by the creditor in the role of judicial collaborator. Then, in accordance with the provisions of Article 57 of Law 24,441, once the state of the property has been verified, the creditor will themselves request, without the need for judicial intervention, the sale at public auction of the property involved, by the auctioneer designated in the usual market conditions.

487. Another assumption legislated in the Argentine law regarding the private sale of goods is the case regarding the execution of a pledge (Article 2229, CCCN). The creditor can sell the pledged property at a public auction, duly announced ten days earlier in the local newspaper where legal publications are printed and where, according to the contract, the property should be found.

If the pledge involves securities or other negotiable goods on public exchanges or markets, the sale can be made in the usual way in these markets at the quoted price.

---

207. http://www.scba.gov.ar/subastas/.
208. https://subastas.justiciacordoba.gob.ar/regdamientos/.
209. http://www.jusentrerios.gov.ar/22/09/2020/el-poder-judicial-aprobo-las-subastas-virtuales/.

Part X. Arbitration

Chapter 1. General

488. The CCCN considers that there is an arbitration contract when the parties decide to submit to one or more arbitrators all or some of the disputes that have arisen or may arise between them for a decision concerning a specific legal, contractual or non-contractual relationship, under private law as long as public order is not compromised (Article 1649).

The ACCPC dedicates Book Six to regulating the arbitration process. According to Article 736 of the ACCPC, all issues between parties, with the exception of those that cannot be the subject of a transaction (Article 737, ACCPC), may be submitted to the decision of arbitration judges, before or after the initiation of a judicial process.

489. There are various criteria for classifying arbitration. In terms of origin, arbitration may arise from an agreement whereby the parties decide to submit a dispute to an arbitration tribunal for their judgment by signing an arbitration agreement; or if this has been imposed by law.

Depending on which party has to make the designation, arbitration may be either institutional, meaning that a specific arbitration institution is chosen to manage the process, or ad hoc, when specific people are appointed to act as arbitrators.

According to the international commercial arbitration Law 27,449 (2018), arbitration is considered international when the parties to the agreement are from different countries at the time of the execution of that agreement. Or when the place selected for the arbitration, in compliance with a substantial part of the obligations inherent to their commercial relationship or the location most closely connected to the object of the litigation, is outside the country where the parties are based.

There are different ways of resolving disputes submitted to arbitration. A distinction may be made between: (i) arbitration in law, in which the arbitrators must abide by the rules of ordinary or summary proceedings, as long as the parties have said nothing and the award is rendered according to the statute of limitations governing the content and form of judicial judgments; and (ii) equity arbitration or involving amiable compositeurs, where the arbitrators are not subject to legal forms and may rule according to their knowledge and understanding, limited only by the need to respect the parties' right of defence (Article 769, ACCPC).

The ACCPC provides in this regard that if nothing is stipulated in the agreement about whether the arbitration should be in law or in equity, or if the arbitrators are authorized to decide the controversy according to equity, it should be understood that this should concern amiable compositeurs (Article 766, ACCPC). However, the ACCC, in line with comparative trends in the matter, tends towards arbitration in law when the parties are silent on the matter (Article 1652, ACCC). Some authors add a third type of arbitration, referring to arbitration expertise (Article 773, ACCPC).

490. The ACCPC dictates that all disputes between parties may be subject to arbitration, except those that cannot be settled in this way (Article 737, ACCPC). This means that disputes concerning family matters, things that do not concern trade or are not subject to conventions, are not arbitrable. The ACCC excludes the following from arbitration contracts: those referring to the marital status or the capabilities of individuals; family issues; those related to user and consumer rights; standard-form agreements whatever their purpose; or those related to employment relationships. Likewise, it provides that the provisions on arbitration may not be applied to disputes to which national or local states are a party.

491. Regarding capacity, the ACCPC provides that people who are unable to dispose of property rights may not agree on an arbitration clause. When the law requires judicial authorization for acts of disposition, this will also be necessary to celebrate the agreement. Once authorization is granted, the award does not need to be judicial approval (Article 738, ACCPC).

Chapter 2. Arbitration Award and Autonomy of the Parties

§1. Arbitration Clause

492. The arbitration clause is the convention drawn up between the parties wherein they stipulate they will submit the conflicts derived from a relationship of substantial law to the judgment of arbitrators.

The ACCPC provides that submission to arbitration may be agreed in the contract or in a subsequent act (Article 736, ACCPC). For its part, the ACCC establishes that the arbitration agreement must be written and may be included in an arbitration clause as part of a contract, or in an independent agreement, a statute or regulation. The reference made in a contract to a document containing an arbitration clause constitutes an arbitration contract, provided that the contract is in writing and the reference implies that this clause is part of the contract (Article 1650, ACCC).

Rendering an arbitration clause has certain effects: (i) it empowers the contracting party to demand that the agreement be signed in court and request an arbitral tribunal; and (ii) it supports any challenges brought in the event that one of the parties has sued the other before the state courts.

§2. Arbitration Agreement

493. The arbitration agreement enshrines the parties' determination of the issues to be decided by arbitration, including the appointment of the arbitrators (or amiable compositeurs) and the requirements to be observed during the proceedings and met with respect to the award. There is an assumption underlying the arbitration process. The agreement must be formalized by public deed or private instrument, in a document signed before the judge trying the case or before the one who would have otherwise have done so (Article 739, ACCPC).

As for content, the ACCPC distinguishes between the mandatory clauses which must be included under penalty of nullity and merely optional ones. Mandatory requirements are as follows: details of the date, name and address of the grantors; name and address of the arbitrators; the issues being submitted to arbitration, stating their circumstances and stipulating a fine to be paid in the event of one party failing to perform the acts required to carry out the agreement (Article 740, ACCPC). The optional requirements set by the ACCPC include the following: (i) the procedure applicable and the location where the arbitrators are to hear and decide (if the location is not given, it should be where the agreement is granted); (ii) the deadline for rendering the award; (iii) the appointment of a secretary for the panel; (iv) the secretarial costs must be paid by the party appealing the award before they can be heard, if they do not waive their right to appeal and there is no annulment (Article 741, ACCPC). The ACCC adds to these the language in which the procedure is to be held, the confidentiality of the proceedings and the distribution of costs (Article 1658).

The arbitration agreement is extinguished by: (i) the unanimous decision of those who contracted it; (ii) the expiry of the period indicated in the agreement or the legal period indicated, in its absence. However, extinction does not exempt from liability for damages either the arbitrators if the corresponding period expired in vain or the parties, who must pay a fine; and (iii) the expiry of a period of three months during which neither the parties nor the arbitrators have done anything to advance the proceedings.

§3. International Arbitration

494. Law 27,449 defines an arbitration agreement as the pact by which the parties decide to submit to arbitration all controversies, or certain controversies that have arisen or may arise between them, with respect to a specific legal, contractual or non-contractual relationship. It can take the form of an arbitration clause included in a contract or a separate agreement. It must be enshrined in writing, recording content that reflects the exchange of petitioner and respondent briefs whereby the existence of an agreement is affirmed by one party without being denied by the other. The reference made in a contract to a document containing an arbitration clause constitutes an arbitration contract, provided that the contract is in writing and the reference implies that this clause forms part of the contract (Article 1650, ACCC).

Chapter 3. Composition and Performance of Arbitrators and Amiable Compositeurs

495. To be appointed as arbitrator, the ACCPC only requires people to be of age and in the full exercise of their civil rights (Article 743). Although all that ACCC requires is for people to exhibit full civil capacity, the parties may stipulate the appointment of people meeting certain conditions regarding nationality, profession or experience (Article 1660, ACCC).

496. The ACCPC authorizes one or more arbitrators to be appointed. The parties are empowered to choose whomsoever they prefer to act as arbitrator and intervene in the proceedings. If more than one is needed, each of the parties may designate one. The third party may be appointed by common agreement or by the other arbitrators appointed. If this is not possible, the court that would have heard the case had arbitration not been agreed upon may intervene (Article 743, ACCPC). The ACCC requires an odd number of arbitrators to be appointed. If the parties have nothing to say on the subject, it may be presumed that there are three, leaving the determination of the selection method in their hands, stipulating a supplementary mechanism in the event that nothing is agreed (Article 1659, ACCC). The ACCC also states that any clause privileging a party regarding the appointment of arbitrators will be void (Article 1661, ACCC). It also states that the parties may entrust the administration of the arbitration proceedings and the appointment of the arbitrators to civil associations or other national or foreign entities whose by-laws allow them to do so. In these cases, it provides that the arbitration regulations of the administering entities govern the entire arbitration process as part of the arbitration contract (Article 1657, ACCC).

497. In international arbitration, the parties may freely determine the number of arbitrators and the procedure for their appointment. If they do not do so, the arbitral tribunal will be composed of three arbitrators appointed in accordance with the procedures established by law. As above, any clause privileging a party regarding the appointment of arbitrators will be void (Articles 22 et seq., Law 27,449).

498. Once the agreement is granted, the arbitrators are informed and must duly accept this responsibility before either the court clerk (Article 744, ACCPC) or by notarial or public deed (Article 739, ACCPC) undertaking to faithfully carry out their duties. The acceptance of the arbitrators empowers the parties to compel them to carry out their duties, under the pain of answering for damages (Article 745, ACCPC).

499. The ACCC establishes certain obligations derived from the contract signed between each of the parties and the arbitrators. These include disclosing any circumstance prior to acceptance or which arises subsequently that could undermine their independence and impartiality. Arbitrators must also remain in the arbitral tribunal until the process is over, unless there is a legally justifiable impediment or a legitimate cause for resignation; they must respect the confidentiality of the proceedings; have enough time to diligently attend the arbitration proceedings; personally participate in hearings; deliberate with other arbitrators; render the award with reason and within the established period. In all cases, the arbitrators must guarantee that the parties are equally treated and respect the principle of contradictory debate, as well as ensuring that each of them receives sufficient opportunity to assert their rights (Article 1662, ACCC). Unless otherwise stipulated, the arbitration contract grants the arbitrators the power to decide on their own competence, including concerning objections regarding the existence or validity of the arbitration agreement or any other which could be an obstacle to their gaining an in-depth understanding of the controversy at stake (Article 1654, ACCC). If any of the arbitrators resigns, is recused, becomes incapacitated or dies, they must be replaced in the manner agreed in the agreement. If nothing has been foreseen, the judge will appoint a new arbitrator (Article 745, ACCPC).

500. The ACCPC states that the grounds for disqualification of judges are applicable to arbitrators and amiable compositeurs and forbids recusal without cause (Article 746, ACCPC). Similarly, the ACCC acknowledges that the parties enjoy the same powers, specifying that they may issue a challenge for the same reasons as those applied to judges, according to the law applicable where arbitration takes place. Any challenge must be resolved by the entity administering the arbitration or, failing that, by the court. The parties may also agree that such a challenge be resolved by the other arbitrators (Article 1663, ACCC).

Law 27,449 establishes that a person notified of their possible appointment as an arbitrator must reveal any circumstances that could give rise to justified doubts about their impartiality or independence. An arbitrator must, as from their appointment and throughout arbitration proceedings, promptly disclose any such circumstances to the parties, unless they have already been informed. The parties may only issue a challenge if there are circumstances giving rise to justified doubts regarding the impartiality or independence of the arbitrators, or if they lack the qualifications formerly agreed by the parties (Articles 27 and 28, Law 27,449).

501. Regarding the fees for their professional services, the ACCPC provides that these are regulated by the judge. Arbitrators may request the judge to order the deposit or attachment of the amount corresponding to them as fees, if the goods that are the subject of the trial are insufficient as collateral (Article 772, ACCPC).

Although the ACCC leaves this up to the parties, it foresees the final determination being taken by the judge, on the basis of local rates charged by lawyers for extrajudicial work (Article 1665, ACCC).

Chapter 4. Provisional Measures and Preliminary Awards

502. As they lack the power conferred by law (imperium) neither arbitrators nor amiable compositeurs may order compulsory or enforcement measures and must request judicial assistance (Article 753, ACCPC). Based on this provision, the power of the arbitrators to take precautionary measures has been discussed.

Accordingly, the ACCC establishes that – except as otherwise provided – the arbitration contract empowers arbitrators to adopt, at the request of either party, the precautionary measures deemed necessary concerning the matter at stake. Arbitrators may require the applicant to put up bail. The court is responsible for executing any precautionary measures and, where appropriate, ordering pretrial proceedings. The parties may also request the judge to adopt these measures without this being considered a breach of the arbitration contract or a waiver of arbitration jurisdiction. Although this does not undermine the powers wielded by the arbitrators, any previous measures adopted by them may be challenged in court if they violate constitutional rights or are unreasonable (Article 1655, ACCC).

503. In international commercial arbitration, unless otherwise agreed by the parties, the arbitral tribunal may issue precautionary measures and preliminary orders at the request of a party.

According to Law 27,449, precautionary measures are any temporary measures taken at any time prior to issuing the award definitively settling the controversy by the arbitral tribunal ordering one of the parties to maintain or re-establish the status quo pending the resolution of the dispute. The arbitral tribunal may adopt measures to prevent any current or imminent damage or impairment of the arbitration procedure, and may order a party to refrain from carrying out certain acts that could give rise to some form of damage. They may also provide some means of preserving assets to enforce an award, or to preserve elements of evidence that could be pertinent for resolving the controversy. A preliminary order may be issued to prevent any party from obstructing the purpose of the requested precautionary measure.

The arbitral tribunal may modify, suspend or revoke any precautionary measure or preliminary order that it has granted, at either the request of one of the parties or, in exceptional circumstances, ex officio, after notifying the parties. Only judges have the jurisdiction to recognize or enforce the precautionary measures taken by the arbitral tribunal before the competent court (Articles 38, 39, 42, 50, 59 and 102, Law 27,449).

Chapter 5. Development of Arbitration Procedures

504. With regard to the performance of the arbitrators, the procedure varies depending on whether it is an arbitration in law or an equity arbitration. In the first case, the parties may agree on the procedure they deem appropriate when signing the agreement or in a later document. If they do not sign a document, they must decide on the applicable rules (of ordinary or summary proceedings), taking into account the nature of the matter (Article 749, ACCPC). In the case of equity arbitration, the amiable compositeurs may proceed without being required to be subject to legal forms, being limited to receiving the background information and documentation presented by the parties and requesting any supporting data deemed appropriate (Article 769, ACCPC).

505. In international commercial arbitration, it is the arbitrators themselves who decide on their competence, including any exceptions concerning the existence or validity of the arbitration agreement itself. Law 27,449 determines the autonomy of the arbitration clause, by which the nullity of the contract does not *ipso iure* entail annulling the arbitration clause contained therein. The arbitration procedure may be freely determined by the parties, while maintaining the guarantees of equality of the parties and ensuring they have every opportunity to enforce their rights. In the absence of an agreement, the arbitral tribunal may conduct the arbitration in the manner deemed appropriate. This allows them to determine the admissibility, relevance and value of evidence (Articles 35, 36, 62, 63 and 64, Law 27,449).

Unless agreed by the parties, arbitration proceedings will begin on the date when the defendant has received the request to submit the controversy to arbitration. The plaintiff must provide a statement of the facts underpinning the claim within the term agreed by the parties or set by the arbitral tribunal, as well as details of the controversial points and object of the claim, while the defendant is required to respond to the alleged points. They must also offer all the evidence they wish to present or offer within this term, and the court must set a hearing to examine it unless otherwise agreed by the parties (Articles 67, 70 and 71, Law 27,449).

Chapter 6. Arbitration Award

506. The award is the final decision in the litigation submitted before the arbitrators or amiable compositeurs. The resolution decides on the issues formerly laid out in the arbitration agreement (Article 499, ACCPC).

The ACCPC requires the arbitrators to pronounce their ruling on all the claims submitted for their decision, within the period set in the agreement, with any extensions agreed by the interested parties. Incidental issues and those which the arbitrators have consented to treat are included among those on which they must decide (Article 753, ACCPC). In this sense, the award must decide on the imposition of costs, in the manner provided by the ACCPC. On this point, it is stipulated that the party that fails to do what is required to resolve the agreement must pay the costs.

Law 27,449 requires the arbitration award to be rendered in writing and signed by the arbitrator or arbitrators involved. Unlike the Model Law of the United Nations Commission on International Trade Law, the likelihood of having the award documented orally, by the conduct of the parties or by any other means is not foreseen (Articles 86 and 87).

507. If the arbitration is in law and the parties did not agree to this, the terms will be set by the judge, taking into account the circumstances of the case, and will be continuous, only being interrupted if any of the arbitrators must be replaced. The judge may extend the term at the request of the arbitrators if the delay is not attributable to them (Article 754, ACCPC). If this is an equity arbitration, and the parties have said nothing, the arbitrators must render the award within three months (Article 770, ACCPC).

508. In all cases, a majority vote is required to render the award. The ACCPC regime indicates that an award signed by the majority is valid even if one of the arbitrators refuses to do so. When there is no majority, the appointment of another arbitrator may be contemplated (Article 757, ACCPC).

509. Those arbitrators who, without justified cause, do not render the award within the terms indicated will not be entitled to fees and will also be held liable for damages and losses. If the arbitration is in equity, in addition, the omission constitutes grounds for the nullity of the award.

Chapter 7. Appeal Against the Arbitration Award

510. Awards may be challenged, although there are certain peculiarities inherent to the mode of dispute resolution governed by the autonomy of those who submit to the process. Hence, in principle, the court's ability to control the arbitrators' decision only operates inasmuch as the parties determine thus, with certain specific limitations.

In *José Cartellone Construcciones Civiles S.A. v. Hidronor S.A.,*[210] the Supreme Court established that the waiver of the right to appeal an arbitration award cannot be interpreted as applicable to cases where the award terms contradict public order. This is because such a waiver cannot contemplate the arbitrators adopting a decision that produces a flaw of this nature, and highlights that although the arbitrators have the duty of evaluating the facts and the regular application of the law ensuring the award rendered is final under these conditions, their decision may be judicially challenged when it is unconstitutional, illegal or unreasonable. This criterion is ratified by the ACCC, which establishes that the arbitration contract cannot contain a waiver of the right to issue a judicial challenge of the final award if this is contrary to the legal system (Article 1656, last part, ACCC).

511. Faced with the award made by arbitrators in law, the ACCPC enables that it may be appealed in the same way as a judgment, unless the parties expressly waived their right to do so in the agreement (Article 758). If these rights have been waived, an award may be rejected without the need for substantiation. However, in order to safeguard the right of defence and effective legal protection, the lawmakers placed limits on the autonomy of the parties by clarifying that any waivers agreed by the parties do not extend to an appeal to clarify the award or to an appeal for annulment. The latter may be based on: (i) flaws intrinsic to the procedure; (ii) whether the arbitrators ruled after the deadline or on issues that are not part of the agreement (Article 760, ACCPC); or (iii) whether the award contains irreconcilable contradictions in its operative articles.

Unless the parties requested arbitrators to intervene in the review process, appeals filed against the award will be heard by the court which is hierarchically superior to the judge who would have been hearing the case had the matter not been submitted to arbitration (Article 763, ACCPC).

In equity arbitration, on the other hand, the award rendered is irrevocable. However, when amiable compositeurs issue a ruling after the deadline or on uncommitted points, the parties can challenge that decision by bringing legal action.

In these cases, an autonomous action for annulment must be filed within five days of notification. Once the claim is filed, the judge will transfer the other party for the same term, after which, whether the transfer is answered or not, the judge will decide on the validity or nullity of the award, without any recourse (Article 771, ACCPC).

---

210. *Fallos* 327:1881 (2004).

512. An extraordinary federal appeal may not be filed directly against arbitration decisions, since one of the requirements of this extraordinary means of challenge is the existence of a final judgment issued by a judicial court, which the arbitrators are not, nor are they part of the judicial power. However, the jurisdiction of the Supreme Court may be accessed by filing an extraordinary appeal when the decision ruled by the judicial court that has heard in the appeal against the award is challenged.

513. When awards are rendered in international arbitration they may only be challenged through a 'request to annul' based on any of the following: the impairment of the capacity of one of the parties; the invalidity of the arbitration agreement; the improper notification of the appointment of an arbitrator or of the arbitration actions; or if they were unable, for any other reason, to assert their rights; when the award refers to a controversy which is unforeseen in the arbitration agreement or contains decisions that exceed the terms of the arbitration agreement; defects in the constitution of the arbitral tribunal or the arbitration procedure; or if the object of the controversy is not subject to arbitration or is contrary to Argentine public order. A request for annulment must be filed within thirty days from the date that the award was rendered (Articles 98, 99, 100, Law 27,449).

Chapter 8. Recognition and Enforcement of Awards

514. As explained earlier, the law equates the award in its effects to a judgment (Article 499, first paragraph, ACCPC). Awards are enforced in accordance with the rules established for the legal enforcement of judgments (Article 499, ACCPC).

515. As for the recognition and enforcement of international arbitration awards, Law 27,449 stipulates that, regardless of the country where it was rendered, they are enforceable and binding, unless there are any reasons for denying the recognition of the award established in the law itself. If a court of the country where the award was rendered is requested to nullify or suspend it, the court requested to recognize or enforce it may, if it deems appropriate, postpone a decision and, at the request of the party filing for recognition or enforcement of the award, also order the other party to provide appropriate guarantees (Articles 102, 103 and 105, Law 27,449).

Chapter 9. Arbitration Expertise

516. Arbitration expertise is a mechanism whereby the parties in a dispute submit a factual matter to the decision of one or more experts.

There are similarities in procedural terms with arbitration and expert evidence, but this instance raises certain differences.

Although the procedure is legally similar to that followed by amiable compositeurs, when it comes to arbitration expertise, the aspects to be decided are exclusively linked to matters of fact. Likewise, this procedure may be applied both within the framework of a judicial file and outside of it. Regarding the agreement, it is sufficient to state the date, names of the grantors and of the arbitrator(s), as well as the facts about which they must render an award. These requirements are however unnecessary when the matter of the pronouncement and the individualization of the parties are determined by the judicial resolution providing for arbitration expertise or may be determined due to the facts giving rise to it.

517. Arbitration expertise is appropriate when: (i) the settlements or accounts are extremely complicated, lengthy and difficult to justify; (ii) expert knowledge is required; or (iii) the laws establish this procedure under the name of the judgment of arbitrators, arbitrators, expert or expert arbitrators, enabling them to resolve factual matter which has been expressly specified on an exclusive basis.

518. The rules of trial by amiable compositeurs apply with the following adjustments: (i) expert arbitrators must be specialists in the factual matter at issue; (ii) they must be pronounced within one month from the last acceptance; and (iii) the judicial decision that, where appropriate, must be pronounced in any trial related to factual matters awarded must be adjusted to that established by arbitration expertise.

Part XI. Mediation

Chapter 1. General Considerations and Legislation

519. Mediation in Argentina was instituted within the national order in 1995 by Law 24,573 as a step prior to the beginning of compulsory judicial proceedings. Born as a kind of pilot plan whose duration was expected to be five years, after successive extensions, Law 26,589 (2010) established it definitively as a prior mandatory instance for all organs in the national and federal justice system.[211] The Argentine provinces have replicated the position adopted at national level, and only La Rioja and Santa Cruz lack provisions on mandatory mediation, beyond the pilot experiences driven by their own Superior Courts or their own rules in certain matters (such as criminal or family law).

520. The mediation model follows the following steps: (i) a request for mediation may be made before or during legal proceedings. Law 26,589 made a few changes, allowing a judge to refer a case to mediation once only during proceedings. This decision can be taken either at the preliminary hearing or when considered pertinent, provided that the circumstances of the case justify it. The court proceedings are thus suspended for a period of thirty days, which may be extended by agreement of the parties (Articles 34, paragraph 1 and 360, paragraph 1, ACCPC, and 16 (d), Law 26,589); (ii) the process is performed in the presence of a mediator, a third party outside the judicial structure who must be impartial as regards the interests of the intervening parties (Article 7 (a), Law 26,589); (iii) the idea is to encourage direct communication between the parties, using techniques to foster the mutual understanding of their interests and positions; (iv) the process preserves the confidential nature of any information disclosed by the parties, their advisers or third parties summoned during the mediation. This extends to the content of papers and/or any other working material prepared by the parties or which they are evaluating for the purposes of the mediation process. The obligation of confidentiality only ceases by express dispensation of all the parties intervening, or when this is necessary to avoid or prevent a crime from being committed. This must be interpreted restrictively and any exceptions are clear. Confidentiality does not require the express agreement of the parties (Articles 7, 8 and 9, Law 26,589); and (v) the process concludes with an agreement resolving the conflict, which in law has the same effect as

211. A broad analysis of mediation in Argentina and its efficacy as well as a detailed study of the results of implementation may be consulted at L. Giannini, *La mediación en Argentina*, Santa Fe, Rubinzal-Culzoni, 2009.

a judgment. It may be enforced under the procedures established for the enforcement of judgments (Articles 56, Law 26,589, and 500, ACCPC).

521. In the RA, for certain types of conflicts, mandatory prior proceedings have been instituted not as an instance of mediation but rather to prompt discussion and/or resolution. Beyond prior administrative proceedings in conflicts or administrative claims against the State (Law 19,549 (1972) and amendments), these instances are mainly handled by the Compulsory Labour Conciliation Service (SECLO, for its acronym in Spanish) and the Pre-Conciliation Service in Consumer Relations (COPREC, for its acronym in Spanish). The first is regulated at national level by Law 24,365 (1996) and refers to all individual and collective claims regarding conflicts in the orbit of National Labour Justice. This body answers to the Ministry of Labour, Employment and Social Security. It is free for workers and their representatives and only charges employers a comparatively low cost. The second is governed by Law 26,993 (2014) and only intervenes in claims of individual consumer or user rights where the amount involved does not exceed fifty-five adjustable minimum living wage payments.

Chapter 2. Rights Subject to Mediation

522. As a rule, all disputes must be submitted to a mandatory pretrial mediation process, unless they are expressly excepted (Articles 4 and 5, Law 26,589). These exceptions have to do with conflicts where issues of public order are at stake or when the particular legal action or claim cannot be submitted to a prior instance without suffering some form of distortion or being denatured.[212]

523. Thus criminal action, personal separation and divorce, marriage annulment, paternity suits, parental authority and adoption are excluded, except in relation to asset-related matters derived from these. In these cases, the judge must divide the proceedings, referring the asset-related issues to the mediator. Outside of the aforementioned conflicts, all disputes arising from family relationships or involving the interests of its members, including those related to the subsistence of the marriage bond, must be submitted to family mediation (Article 31, Law 26,589).

Cases may not be referred to mediation in the following circumstances: when the State or any of its decentralized entities are a party, unless expressly authorized otherwise; when a party is not allowed to resign their right to property on the matter under discussion; processes of disqualification, declaration of incapacity and rehabilitation; *amparos*, habeas corpus, habeas data and injunctions; precautionary measures; preliminary proceedings and advance evidence; probate; voluntary reorganization and bankruptcy proceedings; the call for an assembly of co-owners; conflicts of labour justice jurisdiction; and voluntary proceedings.

The same occurs when rights which use other legal or institutional mechanisms for resolution are in dispute, such as disputes concerning conflictive consumer relationships, which are covered by the Prior Conciliation Service in Consumer Relations.

Also, in certain conflicts, mediation is optional for the petitioner, without the requested party being able to object to the decision adopted in this regard, such as, for example, foreclosure and eviction proceedings.

There are similar regulations in the provinces, where the exceptions envisaged vary in amount or scope. For example, the province of Córdoba excludes collective or class actions from prior mandatory mediation (Article 6 (17), Law 10,543 (2018)).

212. The law does not foresee any specific provision for collective disputes.

Chapter 3. Mandatory Nature of Mediation System

524. The Supreme Court had the opportunity to rule on the constitutional validity of the mandatory nature of the mediation system established by Law 24,573. In *Baterías Sil-Dar*,[213] it ruled in favour of the process's constitutionality. It maintained that the legal imposition to submit to this prior extrajudicial procedure only leads to the duty to appear at the hearing set by the mediator, but not necessarily to remain throughout the proceedings, since it is enough for one or both parties to express their willingness to terminate the procedure for it to conclude, and they may resort to a legal course of action. The Supreme Court considered that mediation as such constitutes a reasonable regulation of the right of defence. After fifteen years, Law 26,589 (2010) definitively established mediation as a prior mandatory instance for all organs in the national and federal justice system.

525. The provinces have followed a similar pattern. For example, the province of Buenos Aires instituted mediation through Law 13,951 (2009), requiring proof of having completed this previous phase as a condition for admitting the claim in court proceedings. The province of Santa Fe did the same through Law 13,151 (2010), leaving behind the earlier voluntary model, while the province of Cordoba, which used a partially mandatory mechanism in the civil and commercial sphere (Law 8858, 2000), replaced this by Law 10,543 (2018) making it obligatory in all areas.

213. *Fallos* 324:3184 (2001).

Chapter 4. People and Institutions That May Act as Mediators

526. Mediators must be lawyers with at least three years' experience and special training as established in the regulations (provided by specific entities created for this purpose). They must pass an exam to test their knowledge and criteria and be registered in the National Mediation Registry which answers to the Ministry of Justice and Human Rights of the Nation. Lawyers who have been disbarred in the areas of commercial, civil or criminal law may not act as mediators, nor those who have been convicted of intentional crime, nor those for whom there are incompatibilities or impediments to practice law (Articles 10, 11 and 41, Law 26,589 and 3, Law 23,187). Mediators must pay annual collegiate fees, and failure to pay for two years will lead to their being struck off the list. Other professionals may only intervene as assistant technicians during the negotiation, under the direction and responsibility of the mediator.

527. The National Mediation Registry is in charge of authorizing and controlling mediators, mediation centres, assisting professionals and training entities. It exercises disciplinary control over the performance of qualified mediators, ensuring compliance with the regulations and applying the corresponding sanctions. It may commission mediators to observe hearings and subsequently draw up a report for the National Directorate of Mediation and Participatory Conflict Resolution Methods, which is in the orbit of the Ministry of Justice and Human Rights (Articles 32, 34, 40, 44, 45 et seq., Law 26,589).

528. As for the appointment of a mediator, this can be agreed upon by the parties, or the name of the corresponding mediator may be drawn by lot. In the first case, the decision may be an express one (when the parties choose the mediator by written agreement) or a tacit one (following a proposal from the applicant to the requested party, in order for the latter to select a mediator from a list). In the second case, when the claimant formalizes the request with the reception office of the Chamber of Appeals in the jurisdiction where the lawsuit has been filed, the office draws the name of the mediator by lot and assigns the courtroom that will eventually hear the case. If the judge refers a case to mediation during the proceedings, the mediator will be drawn by lot from the list registered with the National Registry of Mediation, unless there is a prior agreement between the parties to this effect.

529. Mediators must recuse themselves and may be challenged for the same reasons as judges, in order to preserve impartiality. Any mediator who omits to do so may be disqualified, and if they were drawn by lot, a new draw will take place immediately. If the challenged mediator was proposed by the applicant, they are replaced by the next person on the list in the order proposed (Articles 13, 14 et seq., Law 26,589).

As they have a duty to be impartial, mediators may neither advise nor sponsor any of the parties involved in the mandatory pretrial mediation procedures where they acted until one year has passed after their formal withdrawal from the National Mediation Registry. This prohibition is absolute in relation to the conflict where they intervened as a mediator.

530. The tasks performed by the mediator and the assisting professionals are remunerated. The mediators receive a basic fee for their work, and the amount and payment conditions are regulated by the national executive power. The remuneration of the parties' lawyers is governed by the provisions of the law on professional fees and the CCCN. If any of the parties lacks resources and can prove this, they may request that the mediation be done free of charge. This mediation procedure will be carried out in the mediation centres of the Ministry of Justice and Human Rights or in public mediation centres offering this service.

Chapter 5. Mediation Procedure

531. The mediation procedure is governed by several parameters, including: the principles of impartiality of the mediator, in relation to the interests of the intervening parties; the freedom and willingness of the parties to participate in the process, beyond its mandatory nature; the equality of the parties, with special regard to the interests of children and adolescents, people with disabilities and elderly dependents; the confidentiality of the information disclosed; fostering direct communication between the parties; and overall celerity, depending on the progress of the negotiations and the deadlines involved (Article 7, Law 26,589). Mediation suspends the statute of limitations (Articles 18, Law 26,589, and 2542, CCCN).

532. The procedure begins with the appointment of the mediator, either by lot or by following the agreement of the parties.

When the mediator is drawn by lot, the reception office of the Court of Appeal in the jurisdiction concerned must deliver the applicant two copies of the mediation form and send another to the court selected to hear the case if the mediation fails. With these copies, the petitioner must, within three business days, pay the mediator a sum in advance to cover administrative expenses. The mediator keeps one of the copies and returns the other, sealed and signed. When the petitioner does not go to the mediator's office within that period, they must pay the starting fee again and request the same mediator to be appointed.

When the request for mediation is carried out at the request, or by agreement, of the parties, the applicant must notify the other party by reliable means of the identity of the mediator they propose, as well as a list of no less than four other mediators and their contact details, so that the other party can choose from these within five business days of being notified. This notification may also be made by the proposed mediators themselves. If the requested party exercises their option and chooses a mediator from the alternative list sent by the applicant, they must notify the latter of their decision at the address given for that purpose. The mediator chosen by the requested party is the one who will carry out the mediation. However, the silence or the refusal of the requested party is taken as confirmation of the mediator proposed by the requesting party. If there is more than one requested party, they must agree on their choice otherwise the mediator proposed by the requesting party will be confirmed (Article 13, Decree 1467/11).

533. The second significant moment in the process involves the mediation hearings themselves, which are usually held in the office of the mediator, unless there is a well-founded objection. The mediator may convene as many hearings as deemed necessary, within the timeframe established. The first hearing must be held within fifteen days of the notification of their appointment, made either by reliable means or personally, at the choice of the parties or their lawyers (Articles 24, Law 26,589 and Decree 1467/2011). The mediator may themselves or at the request of a party decide that a third-party intervention is necessary and summon them accordingly. In all cases, the agreement of the parties is required.

The term for mediations is up to sixty calendar days as from the last notification to the requested party or a third party, except when the mediation is optional, in which case the term is thirty days, although in both cases, the term may be extended by agreement of the parties.

The parties must be present at the mediation hearing and may not send a proxy, except for officials authorized to make a statement ex officio (Article 407, ACCPC), legal entities and those domiciled more than 150 km from the city where the hearings are being held.

Legal representation is mandatory. The law establishes that a party who attends the hearings without their legal representative will be deemed not to have appeared, unless a new date is agreed to correct this error.

The parties may contact the mediator appointed before the date of the hearing in order to make the scope of their claims known. If either party does not attend the first hearing with just cause, the mediator will set a new date for the hearing. When the requested party is absent without just cause, the requesting party may either choose to conclude the mediation procedure or call a new hearing. If it is the applicant who is absent, the mandatory pretrial mediation proceedings must be restarted.

534. At the first hearing, the mediator must inform the parties of the principles governing the mediation procedure, in particular, the confidentiality of the proceedings. The mediator is endowed with broad prerogatives to administer the forms and modes of meeting, and can do so jointly or separately, as long as they maintain their impartiality and do not favour one party over the other. The main objective is to encourage the parties to communicate directly with each other in a creative and cooperative search for a solution to the conflict. Hence, both mediator and any of the parties may propose the intervention of professional assistants, whose participation is subject to the agreement of all the parties, and who are appointed by the mediator.

In the light of the emergency situation following COVID-19, the Ministry of Justice and Human Rights has enabled mediation hearings to be carried out virtually in a videoconference setting online, provided that the identity of the intervening parties can be guaranteed and the principles governing the mediation procedure are respected. To this end, a guide for conducting online mediations has been approved.

535. The procedure can conclude with an agreement, without one, or by default of the parties (Articles 27 and 28, Law 26,589). In all cases, a record is drawn up stating the cause and, where appropriate, the terms of the agreement, its absence or the negative result of the proceedings arising from the unjustified absence of any of the parties or the impossibility of notification. The record must be signed by all the participants. When mediations are carried out following the referral of a judge, a copy of the record must be sent to the judicial body referring the case to mediation.

When there is no agreement or the mediation is concluded by default, the requesting party is empowered to begin court proceedings accompanied by their copy of the mediation record. In such cases, it is expressly forbidden to record the details of the hearings held. The lack of agreement also enables court proceedings for the counterclaim that the requested party may file, if they expressed their claim during the mediation procedures and it was duly recorded. A party who does not appear must pay a fine whose amount will be equivalent to 5% of the basic salary of a national judge of first instance.

If, after the mediation process fails, the plaintiff files a claim against a person who was not summoned or against a third party, another mediation procedure must be opened with the new party introduced into the proceedings. All mediation proceedings concluded must be reported to the Ministry of Justice and Human Rights for the purposes of their registration and the certification of the pertinent instruments.

Chapter 6. Mediation Agreement

536. The proceedings are held to have concluded successfully when the parties are able to reach an agreement resolving their differences which puts an end to the conflict. In this case, a record must be drawn up identifying the parties involved in the controversy as well as issues such as: the existence of an agreement; the appearance of the requested party or named third parties who have been reliably notified; the object of the dispute; the addresses of the parties; their signatures, those of their lawyers, the mediator (which must be certified by the Ministry of Justice and Human Rights) and that of any attending professionals who may have intervened. The mediator must draw up the agreement reached, clearly stating its scope (total or partial), the terms, items or points agreed and the conditions for compliance, which include the costs involved. Within the concept of judicial costs, the expenses that would have been incurred to avoid the lawsuit are also included, including those of the mandatory pretrial mediation procedure (Article 77, ACCPC).

Chapter 7. Endorsement and Enforceability of the Agreement

537. In the national regime, an agreement does not require judicial approval, unless the interests of children, adolescents or *persons* with restricted active legal *capacity* are involved. In these cases, the legal representative must, with the intervention of the Public Ministry, request that the judge drawn by lot at the beginning of the procedure or whoever is deemed competent according to matter at stake, approve the agreement. These actions are exempt from the payment of court fees. The judge must ensure that the agreement reached does not violate public order.

538. In some provinces, all agreements have to be subject to judicial approval. For example, in the province of Buenos Aires, the judge is required to verify that the agreement reflects a fair balance of the parties' interests (Article 17, Law 13,951 (2009)). This has led to numerous objections in that it imposes a standard of control that goes beyond verifying the availability of rights or the non-violation of public order, as it requires an analysis of the fairness of the resolution, undermining the principle of confidentiality which should characterize the instance. Judicial control of the agreement also undermines the system's innate ability to achieve self-resolution in a speedy fashion which is purportedly its objective.

In the province of Cordoba, endorsement is not required, except in those cases involving property registration or, as regards the principle of national order, where children and adolescents or people with restricted active legal *capacity* are involved. The endorsement process is exempt from legal fees, contributions and all other expenses, without prejudice to what must be paid for these concepts as part of the mediation process when concluded by agreement of the parties. This is 50% of the amount to be paid in court, taking into account the nature, type and amount of the claim being made (Articles 26, 28 and 29, Law 10,543).

539. An agreement implemented in a document signed by the mediator or judicially endorsed in those cases where this is required, is enforceable through the judgment enforcement procedure (Article 500, subsection 4, ACCPC). This transforms the agreement into an enforceable title, giving the regime more agility and freeing up the system. However, the legal comparison between a mediation agreement and a judgment has raised constitutional objections, which could be relevant if the agreement were enforceable in a way similar to that of any extrajudicial title (Article 523, ACCPC). As for enforcement at the request of a party, the judge may impose a fine on the unwilling party for reckless or malicious behaviour (Article 45, ACCPC).

Selected Bibliography

Arazi, R. Derecho procesal civil y comercial, Buenos Aires: Rubinzal-Culzoni, 2018.

Arazi, R. La prueba en el proceso civil, Buenos Aires: Rubinzal-Culzoni, 2008.

Berizonce, R. O. Tutelas procesales diferenciadas, Buenos Aires: Rubinzal-Culzoni, 2009.

Berizonce, R.O. Derecho Procesal Civil actual, La Plata: Librería Editora Platense, Abeledo Perrot, 1999.

Corte Suprema de Justicia de la Nación, Supreme Court of Argentina https://sj.csjn.gov.ar/sj/suplementos.do?method=ver&data=fr20182eb.

De Lázzari, E. *Medidas cautelares. Disposiciones relativas a la materia contenida en la parte general del Código Procesal Nacional (Arts. 195 a 237),* La Plata: Librería Editora Platense, 1995.

Falcón, E. Código Procesal Civil y Comercial de la Nación : comentado. Concordado. Anotado, Buenos Aires: LexisNexis ; Abeledo Perrot, 2006.

Falcón, E. Tratado de la prueba, Buenos Aires: Astrea, 2009.

Falcón, E. Sistemas alternativos de resolver conflictos jurídicos : Negociación, mediación, conciliación, Buenos Aires: Rubinzal-Culzoni, 2012.

Falcón, E. Tratado de Derecho Procesal Civil y Comercial, Buenos Aires: Rubinzal-Culzoni, 2006.

Fallos (Official Collection of Argentina's Supreme Court of Justice Decisions) http://sj.csjn.gov.ar/sj/tomosFallos.do?method=iniciar.

Garay, A.E. Cómo interponer un Recurso Extraordinario y su Queja (A partir de la acordada 4/2007, CSJN), Buenos Aires: Abeledo Perrot, 2010.

Garay, A. La doctrina del precedente en la Corte Suprema, Buenos Aires, Abeledo Perrot, 2013.

Gelli, M.A. Constitución de la Nación Argentina, Comentada y Anotada, Buenos Aires: La Ley 2004.

Giannini, L. La mediación en Argentina, Santa Fe, Rubinzal-Culzoni, 2009.

Hitters, J.C. & O. Fappiano. *Derecho internacional de los derechos h*umanos, Buenos Aires: EDIAR, 2007.

Hitters, J.C. *Técnica de los recursos ordinarios*, Buenos Aires: Librería Editora Platense, 2004.

Morello, A. M. et al., Códigos Procesales en lo Civil y Comercial de la Provincia de Buenos Aires y de la Nación: comentados y anotados, La Plata: Librería Editora Platense, Abeledo Perrot, 2015.

Selected Bibliography

Morello, A.M. & R. Rosales Cuello. Práctica del recurso extraordinario, Buenos Aires: La Ley, 2008.

Oteiza, E., et al. *Sendas de la reforma de la justicia a principios del siglo XXI,* Madrid: Marcial Pons, 2018.

Palacio, L.E. Derecho Procesal Civil, - Buenos Aires: Abeledo Perrot, 2011.

Index

The numbers here refer to paragraph numbers.

Index

Index

www.ingramcontent.com/pod-product-compliance
Lightning Source LLC
Chambersburg PA
CBHW071436230926
51846CB00001B/255
9789403539522